CAN FAITHS MAKE PEACE?

CAN FAITHS
MAKE PEACE?

Holy Wars and the Resolution

of Religious Conflicts

Edited by

PHILIP BROADHEAD & DAMIEN KEOWN

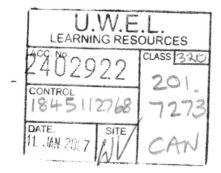
I.B. TAURIS
LONDON · NEW YORK

Published in 2007 by I.B.Tauris & Co Ltd
6 Salem Road, London W2 4BU
175 Fifth Avenue, New York NY 10010
www.ibtauris.com

In the United States of America and in Canada distributed by Palgrave Macmillan
a division of St. Martin's Press, 175 Fifth Avenue, New York NY 10010

International Library of War Studies 9

ISBN: 978 1 84511 276 9

A full CIP record for this book is available from the British Library
A full CIP record for this book is available from the Library of Congress

Library of Congress Catalog Card Number: available

Printed and bound in Great Britain by TJ International Ltd, Padstow, Cornwall
Camera-ready copy edited and supplied by the editors

CONTENTS

ACKNOWLEDGEMENTS

The editors are grateful to the History Department of Goldsmiths College, London, for sponsoring the 'Can Faiths Make Peace?' conference in July 2004, and for assistance towards the production and publication costs of this volume. We would like to thank our contributors for the care they have taken in the preparation of their chapters and for adhering closely to the production schedule. The editors are grateful to Katherine Holmes of *ProjectPublish* for managing the production of the volume; her meticulous work in copy-editing, compiling the index, and preparing the final camera-ready manuscript meant that the project remained on schedule throughout. Finally, our thanks go to our editor Alex Wright and the staff of I.B.Tauris for enabling our deliberations to reach a wider audience in such an efficient and professional manner.

INTRODUCTION

Philip Broadhead

The value of peace is emphasized in the teachings of all the major religions currently practised in the world. It is nevertheless the case that over past centuries, and
down to the current time, religion has proved to be one of the most significant
causes of war and conflict across the globe, as the followers of the world's faiths
have fought amongst co-religionists and against those with different beliefs. The
chapters which follow are an attempt to examine this paradox from a range of
perspectives, and include contributions by historians, sociologists and writers on
religion, politics and philosophy. They are the outcome of an interdisciplinary
conference entitled, Can Faiths Make Peace? Holy Wars and the Resolution of
Religious Conflicts from Historical and Contemporary Perspectives, organized by
the History Department at Goldsmiths, University of London, and held between
12–13 July 2004. Unsurprisingly they do not produce a consensus or ready solutions to the problems of persistent warfare and distrust between people of different
faiths, nor yet to the constant divisions between sects and denominations, which
lead to internecine hatred and violence. If resolutions to these conflicts were to be
so easily found, they would have been discerned long ago. Nevertheless, several
significant themes and questions emerge, which cut across disciplines, faiths and
regions, and are relevant for religious wars from a range of different periods and in
a variety of contexts. Several of the most crucial issues which are at stake in religious conflicts are identified, as are some recurring features of the religious, cultural,
political and social environments in which religious war flourishes and which need
to be addressed in any attempts to establish lasting peace.

In general, religious conflicts differ from other wars and are more complex
than disputes over territory and political or economic dominance. In these cases

consideration of military advantage or weakness can be weighed against the value of potential gains or the dissipation of resources involved in fighting, and may be used to decide whether combatants persist in war or opt to seek peace. From a modern social anthropological point of view, religions are myths and rituals created by humans to give meaning to their existence in the world and to provide explanations for the otherwise inexplicable forces of nature.[1] By their adherents, however, religious teachings are held to be sacred truths, revealed by a divine force through signs and holy texts, and confirmed not only by the witness of teachers, saints and martyrs, but also through portents and prophecy and the exercise of supernatural power in the world. For their followers religions are credible and convey meaning and truth. Even though different faiths approach and express the concept in a variety of ways, in general they see their beliefs as representing, or leading towards, goodness and perfection. This situation militates against a search for middle ground, especially when it is presented in terms of compromises between truth and falsehood, good and evil. There are, therefore, conflicts that are intrinsic to interfaith relations and which encourage suspicion and hostility through their incompatible claims to represent the only true deity or deities and the only correct beliefs. For one religion to recognize the validity of another risks casting doubts on its own authority, an act that could be seen as undermining faith, and being a form of apostasy that carries with it the danger of the loss of divine favour, which could bring terrible retribution.

Religious conflict also carries with it the sense of divine mission, which can serve as a counterweight to military reversals and unfavourable odds in battle, for steadfastness in such circumstances is seen as a test of faith and commitment. This position is exemplified in the status attached to martyrs, who earn spiritual rewards from their death. Religions which under normal circumstances condemn the taking of human life, find it expedient to justify fighting under particular conditions, that are deemed to constitute just wars. Never is this more true than when that war is to defend the existence or honour of their faith and the freedom of its clergy and followers to worship. In all these circumstances ultimate victory is believed to rest on right, not might, and it can be anticipated even when, in human terms, it appears impossible. Were religious groups each to operate in their own space, such intrinsic and implacable differences would be of little account, but the movement of people and ideas, creates flashpoints of difference, particularly where there is competition over shared sacred sites. At the sites contested by Muslims and Hindus, for example at Ayodhya in India, or between Jews, Muslims and Christians in Jerusalem, there is frequently a sense that their occupation by non-believers amounts to a humiliating desecration.

Against this background of apparently unavoidable religious conflict, stand many examples of followers of different faiths setting aside or controlling and containing rivalry, in order to live side by side in peace. The Indian subcontinent in the reign of Akbar, the bi-confessional cities of the Holy Roman Empire between the sixteenth and eighteenth centuries, France during the period when the Edict of Nantes was in force, have each demonstrated different approaches to creating religious toleration. The concept of toleration, based on the premise that people have a right to follow their own religion, even if others disagree with what they believe, ultimately provides the most fundamental argument for avoidance or cessation of religious conflicts. This view of toleration, and the cultural relativism it implies, might be seen by some believers as a sign of weakness and indifference. By permitting a variety of belief, a dominant group could be portrayed as having lost its authority. On the other hand it can be represented as a sign of religious strength and confidence, that a faith and its followers do not feel threatened by those, either with different belief, or none at all.

The concept of religious toleration has developed from a number of impulses, of which in the West two have been of particular significance. Firstly, that religious faith is a personal matter and can not be forced on individuals or societies by legislation or persecution. This position was, for example, described by John Locke, who saw the imposition of beliefs as being an impediment, rather than a means to salvation.[2] Another impulse towards religious toleration comes from a conscious decision that the state has no role in imposing uniformity of belief, not least because diversity and individual freedom have positive value for society. This view, espoused by Mill in the nineteenth century, has been influential in shaping modern liberal attitudes towards toleration, but as these papers show, is contested by many followers of all the main religions.[3]

The belief that the rise of rational thought, the discoveries of science, and changes in the social order, would permit a 'modernization' of attitudes towards religion, either by evolutionary processes or revolutionary action, are now questioned. Religions have shown themselves to be remarkably resilient and are seen in these chapters as, not only able to survive, but also to thrive in the modern world. Unlike the vague and often alien concepts of modernization, secularization and liberalism, they offer a sense of identity and belonging, which can be harnessed to protect local interests, but more importantly to defend ideals of humanity, individual worth and human dignity, against forces of change and unbridled materialism. Religions have also proved capable of adaptation, by being able to engage with and use technology and education, yet at the same time to retain the support of populations which have experienced and accepted the beneficial aspects of modern society. In the chapters that follow, we see the continuing importance of religious belief in developing countries, for providing stability during periods of change when traditional identities and ways of life are under threat.

What is evident from this collection is the complexity of religious conflicts, both in the past and at the present time, and the consequent need for effective peacemaking to recognize and address those religious aspects which shape and direct disputes. One of the problems identified is that of recognizing the differences within religions and between their followers. While all Christians, or Muslims, or Jews or Hindus share beliefs with their co-religionists, there are differences between them which shape the way in which they engage with the world and with other religions. Most recently this has been portrayed as a distinction between moderates and fundamentalists or extremists, but an understanding of the different concerns within religious groups is a prerequisite of finding peace. It is also the case that what is ostensibly religious conflict is seldom fuelled solely by inter-denominational or interfaith disputes. Whether in Northern Ireland, Bosnia or Sri Lanka, religious differences are bound up in a range of secular grievances, which are frequently rooted in history, but have implications for the present.

A constant of religious wars which stretches from ancient times to the present is shown by Robinson to be the defence of honour. While this cause might be found in most, or even all wars, it is shown to have particular significance when religion is involved, for defending the honour of one's religion brings divine sanction and is depicted as a holy mission. This might explain why religious wars have proved to be some of the most savage and the most difficult to settle. He shows too the danger of notions of 'just wars', which rescind normal religious and moral res-traints on killing, and can also imply that religion is served better, at least in certain circumstances, by war than by seeking peace.

The role of historical experience for faith groups emerges repeatedly here, al-though ambiguities are identified. Tallett and Atkins show that the policy of de-christianization during the French Revolution was not a success, but it did perma-nently establish a new policy, in which membership of the civil community in France was based on secular and not religious affiliations. Abse in his study of papal attitudes towards Italian Jews asserts that anti-Semitism remained significant in Italy as ideological positions of the past were unchallenged by the papacy in the period prior to and including World War II. He identifies a feature which recurs in other chapters, that minority religious groups are particularly vulnerable to perse-cution during periods of political upheaval, for it is at these times, when there is competition for influence and power, that the safeguards of tolerance are challenged.

This is shown by Carmichael to have been evident in the breakdown of religious co-existence, which occurred in the final half century of the Russian and Ottoman Empires, as political change prompted the growth of latent hostilities between religious groups. Here religion is shown as a key sign of difference between various groups in society. Acts deliberately intended to outrage religious sensibilities were particularly effective in causing separation between faiths, and in prising open latent hostilities. It was in this context that all groups committed acts of religious genocide which deepened the fissures in society.

Religious conflict has re-emerged as a significant force in the region following the collapse of the Soviet Empire in the late twentieth century. Anderson demon-strates that as the new states which have been formed from the USSR seek to establish their independence and identity, religion has both become important in defining difference between groups competing for control, as in Uzbekistan, but also in establishing the changes from the previous political order. Despite the emphasis upon religious issues, he notes the significance of political religion in the region, as it is mainly secular goals which are contested by the local populations.

In dealing with the most serious on-going example of religious conflict, Wilkes focuses on the lack of success of previous attempts to establish a negotiated settlement in the Middle East. He sees this as stemming from the failure to recognize the extent to which attitudes related to such problems as land rights and sacred sites, are an intrinsic part of the conflict. Efforts to establish peace based solely on secular concerns are therefore incomplete and have only a limited chance of success. He suggests that the impasse of religious war could be bridged by identifying shared religious values between Jews and Muslims, in particular the common importance attached to the preservation of human life. Herbert too draws attention to similar underlying ethical and moral values, which are based on shared attitudes to humanity. His chapter shows that there are practices and traditions within Islam, which facilitate reconciliation between enemies. He also identifies weaknesses in modernization theories, by demonstrating the ability of Islam to deal with change in the world, by positive engagement. Taken together therefore, he identifies attitudes which could form a religious context for peace in the Middle East. Seidler begins to unravel the closely bound roles of religion and history in the contemporary conflicts of the Middle East. He shows that violence is seldom random or unpredictable, but flows from long-held attitudes and experiences, which condition, and are used to justify religious violence. Memories of the persecution of Jews under the Nazis, the attacks on Palestinian communities by the Israeli army, or the destruction of the World Trade Centre, create a perpetual and escalating cycle of violence and mistrust. Seidler suggests solutions to religious conflicts should be sought not in trying to remove the religious elements from discussion, but in a greater willingness by all sides to listen to their opponents, and by so doing, prepare themselves to engage constructively with the hurt and grievances they encounter.

The need to deal with religious issues in finding peace, are similarly revealed in the contributions on Sri Lanka. Deegalle shows that efforts to settle civil conflicts between Tamils and Sinhalese have been hampered by a general unwillingness to admit, and therefore address, religious and ethnic causes of violence. Just as in the examples used by Carmichael from Europe, he shows ritual acts of desecration as being used to inflame hostility and define the identity of the opposing forces. As a result, even the pacifist ideals of Buddhist monks have been compromised by their desire to defend religious honour. Even if it is at root a war over secular power, Deegalle sees a need to recognize the religious dimension in a search for peace. As in the disputes between Jews and Muslims in the Middle East, Harris sees reconciliation in the divisive conflicts of Sri Lanka to be most likely found in a reexamination of religious values. In particular, by showing that those beliefs which divide followers of different faiths, can be balanced by shared attitudes towards such things as compassion for suffering and the value of human life.

Doctrinal divisions between members of the same faith continue to be the cause of conflict, especially when they become intertwined with secular motives. The divisions of the Christian Church in Europe, particularly in the post-Reformation period, have provided many examples of destructive interdenominational strife. In comparison Khan shows that in contemporary Pakistan, division between different Muslim groups impacts on the state and the unity of the nation. Whilst successive governments have found it convenient to ally with certain groups, gaining their political support in return for excluding religious rivals, the effects have been to encourage sectarianism that is a barrier to the political unity which is sought by the government. Ordinary people are shown to be successful in assimilating a range of religious beliefs and adopting them to their own needs in the examples of women converts to Islam in South Africa examined here by Lee. Comparing and contrasting the experiences of male and female converts, she finds that in the increased cross-cultural and interfaith contacts of post-apartheid South Africa, some black women have been drawn to convert to Islam, as they recognize in it a religious message and purpose which fits with pre-colonial religious traditions and belief systems. At the same time they have little sense of rejecting Christian belief, and instead have assimilated features of different religious cultures.

These chapters make no claims to offer solutions to religious conflict, but instead provide indications from history, from religious teachings and sociological and anthropological research, which show where better understanding might be obtained. Central to this, is an awareness that religious passions and divisions are most frequently inflamed in times and places where normal controls have broken down. In the wider fight to establish control over authority and resources, religion becomes central to establishing group and individual identity and rights. Additionally it emerges that where conflicts have a religious dimension, it must be reflected in efforts to establish peace if they are to have a significant chance of success. If religious ideology is a cause of war and violence, it can also be part of the solution. Above all, those who seek a solution to religious war need to look beyond the issues which divide, to core humanitarian values which are shared by those of different faiths.

1

RELIGIOUS ATTITUDES TO THE MIDDLE EAST PEACE PROCESS

George R. Wilkes

Religion, one of the most widely evoked features of Arab-Israeli conflicts, has also been a recurrent feature of high-level peacemaking initiatives in the Middle East. Before Anwar Sadat decided to make peace with the State of Israel in 1977, he secured the support of the leading Egyptian cleric of his day, Mohamed Sha'rawi, bringing Sheikh Sha'rawi to Jerusalem to pray with him at the Al-Aqsa Mosque.[1] This made sense in the context of the domestic pressure on Sadat exerted by advocates of greater Islamization in Egypt, an oppositional force which gathered strength from that time. But Sadat was also a religious man, and made clear in his speech to the Israeli Knesset that he was engaged in a religious mission:

> I come to you today on solid ground to shape a new life and to establish peace. We all love this land, the land of God, we all, Moslems, Christians and Jews, all worship God... But to be absolutely frank with you, I took this decision after long thought, knowing that it constitutes a great risk, for God Almighty has made it my fate to assume responsibility on behalf of the Egyptian people, to share in the responsibility of the Arab nation, the main duty of which, dictated by responsibility, is to exploit all and every means in a bid to save my Egyptian Arab people and the pan-Arab nation from the horrors of new suffering and destructive wars, the dimensions of which are foreseen only by God Himself. After long thinking, I was convinced that the

obligation of responsibility before God and before the people make it incumbent upon me that I should go to the far corners of the world, even to Jerusalem to address members of the Knesset and acquaint them with all the facts surging in me, then I would let you decide for yourselves...[2]

At the time of the Camp David Summit in 1978, the Israeli religious settler movement confronted Sadat's opposite, Menahem Begin. As the summit began, Begin announced that he would lose his right arm before agreeing to transfer the settlements in the Sinai to Egypt.[3] Though Begin was in many ways just as prone to adopt religious language as Sadat,[4] within days he had agreed to the transfer, and engaged his extremist contacts to ensure that the settlements could be removed.

Can faiths or religions make peace between Israel and its neighbours? Or are they merely obstacles for a peace process to overcome? We are immediately plunged into calculations about the strength commonly attributed to religion in Middle Eastern societies and politics, and about the degree of secularization also affecting these rapidly changing countries. During the opening session of the intergovernmental peace conference at Madrid in 1991, speaker after speaker underlined at some length the significance of peace in their own religious cultures.[5] By contrast, when they made their closing remarks the next day, God and the religions of peace were not mentioned at all.

Is religion indispensable for making peace in the Middle East, as religious scholars and peace activists like Yehezkel Landau and Marc Gopin argue?[6] Or is it at best window-dressing, a source of the kind of flowery rhetoric which many secularist supporters of the peace process, with Hanan Ashrawi and Shimon Peres, have rejected in favour of more tangible calculations about security, prosperity and self-interest?[7] How do the religious populations of Israel and neighbouring Arab countries respond to this secularist dichotomy between real and religious interests?

Is religion only of use for those opposed to a peace process, a force for conflict and violence? If Hamas, Islamic Jihad and the various extremist movements on the Israeli Right give secularists like Ashrawi and Peres grounds for such a concern, students of the Middle East peace process will find much opinion which contradicts this view, and which throws the sharp division between religion and secularism on its head. Thus, leading moderates from all three religious traditions have insisted that 'true' faith and religion are not causes of conflict or violence. Moreover, scholars of both Palestinian and Israeli religious politics have underlined how often they rely on secularist argument and support from sections of the populace who are not ostentatiously religious in public. Just as many Palestinians who tell pollsters they support Hamas do not regularly attend mosque,[8] so too the uncharacteristic call for harsh military responses against Arabs from the ageing spiritual guide of the Israeli Shas Party, Rabbi Ovadia Yosef,[9] struck a chord among many faithful Shas voters who are not synagogue-goers.[10] The task of identifying the role of religious opinion is made vastly more complicated by the private nature of much Israeli and Palestinian religious activity. Christians now make up a tiny proportion of the people of the region – just two per cent of the Israeli and Palestinian populations. They mainly appear below in the context of religious peacemaking initiatives, in which they have been prominent. For many in the Christian population, faith and religious identity provide a link with a social and also a political community, whether or not they are regular church-goers. There are now generations of secular or secularist Christians, Ashrawi being a prominent example, they being often defined as much by who they are not as by the family tradition with which they identify.

Religion in a Political Context

The search for a framework for understanding the role of religion in the conflict and peace process between Israel and its neighbours thus calls for reflection on what faith and religion refer to in these contexts. While we will see that there are grounds for an interpretation centred on ideology, according to which individuals define themselves either in relation to traditional religious authority structures or in terms of their own private faith and secular aspirations, I will also explore a perspective in which religion is the object of very realist, political calculation on the part of religious leaders, the leaders of the religious parties, the people for whom they speak, and the self-identified secularists who oppose the encroachment of religious authorities and parties on political life.

The divide between Jewish secularist and religious communities defined debate over Zionism within the Jewish community as soon as the first modern Jewish communities settled in what is now the State of Israel in the 1880s. Among Israeli Jews, the dominant political parties, anticlerical or more moderately secularist, have nevertheless adapted religious texts and tradition for use as their own symbols and arguments. The Likud Party in particular has attracted a sizeable proportion of the population which identifies either as religious or as 'traditional' (*masorti*), meaning 'moderately' or personally believing, and preferring 'Orthodox' religious authority to Western modernist Judaisms. The small political parties representing the more strictly Orthodox Jewish populations have famously commanded a strong position in building government coalitions, partly as a corollary of their flexibility with respect to the main issues dividing the Israeli Left and Right. The 'non-Zionist' religious parties, notably the Sephardi Shas Party, classically gave no religious sanction to the State of Israel but have found after decades of political engagement that opposition to Zionism appeals less and less to disaffected sections of the population. While the National Religious Party (NRP) has always reflected the interests of a committed Orthodox, religious Zionist population, after the 1967 war, and particularly after the rise of Likud in the 1970s, the NRP transformed from a broad-based party with leftist sympathies into a rightist party competing with a score of other factions particularly for the votes of Jewish settlers and their supporters, many of whom are not religious in traditional terms.

Regardless of the much-noted weakness of democratic institutions in the surrounding Arab states, the relationships between religion and secularism forged in the struggle for political control elsewhere in the Middle East bear some comparison with the Israeli situation. The first Arab anti-Zionists were either Islamist or were nationalists who called for a new Muslim-Christian political alliance – following the lead of the Grand Mufti of Jerusalem, Hajj Amin al-Husseini, there was briefly an alliance between the two streams in the 1930s. After the creation of the State of Israel, more determined secularist Arab nationalist movements gained hegemony and this only began to be effectively challenged by a resurgent Islamist opposition in the 1970s.[11] As in Israel, the religious opposition – which in most surrounding states has been based on the Muslim Brotherhood – is largely non-nationalist in origin, but has increasingly made accommodations with nationalist ideology and objectives in an effort to increase its political credibility. In the Palestinian territories, the Brotherhood established a political and military wing, Hamas, in 1987–88, as a token of its renewed commitment to the national cause.[12] As a result, Islamists have won sympathy and support from a wide section of the population which is not inspired by the need for an Islamic society on other grounds. In turn, secularist parties and factions across the region have joined in alliances with the Muslim Brothers, and often combine anticlericalism with a renewed recourse to religious language and inspiration. This coalition of religion and nationalism has coloured the competition between public figures in government and in opposition, each anxious to show themselves more anti-Zionist than their competitors – a rhetorical game which many Palestinians have long viewed with suspicion.

Religion, Conflict and Violence

The clash of interpretations that I have introduced also shapes much commentary on the relationship between religion, violence and political conflict. There is thus no consensus across or within communities over where violence begins and purely political conflict ends, let alone about the relationship of the three religions to the conflict.

A more determined liberal perspective prominent in literature on the contribution of religion to the conflict suggests that the models of the relationship between Judaism, Christianity and Islam as traditionally expressed in one or all of the faiths constitute a primary cause of the violence between them – the ethnic exclusivism imputed to 'traditional' Judaism, the faith-based supercessionist exclusivism associated with traditional Christianity and Islam, and the more intolerant political uses of each religion in this region which have historically subjected minority communities to subjugation and persecution.[13]

And yet prominent figures in each community present 'orthodox' Judaism, Christianity or Islam as eschewing violence, either altogether or in all situations except those in which immediate self-defence is the only option. From this perspective, the traditions are resources for distinguishing natural and even healthy conflict from violence. The *Qur'an* (5: 48) suggests that Allah differentiated the three faith communities so that they could come to recognize each other and compete in good works – a verse little acknowledged by extremists and which thus does not appear in the Hamas Covenant, although the very next verse from the *Qur'an* does.[14] Leading thinkers of all three communities have argued that the Abrahamic faiths have a special religious basis on which to draw together in mutual recognition – as a family, with shared origins and values – without giving up traditional claims to an exclusive claim on the revealed truth.[15] This may define them as supporters of interfaith reconciliation, but it does not necessarily make them 'moderate' or 'liberal'.

Classic liberal categories of thought may be of some help in the context of communities for whom the right to self-defence is associated with defence of religion against the onslaught of the unbelieving world, and of threats related to modernity in particular. For this reason, the most active exponents of the use of force in the name of religion on both sides – in Hamas and within the National Religious bloc in Israel – are ideologically committed to confronting modernity head on, taking what is useful and rooting out what is harmful. In both cases, the most prone to support violence in the face of the onslaught of the modern world argue that the contemporary period is an apocalypse, with the challenge to faithful conduct being foremost a political task. In much Hamas literature, the Zionist entity presents a demonic force: 'the Jews' are at once descendants of the Jewish adversaries of Mohamed described in the *Qur'an* and at the same time a forward column of the contemporary forces of evil preventing true Muslims from gaining their rightful position in the world.[16] In the pronouncements of an extremist settler fringe – represented by small parties like Moledet in the Knesset, but also gravitating around outlawed underground movements like Kach – the Al-Aqsa Martyrs Brigade, Hamas and other terrorist groups are portrayed as the natural response of the evil within humanity to the appearance of a political state based on divine love and providence, a product of a modern chaos born of the rejection of the core truths taught in the revealed religion.[17]

Both Hamas and the violence-prone settler fringe have had to overcome a series of established traditional obstacles to religiously-inspired violence: notably the call to wait for divine intervention in favour of such violence, and the absence of authorities sanctioned to declare collective violence religiously legitimate. A number of streams have solved this by enfranchising the secular state as defender of the nation, reading this in different ways as an obvious response to the emergency situation which exists in these apocalyptic times. Aviezer Ravitsky has described how in this new situation the 'messianic' tendencies within the National Religious settler movement have overcome a long-held Orthodox distance from employing secular force by casting the creation of the State of Israel and the 1967 victory as miracles portentous of a divine declaration that the end of history and the beginning of the messianic era has arrived: thus, all obstacles to 'forcing' or 'hastening' the Messiah are now bypassed.[18] Compare developments in fundamentalist Islam in the region since the beginning of the twentieth century. The focus of the moderate stream within the Muslim Brotherhood has historically been on political opposition through a non-violent 'steadfastness', strengthening themselves religiously through inner struggle – the greater *jihad* – until such time as the Muslim movement may be ready to face its enemies with confidence. Many in Hamas and Islamic Jihad, by contrast, inspired by the more militant tendency within the Brotherhood initiated by Sayyid Qutb, argue that the world is now ruled by hostile nfidels, by ‘*shirk*’, and that an emergency situation arises in which ‘steadfastness’ by itself cannot be the only response.[19] Specifically, many reject the reliability of the *hadith* enjoining Muslims to prefer inner struggle to military combat, the ‘lesser *jihad*’.[20]

Not all religious Jews or Muslims who engage in self-authorized violence need see themselves as inspired by an ‘apocalyptic’ or ‘messianic’ vision of the times we live in, though some evidently do. In common, the statements which claim to represent the views of Hamas, Kach or Moledet supporters employ a discourse in which there is no doubt as to the divine legitimation given to the statement’s authors, nor of the existence of a clear enemy, which is hostile to the nation and to its revealed religion. In so far as delegitimation of the other lies at the root of much of the incitement on both sides, such an approach to religion plays a distinctive role in creating the conditions for violence.

Religions, Politics and the Middle East Peace Process

To track religious attitudes to the peace process, the observer must engage in a three-level analysis: first, of the statements of religious authorities, second, of the development of party political positions, and third, of the shift of opinion among the religious population, particularly as they have moved from one party or faction to another.

As at the time of the peace accords between Israel and Egypt, the revival of the Middle East peace process in the 1990s again drew religious authorities into public statements of the conditions under which making peace is legitimate. There is more commonality on the two sides of the conflict than is often acknowledged. On both sides, the more uncompromising religious opponents of the peace process per se have fallen back on well-known red lines which the Israeli government and Palestinian Liberation Organization (PLO) could not by their nature fulfil: that no secular authority has the right to give up on Jerusalem, nor on the rights of Jews or Palestinians to live freely on the land given to them by God.[21] A portion of both the Israeli and Palestinian religious extremists argue that they themselves also have no mandate to trade away land given to them by God. However, there are competing authorities on both sides for whom saving lives is in most situations more important than keeping land. This is a basic tenet of OzveShalom (Peace and Strength), a Modern Orthodox Jewish religious peace movement formed in the Lebanon War which subsequently spawned the dovish religious peace party Meimad.[22] In the light of this, the debate between leading Israeli and Arab religious figures over the legitimacy of the peace process has focused on the meaning given to the common contention that concessions can only be sanctioned on the basis of whether they lead to a ‘real’ or long-term peace. The advantages which can accrue from a temporary truce (*hudna*) also form a prominent feature of Islamist assessments of the prospect of peace initiatives, not a prominent feature of debate amongst Israeli religious figures.

The fact that religious parties and factions are primarily acting as disempowered forces of opposition across the region further complicates the project of identifying how their stances relate to popular religious opinion towards the peace process. In the mid-1990s, a bloc of Israeli non-Zionist religious parties moved in favour and against the peace process in response to calculations about what would maximize their domestic influence.[23] The Israeli National Religious Party and Palestinian Hamas have similarly presented a 'pragmatic' acceptance of an Arab-Israeli settlement where the alternative was to risk their popular support shifting to the Likud or Fatah – simultaneously both have insisted on giving no legitimation to the representatives of their erstwhile adversaries, the Palestinian Authority or 'the Zionist entity'.[24] Leaders of both are aware that a permanent settlement agreement would spell disaster, not least for their own political cohesion and public support. They may have a vested interest in conflict now, but if a successful settlement could be forged – which both extremes doubt – their interests would become far less easy to calculate.

A small minority of religious figures have been willing to lend their weight forcefully to the prospect of making definite commitments in the peace process. The self-identified peace bloc within the religious Jewish community in Israel has remained small, despite a significant boost at the time of the Lebanon War with the creation of OzveShalom. Disgusted with what they subsequently saw as the self-serving responses of the religious parties to the Oslo peace process, leading moderates from this wing established a political party, Meimad, led by Rabbi Michael Melchior, with the avowed intention of removing religion from party politics and expressing consistent support for the main centre-left parties committed to the peace process.[25] Though OzveShalom and Meimad are small, they have both proven to be influential political actors, and draw a significant proportion of their support from moderates within the religious settler establishment. Melchior has been a key player within the international efforts at forging agreements between Middle Eastern religious leaders within the Alexandria Process, a Church of England-initiated inter-religious dialogue programme formally launched in Alexandria in 2002, co-sponsored by Muslim authorities in Egypt and the Gulf and drawing in religious figures of the three faiths from across the region. The programme's Muslim dialogue partners in the Palestinian territories, such as Bassam Jarrar, represent the tendency within the Islamist movement most open to working with the Palestinian Authority to forge a settlement with Israel.

Religion and the Search for Peace through Religious Dialogue

One of the prizes sought through this marriage of inter-religious dialogue and political negotiation is a workable resolution of the conflict over Jerusalem. To their surprise, the Palestinian delegation at the second Camp David meeting of 2000 found that the secularist Israeli Labour Party under Ehud Barak vehemently rejected the suggestion that Israeli Jews have no real religious or historic feeling for the Temple in Jerusalem.[26] Barak himself appeared equally surprised by the forceful rebuttal he received from his secularist Palestinian counterparts when he suggested a synagogue be placed within the Temple Mount complex.[27] Continuing disagreement over the Jewish holy sites in Jerusalem is one of only two major issues unresolved in the final status negotiations, together with a solution of outstanding problems relating to the rights of Palestinian refugees.

One of the key initiators of the Alexandria Process, Rabbi Menahem Fruman, has been the most prominent proponent of the need for a religious 'negotiating track', particularly to solve the problems associated with assigning sovereignty to the different parts of the Temple Mount complex. While key advisers to the negotiators have sought to defuse the potential for conflict by dividing the complex into separate areas and balancing national claims to each, Fruman argues instead for a joint administration of the entire complex by a committee of representatives of the three religions, on the basis that sovereignty of the holy sites belongs to God.[28] Israeli negotiators have not been favourably disposed to Fruman's concept. However, the proposal has received a certain amount of appreciative attention from religious peacemakers for whom the proposal reflects the value of religious symbols in conflict resolution.

Historically, a number of religious figures have presented themselves as mediators with respect to other aspects of the political conflict. From the 1930s, the most prominent group were the European Jewish exponents of inter-religious dialogue surrounding Martin Buber and Judah Leib Magnes, favouring a religious renewal in the context of a binational Jewish-Arab state.[29] The binational option, which had never drawn support from more than a minority on either side, was effectively buried in the aftermath of the 1967 war. When religious peace movements again began to flourish within all three communities in the 1980s, they coalesced instead around the need to press for a two-state solution and focused on human rights activities which demonstrated the adverse effects of occupation on both Palestinian and Israeli society.[30] The Palestinian Christian communities, increasingly embattled within both Israel and the territories, also increasingly presented themselves from this time as natural mediators, as bridges between Israel and Palestine.[31] It is a difficult role for a small minority to take on in such circumstances, and one for which they have found relatively little appreciation among Jews in Israel or Muslims in Palestine.

Some of the more innovative religious peace initiatives, however, have focused not on the political process of negotiation and agreement, but on the task of creating an atmosphere or culture of mutual respect and acceptance. Indeed, for many Palestinians and Israelis – particularly within the Christian and more secularist Muslim and Jewish communities – the need to separate religion and politics follows from the threat from theocratic parties. By contrast, the partners of the Interfaith Encounter Association agree to avoid 'political' topics in order to be able to draw figures from the religious and political extremes into the process of learning to recognize each other as independent partners to a dialogue based on fuller respect and acceptance.[32] The *tariqat ibrahimiyya*, a more recent initiative, has brought orthodox Jews and Palestinians together in a regular Sufi prayer and dialogue gathering in an attempt to create a symbol of the religious basis on which full mutual acceptance is possible.[33]

The Alexandria Process initially concentrated on drawing religious leaders from Israel and its Arab neighbours together to condemn the killing of civilians by religious extremists.[34] Leading Israeli and Palestinian partners in the Alexandria Process are now concentrating on broadening the circle in which encounters take place with younger religious leaders whose influence may better be felt through their role in their own communities than through engaging from the outset in public declarations. This less political dialogue is designed to impact upon groups on both sides which have become habituated to the common notion that the other party to the conflict only understands the language of force or violence. A sort of dialogue, conducted at a distance between extremists on both sides, has always maintained that the conflict is a result of fundamental differences between religious cultures: Israeli Jews, according to one version, value peace and life more than Muslim Arabs; Muslim ideologues correspondingly argue that their willingness to die for their cause will prove stronger than the will of their Jewish enemies to live amidst such a high level of civilian and military casualties. The deaths of civilians on both sides in the two *intifadas* have led to a widening circle of Jews, Christians and Muslims willing to make sympathy visits to the families of victims on 'the other side', notably including settlers and their Arab neighbours, designed to counter the cycle of violence associated with this competition between religious civilizations.[35] The initiator and many of the members of the Bereaved Parents' Circle, which encompasses parents whose children were engaged in military or other violent activities, are also religious Jews and Muslims.[36] While the funerals of martyrs on both sides are used by hardliners to stoke conflict, some 500 families have banded together within the Parents' Circle to show that their suffering and loss may also provide a mandate for making peace.

Conclusions

The credibility of the notion that religions can make peace in the Middle East turns to some extent on whether we focus on the battle over modernity or the choices religious actors can make. The notion of a combat between the liberal, secularist world order and fundamentalist opposition movements is strengthened in so far as advocates of a liberal or fundamentalist perspective believe there is no alternative to force, that the enemy only understands the language of force – a mantra for extremists on both sides of the conflict. But this may be understood differently in the context of the war of words among Israeli political forces and amongst their Palestinian and Arab counterparts. The most extreme religiously-inspired groups prove to have the most eclectic propaganda programmes, validating material and perspectives from secular nationalist factions which they otherwise oppose. They compete with these forces for popular support, and on this ground they have historically shown themselves capable of pragmatic change. If religious peace initiatives have thus far had little impact on the political peace process, it reflects in part the difficulty of maintaining a faith in the peace process at the present time, but it also reflects the domination of negotiations to date by determined secularists. Distinctive religious visions of a faith-based peace, drawing on the symbols of the three faiths, impress some Middle Easterners more than others. The success of religious peace initiatives in the Middle East depends rather more on the degree to which religious proponents of further peace initiatives gain acceptance as responsible political actors, capable of realistic assessment of the general interest as well as that of their own communities.

2

ISLAM AND RECONCILIATION: TRADITIONS, CONTEXTS AND CONTEMPORARY PRACTICES

David Herbert

But indeed if any show patience and forgive, that would truly be
an exercise of courageous will and resolution in the conduct of affairs.
(Qur'an, Surah 42:43)

This quotation is cited by Muhammad Abu-Nimer (2003) as one of three Qur'anic texts recited at the opening of a reconciliation ceremony (*sulhah*) that he witnessed between two clans in a rural Palestinian village in 1998. Hundreds of villagers gathered in the main square to witness the ceremony, which served to re-integrate members of a clan who had been exiled seven years previously, after one of them committed a double murder.[1] The reconciliation ritual represented the culmination of a three stage process, which began with the victim's family receiving an *atwah*, a sum of money indicating their acceptance of a state of truce (*hudnah*), during which the affair was investigated, and undertaking not to seek revenge during this period. After the investigation, negotiations were able to take place leading eventually to the re-acceptance of the family of the offender.

'Clan' or 'family' in this context is defined as a patronymic extended family of five generations descended from a single grandfather.[2] In this context, a central social value is honour/shame (*'ird*), which might be understood as a right to respect or equal dignity, and in which public recognition of this right plays an important role.[3] If honour is lost – for example by the violation (e.g. murder, rape) of a relative, the victim's family is dishonoured, and to restore face must take revenge. But here a cultural system of dispute resolution has developed, drawing heavily on Islamic texts and traditions but building on pre-existing tribal traditions, and which seek to contain the dangers of spiralling revenge killings through practical and symbolic methods. These include the acceptance of a payment as part compensation and agreement to a process of arbitration, the public giving of an apology by the perpetrator's family, and often the voluntary waiving of further payments by the victim's family in return, itself interpreted as a sign of strength.

This vignette provides one answer to the question asked in the title of this volume: *Can Faiths Make Peace?*, suggesting that in textual sources, historic practice, and in at least some contemporary cultural traditions 'Islam' can indeed be mobilized to make peace. Indeed, Abu-Nimer (1996, 2003) points to a range of parallel examples across the contemporary Middle East, as well to many cases of attempts to work with Western-developed methods of conflict resolution developed in Middle Eastern contexts. However, this kind of answer to the question also raises a number of further questions.

How does the structure of clan hierarchy and the power relations embedded in it translate into urban and urbanizing contexts, in which traditional family relations are challenged by new economic circumstances, and the presence of alternative value systems? These traditional practices rely heavily on respect for elders as third party mediators in disputes. This means that they normally have a conservative orientation, aimed at restoring rather than changing existing power relations, and hence, as Abu-Nimer acknowledges, tend 'to function primarily as a social control mechanism.'[4] This can particularly disadvantage poor families and women.

What if the feuding parties aren't Muslims, as they may well not be in a Palestinian, Syrian or Egyptian village? How do other parties – such as state authorities and Islamist groups – view these traditional practices? How does the discourse of reconciliation here articulate with the discourses used to express and order peaceful relations in modern state and international systems, such as those of human rights? And how does the local level of reconciliation here – between clans – relate to the level of reconciliation perhaps suggested by this volume's sub-title, 'Holy Wars and the Resolution of Religious Conflicts', which seems to imply a larger, political, perhaps even international field of operation?

In this chapter I shall argue that the answers one produces to these questions depend in part on the broader framework one uses to understand the relationship between religion and modernity. I recognize that monolithic concepts of modernity and modernization, and indeed of religion, are highly problematic if not entirely discredited, not least by data gathered from the Middle East. For example, the theory of secularization which links religion and modernization predicts that the processes of social differentiation, societalization and rationalization attendant on urbanization, industrialization and the spread of rationalized transport and communication systems, will progressively erode the social functions of religion.

Yet, even allowing for the exceptions of cultural transition and defence written into some recent versions of this theory, it would appear to founder against the rock of resurgent religious activism in political, social and even economic spheres across the Middle East, for these seem to be neither purely defensive nor transitional phenomena. However, I shall argue that while the secularization thesis is too monolithic in its conception of the interaction between modernization processes and cultural traditions, nonetheless what sociologists traditionally do, which is to seek to discern from a range of sources patterns of interaction between structural and cultural phenomena within and across societies, can still be helpful in enabling us to get a grip on the myriad questions that lurk behind the question 'Can faiths make peace?'

Religion and Agency

First, it will be useful to think about the ways in which agency is ascribed to religion in different discourses. The volume title question again provides a useful starting point. The question 'Can religions make peace?' may be taken to imply further questions about the capacity, coherence and disposition of religious traditions. Thus, 'Do religions have the capacity to make peace?' (assuming that they would want to), and 'Would they want to?' (assuming that they have sufficient agreement, organization and coherence for such a question to be meaningfully answered). Certainly, in spite of the increasing prominence given to religions (and especially Islam) in the analysis of contemporary conflicts, the political significance of religion as an independent variable remains strongly contested, both in terms of capacity and coherence. For example, Fred Halliday, a leading international relations scholar writes:

> [N]o...essential Islam exists: as one Iranian thinker put it, Islam is a sea in which it is possible to catch any fish one wants. ...[t]he answer as to why this or that interpretation [is] put on Islam resides...not in the religion and its texts but in the contemporary needs of those articulating an Islamic politics.[5]

The implication of this for answering this volume's title question would seem to be that religions do not themselves make anything, peace or war – religions are rather the masks worn by actors with real, political interests driven by contemporary needs. In this account there is no hermeneutical circle for contemporary Islamists, just a one-way raid of the Qur'anic treasure trove. But is the Islamic tradition such a passive victim of its interpreters, whether jihadists or democrats? Does the presence of fundamental disagreement over the reading of a tradition necessarily imply that the interpretations of readers are reducible to their political interests or socio-economic background?

In his study of what he describes as the 'Islamic Trend' in Egypt in the mid-1990s anthropologist Gregory Starrett provides what seems to me to be the best rebuttal of this kind of reductionism, and the basis for the kind of analysis which can reinvigorate sociological tradition by linking ethnography with a careful consid-

eration of wider structural trends. In a manner reminiscent of the approach of
cultural anthropologist Clifford Geertz,[6] Starrett shows that religion is more than
just a resource used by people for other ends, which are presumed to be secular.
Rather, religion may also frame how people conceive of life, thus setting the stage
for how they act upon it. Thus Starrett writes:

> If we are to make sense of [the growth of the Islamic Trend] within the
> institutional context of Egyptian society, we cannot dismiss religious
> concerns as benighted survivals of earlier social stages, or merely
> "inflammations" symptomatic of social pathology and political strife.
> Instead, we must see them as perennial questions which persist in an
> active manner, adapting and reproducing themselves within and be-
> tween generations through increasingly complex interactions with insti-
> tutions and communications media whose own advent was supposed to
> reduce rather than increase the influence of religious ideas in society.[7]

How has this process come about? Starrett rejects accounts which focus on
rural-urban migration per se, in the spirit of Ferdinand Tonnies' (1855–1936) and
Max Weber's (1864–1920) *Gemeinschaft/Gesellschaft* distinction,[8] first because such
distinctions break down where new technologies and rationalized practices
penetrate the rural environment, and second because the Egyptian data does not
reveal any significant correlation between those drawn to religious activism and
distinct class interests.[9]

Instead, he focuses on the role of education, noting that 'the Egyptian public
school gives both urban and rural children the opportunity for a "traditional
upbringing", presenting to growing citizens models of personal virtue, social
cohesion and political triumph that tie Islamic symbols in a systematic way to the
complexities of modern life.'[10] In the process, 'although immense disparities remain, schooling can in fact flatten out some of the differences between the experiences of different social classes in a way that Weber…could not have foreseen.'[11]
Thus he traces the modernization of Egyptian education back to Muhammad Ali's
reform of the *kuttab* (village schools for religious instruction) in the early nineteenth century, in a way that eventually produced a supply of literate and technically educated recruits for the military and civil service.

Later, colonial administrators brought practices from late Victorian Britain, in
particular the use of religious education to instil the virtues of hard work and
obedience to authority, following the lead of educational reformers such as the
Quaker Joseph Lancaster, who argued that 'the Koran [sic] might be made, like the
Bible, a means of imparting moral truth combined with instructive history.'[12]

Although the path was not a straightforward one, the extent to which this
strategy was ultimately successful is manifest in the current curriculum in Egyptian
public schools, in a process that Starrett describes as the 'functionalization' of
religion, in which:

[t]he ideas, symbols, and behaviors constituting "true" Islam [come] to be judged not by their adherence to contemporary popular or high traditions, but by their utility in performing social work, either in furthering programs of social reform or in fulfilling the police functions that Europeans attributed to education as such.[13]

In this curriculum, children learn the *Qur'an* not in the traditional sequence, but in bite-sized chunks which are thematically grouped,[14] often linked to a key moral lesson. There is a developmental sequence programmed into learning, following the same evolutionary logic of developmental psychology built into Western educational systems. Throughout the curriculum, and indeed more widely in a range of literature, the complementary relationship between Islam and modern science is stressed. Starrett highlights three ways in which this occurs. First, the use of new technologies to support the religious system, examples of which include loudspeakers for prayer, audio cassettes of Qur'anic recitation and teaching, and using science to calculate the exact times of prayers.[15] Second, new technologies are legitimated by Islamic principles: medical technologies including 'in vitro fertilization, plastic surgery and birth control' may, when 'properly bounded with certain limits...protect or further divine interests by correcting accidental errors or by satisfying other legitimate goals of the individual, family or community.'[16] Third, Islamic concepts and practices are presented as being confirmed by modern science, including *wudu* (ritual washing).[17]

Thus far it would seem that the colonial administrators have mostly had it their own way, as their policies were pursued by successive post-independence governments to the same end of producing a compliant and technically competent work force. A process of 'internal secularization' would seem to have occurred, in which the religious system has been rationalized and harmonized in line with modern educational and scientific principles. Religion has remained influential in other social systems, but only at the expense of the transformation of its contents to fit the rationalized structure of the modern world system. However, all is not as it seems. First, competence in the use of modern technologies does not necessarily entail a decline in belief in supernatural agencies. Rather, people seem perfectly capable of managing to believe both in the spirit world and in science. So also in Egypt:

> functionalization occurs without the desacralization of the material, so that the process described by Durkheim described earlier in this century as one of the goals of the modern educational system is subverted. Naturalistic and materialistic explanations coexist with supernatural ones, for Muslims perceive the two as noncontradictory. The "real" reasons for religious practices do not strip off their theological cloaks. Since God is concerned with the welfare of the Muslim community, the presumptions of Islam are not only beneficial, but manifestly rational.[18]

Furthermore, as well as creating a workforce fit for service in a modern industrial society, teaching the population to apply Islam to everyday life – or 'putting Islam to work' in the title of Starrett's book – has had, other, unforeseen consequences. One dramatic manifestation is that – and remember the context is the mid-1990s when Islamist terrorism in Egypt remained a significant threat – '[t]he young men who bomb and shoot tourist buses, government ministers, and police tend also to be modern educated, with degrees and diplomas in technical subjects.'[19]

According to Starrett, this functionalization of Islamic discourse for opposition political purposes would not have been possible without its prior functionalization within the state education system. But, another, structural change was also necessary for the proliferation of functionalized Islamisms that characterize contemporary Egypt: the rapid expansion in availability and use of communications media that Marshall McLuhan had predicted would have a secularizing effect.[20] Thus, in a process that has been paralleled to the European Reformation, mass literacy, cheap audio-recording, printing, photocopying and the internet has resulted in a proliferation of interpretations of this functionalized Islam.[21] As a result, while the authority of the traditional *ulama* (religious scholars) has not been entirely undermined – and indeed surveys suggest that trust in the *ulama* remains higher than that in most state or commercial institutions – the whole field of religious authority has been substantially reconfigured. As Starrett writes:

> This combination of religion and modern education has proved dangerous to the religious establishment and the government that relies on it for legitimacy, because in the world of mass literacy, mass marketing and mass (not to mention international) communication, the exclusive interpretive authority of local, state-based ulama has been permanently broken. Authority is now more a characteristic of products themselves (sermons, lessons, advice, books, magazines, cassette tapes, computer software) than productive processes (apprenticeship, certification, jurisprudential skill). Who the producer is – when that can be determined – is less important than the marketability of what he has to say.[22]

It would seem that new technologies do not necessarily undermine religious worldviews, nor does an increasing plurality of voices necessarily produce a liberalizing or relativizing effect; for example the growth of publishing in the Arab world resulted in at least five different editions of the infamous European anti-Semitic tract *The Protocols of the Elders of Zion* being available on the streets of Cairo in the early 1990s.[23]

In short, the means of control have turned into the means of dissent, with the result that the tactic of successive governments to pacify and equip the population for modern industrial life by the inculcation of a rationalized form of Islam through a public educational system has embedded Islam in the social system as a central medium of public communication, one which is accessible to a mass public, who increasingly deploy it for their own diverse ends through an increasing variety of communications media.

So where does this extended case study take us in terms of developing an account of the pattern of relationships between religion and modernization processes, in which post-secularization theory might help orient our debates about the capacity of religious traditions for influence in contemporary social systems, and especially of Islam's capacity to make peace in the Middle East? It implies that an understanding of religion as a discursive system providing an orienting framework to make sense of the world and capable of adaptation to incorporate other systems of meaning (e.g. science) and changes in environment (e.g. mass literacy, urbanization, new communications media) is better able to grasp the capacity and limitations of religions to make peace than the political reductionism exemplified by Halliday.

Other studies have also taken the view that religion has a significant role to play in contemporary world systems: for example Manuel Castells (1997) argues that religions can be a source of 'project identity' which can challenge the values of dominant world systems. From a similar systems perspective, Peter Beyer (1994) argues that as holistic systems of meaning not tied to any one functional world system, religions can act as a source of critique of the 'residual problems' of these systems. What Starrett's work adds to these models is an account of how religion can functionalize within modern systems – in this case the educational system, and then electronic communications systems. Indeed, in Egypt the process is much broader, with the growth of Islamic health and welfare organizations and the progressive and controversial Islamization of the legal system. In Habermas' (1987) terms this is not so much a defence of the life-world against colonization by functional systems as a sustained reverse invasion or counter-attack, in which a religious tradition has been vigorously re-articulated across a range of rapidly changing social systems, systems whose extension was supposed by secularization theory to progressively marginalize religion's role.

Are there any limits to this capacity for functionalization? Beyer (1994) has argued that Iran's economic problems in the 1980s and early 1990s suggested limits on the capacity of an integralist[24] Islamic system to function in the global economy. But perhaps more important than answering this question quantitatively in terms of Islam's sheer mobilizing power, is to answer it qualitatively in terms of how that power is exercised. Thus, what space is available for groups who identify themselves as secular or as religious minorities in societies in which Islam is or may become discursively hegemonic? Normatively, Islam's dominant political position in its sphere of influence during the formative classical period, and reflected in the *hadith* literature and early legal tradition, poses a significant ongoing challenge. And the exodus of historic Christian communities from much of the Middle East, numerous examples of attacks on and discrimination against these minorities, and the repeated reference in Islamist writings to the *dhimmi* system, which recognized but systematically subordinated Christians in the Ottoman Empire, are all causes for concern. On the other hand, the treatment of Christians in trades unions run by Islamists in Egypt and the emergence of the Centre Party from the Muslim Brotherhood,[25] are signs of an emergent and more pluralistic Islamism. But are there examples of these kinds of interpretations of Islam exerting social influence at grassroots level?

Islam and Peace Building in Palestine

Modern conflict resolution and peace-building methods, that is those supported by theories and traditions of practice which generally assume a cultural framework characterized by strong individualism, equality between citizens, and often the presumption of a reasonably effective state, have also increasingly been introduced to Muslim majority societies, especially since the end of the Cold War.[26] Sometimes responses to these initiatives by Islamic leaders are very positive; Abu-Nimer cites the example of a professor from the Islamic University in Gaza, who commented at one such workshop, '[t]hose values are often repeated in weekly preaching in the mosque. Your training workshop is only a way of systematically operationalizing those skills, so they become accessible to all segments of society.'[27]

However, Abu-Nimer[28] also lists a number of frequent obstacles and objections encountered in running such workshops in North Africa and the Middle East. The first group of obstacles relates to political and organizational cultures: bureaucratic and patronage-based recruitment policies,[29] patriarchal and other hierarchical assumptions which run contrary the egalitarian ethos of peace-building methods,[30] and a tendency, in imitation of governments, to avoid critical self-examination, focusing instead on blaming external factors for current problems: '[i]nstead of examining the shortcomings and internal problems of schools, factories, government institutions, and family and tribal structures, the masses, at the prodding of the elites, focus on external factors such as colonialism, imperialism, Zionism, and, more recently, globalization.'[31]

Previous periods of Islamic history may be idealized, deflecting attention from practical and critical analysis of the present.[32] The possibilities for local and small scale action may be missed because of the apparent hopelessness of political situations, and a focus on elite political action.[33]

A second raft of issues relates to scepticism about the effectiveness, underlying ideologies, and cultural appropriateness of peace-building and conflict resolution methods. Such methods may be associated with Western countries and agencies, and can be embedded in Western or Christian cultural assumptions. Furthermore, participants may fear that by rejecting violence the individual or community surrenders their rights and search for justice, and is thus caving into Israeli or American pressure.[34] The relative lack of 'justly resolved political conflicts' in Muslim majority societies also creates a credibility problem.[35] Also, a belief in the efficacy of violence – for example, the Arabic saying 'what was taken by force can only be returned by force' was often cited in the Israel/Palestine context.[36]

In spite of these difficulties Abu-Nimer's workshops achieved some successes. Prejudice against non-violent methods has been overcome by pointing to the example of the Prophet, and by explaining that these methods do not rely on idealizations of a conflict-free society, nor require individuals to abandon their search for rights or justice. Furthermore, the disempowerment experienced by participants who find their individual efforts swamped in corruption and politically dead-locked situations can sometimes be countered by focusing on the kinds of helpful actions that are possible. For example, in a workshop in Gaza in 1994, in the wake of deep disillusionment after the failure of the Oslo process to achieve effective progress towards Palestinian autonomy:

> The training team spent one day listening to and identifying problems. After the participants had identifies 113 different problem categories, the training team posed these questions: On which of those problems do the Israelis have the least impact? Can those problems be dealt with? In which areas can you as an individual make an immediate impact? After rearranging their priorities, the participants realized their potential range of influence and agreed to act on that basis.[37]

Appropriately facilitated, such workshops can empower participants by enabling them to break out of established patterns of thinking, and hence possibly also behaviour. Activities aimed at encouraging non-violent methods and constructive engagement in situations of protracted conflict like Israel/Palestine can be seen as preparation for possible future reconciliation.

Abu-Nimer and Groves[38] also relate a story from the West Bank city of Hebron in 1989, which exemplifies the cultural capital in Muslim societies on which peace-building practices can draw. An Israeli patrol had shot and killed a stone-throwing youth, and a member of the patrol had subsequently become separated and found himself surrounded by an angry mob. Frightened, he beat on the door of the nearest house with his rifle, and was admitted by a woman who served him coffee, and waited until it was safe for him to leave. It was the woman's son that the patrol had killed. The story was recounted to a researcher by a Palestinian man who had been asked about the role of religion in the *intifada*. His initial response had been, '[r]eligion and culture enable us to preserve our humanity', and he told the story when prompted to explain, adding '[w]e will never become like the Israelis and hate our enemy; we will offer him hospitality. That soldier could come back again, and the woman would offer him coffee again.'[39] The story illustrates the importance of religiously supported practices which witness to a common humanity and offer a sign of a world of possibility for relationships beyond the military, physical and political barriers separating Palestinians and Israelis.

More formal interfaith groups have also been established, often on Jewish-Israeli initiative, which seek to bring deeply hostile parties into some kind of dialogue. Indeed, there is also a tradition of interfaith dialogue that runs back to the British Mandate period.[40] While this was initially restricted to academic circles, contemporary organizations such as the Israel Interfaith Association and Interfaith Encounter Association (IEA) have much wider reach; for example, the IEA have brought together settlers from the strongly Jewish nationalist National Religious Party with Hamas supporters.[41]

Between individual hospitality and formal attempts to create interfaith dialogue lies a range of ways in which religion plays cultural, social, and political roles that have the potential to promote reconciliation. The main organization responsible for the co-ordination of the *intifada* – the Unified National Leadership of the Up-rising (UNLU) – makes considerable efforts to include and represent both Muslims and Christians in its campaign of resistance to the Israeli occupation. Examples of joint actions include a campaign of fasting led jointly by Orthodox Christian priests and Muslim *imams*, protest marches led by both religious leader-ships, and UNLU publications use of the phrase 'church and mosque' to emphas-ize unity.[42]

Conclusion

In conclusion, I have tried to develop a framework for understanding religious influence in the contemporary Middle East within which it is possible to answer the question 'can Islam make peace?' in a context-sensitive way, but which none-theless links particular contexts to broader social processes. I have argued that understanding religions as evolving cultural systems shaping the life-worlds of individuals and communities, and able to functionalize within modern social systems, makes sense of the contemporary mass-mobilization of religion in a society like Egypt in a way that neither secularization theory nor political reduction-ism can. Such an approach recognizes the shifting grounds of religious influence, away from the main historic institutions, though these remain important, and towards forms of 'discursive' religion communicated through a range of media, and functionalized across society in a number of institutional settings.

Thus I have tried to make some sense of a world in which no new Urban II is likely to call for a fresh Crusade, yet in which the words of a civil engineering grad-uate, Osama bin Laden, can find enough resonance to inspire spectacular acts of violence across the world, and initiate a conflict described by the American president as a 'monumental struggle of good and evil.'[43] It is a world in which the potential for Islam to make use of the resources for reconciliation within its tradi-tion is substantial, but in which the obstacles to realizing that potential are also formidable. Understanding that religion is a powerful and ambivalent cultural force that can shape the human imagination and reproduce itself in modern social sys-tems is one step towards understanding how that positive potential might best emerge.

3

RELIGIONS, HATREDS, PEACEMAKING AND SUFFERING

Victor J. Seidler

Histories

Religions can find it hard to make peace within their own traditions so that historically they have often projected their fears and uncertainties onto 'other traditions' against which they define themselves. Within the West there has been a particular intensity in the struggles between different Abrahamic traditions – Judaism, Christianity and Islam – that have often disavowed their connections with each other and so shaped a fear of the other. A dominant Christianity has often denigrated and preached contempt for those it later recognized as brothers, though only after traditions of Christian anti-Semitism helped produce conditions that made the Holocaust possible. Finding it difficult to learn from Eastern spiritual traditions, Western traditions have been deeply implicated within imperial and colonial projects that have sought to convert 'uncivilized others' whose spiritual traditions had been defined as lacking. Not only have the difficulties Western traditions have faced in coming to terms with their own histories of empire and colonial violence been displaced into conflicts in other parts of the world, particularly in the Middle East, but echoes of the Crusades still haunt relationships between Islam and the West.

Religious traditions have sometimes proved helpful to peacemaking especially where they have been able to acknowledge the violent histories they carry. But they have also shaped their own fundamentalisms that too often denigrate 'the other' as an enemy that has to be defeated. It is only through beginning to take historical responsibilities for destructions carried out in their names, that diverse religious traditions can begin to hear the voices of those who have suffered. Often they were framed within patriarchal traditions that have too often assumed they were the bearers of a singular truth. This has made it difficult to make real the tolerance and pluralism they otherwise value. Given that European modernities have too often been shaped within the terms of a secularized Christianity, they have also devalued the voices of others who have been regarded as 'less than human' because of their 'race', gender or sexuality. Sometimes it is a mother's pain that can remind ruling masculinities of the sufferings they are otherwise deaf too. But this means learning to listen to different voices.

Voices

Amoz Oz, writer and novelist was quoted in *The Independent* on the 60th anniversary of the 'liberation' of Auschwitz saying 'I don't like the word Holocaust because it signifies a natural or divine event. It was the largest organized crime in history – and the crime begins with words. A language of hatred is a danger, not necessarily for Jews, but for whoever is targeted. Each time language is used like an axe we should act because soon killing will follow.'[1] For Raul Hilberg, author of *The Destruction of the European Jews*, it was the critical distinction in Hitler's Germany drawn between 'Aryan' and 'non-Aryan' that proved lethal as it became used like an axe. The crimes began as administrative decisions that were made on the basis of language.[2]

But for years leading up to the Second World War anti-Semitism was deemed a respectable opinion in the ruling houses of Europe, and political parties were able to campaign on anti-Semitic terms. Anti-Semitism did not have to be masked or invoked in coded language because people could be quite open about racial and anti-Semitic language. Racial categories were part of a European cultural inheritance, as Kant's *Geography* makes clear. If it remained in tension with a universal discourse of human rights and Kant's moral theory, this was far from obvious.[3] In the shadows of Auschwitz we have learnt something different, but we are still reticent to rethink the language and cultural inheritances that made Auschwitz possible in the heart of Europe. Traditions of Christian anti-Semitism had their part to play in teaching a tradition of contempt and refusing to explore their own languages that saw Judaism as having been 'superseded' and thereby unable to present a viable spiritual response to the present.[4]

As Jean-Paul Sartre began to grasp in *Anti-Semite and Jew*,[5] there was an implicit intolerance to forms of collective identity within the tolerances being claimed within a rationalist European modernity. This meant Jews would be welcomed out of segregation in ghettoes as 'free and equal' individual citizens as long as they were ready to disavow their collective existence as a people. Within Western Europe at least, as Emmanuel Levinas explored, Jews could belong as individual citizens as long as they were ready to become 'like everyone else'. Jews as 'others' could become 'the same' as long as they accepted that their Jewishness was a matter of individual religious belief that could be practised in private alone.[6] Was this itself a mask for anti-Semitism – a way that Napoleon recognized that Jews as individuals could belong as long as they disavowed their collective identities as Jews? But this was effectively no different to the suspicion that fell, within traditions of Enlightenment rationalism, on other forms of collective consciousness, since class, gender, 'race' or ethnic consciousnesses were equally anathema. Paradoxically though the 1970s and 80s were characterized by a revival of identity politics, postmodern social and cultural theories have often aspired to think beyond categories of 'race', 'gender' and 'sexuality', fearing that they so often foreclose possibilities for individual change and transformation. But this can threaten an historical awareness of how memories also silently shape conflicts in the present.

Another Israeli voice, the peace activist Uri Avneri, talking in the difficult days of the present, after years of *intifada* and Palestinian resistance to occupation, recognizes that:

> The Holocaust overshadows everything the Israeli people think and do. Our attitude is conditioned by the Holocaust. It conditions Israel to justify any means because compared with the Holocaust any bad things we do are negligible by comparison. It is a standard of comparison that gives a kind of moral permit to do anything. In a way we are still victims of the Holocaust today but in a different way. It twists our outlook on things.[7]

This is to recognize anti-Semitism as a mask for perpetrating injustice in relation to the occupied territories. It is the way that the Holocaust still works to disfigure, partly because of the difficulties of coming to terms with its traumatic histories. Sharon is able to use this to his own advantage in suggesting that anti-Zionism has always to be understood as a mask for anti-Semitism.

On the 60th Anniversary he did this by pointing to a painful reminder and then drawing his own somewhat paranoid conclusion: since they will always hate us, we should not concern ourselves with international opinion. As he framed it, '[t]he Allies knew of the annihilation of the Jews and did nothing. Israel learnt that we can trust no one but ourselves. The phenomenon – of Jews defending themselves and fighting back – is an anathema [to] the new anti-Semites.'[8] The West was ready to remember 60 years later, but it did not really want to remember how little was done to rescue European Jewry at the time. Jewish communities so often felt abandoned by their neighbours and the states that were supposedly committed to defend them. Somehow as citizens they seemed dispensable. Was this a mask for anti-Semitism?

For years before 1948 there were many views in Jewish communities in relationship to Zionism and there were numerous movements, for instance, Bundist movements in Eastern Europe that were fiercely anti-Zionist. There are many Jews who consider themselves to be anti-Zionist but after the experiences of the Holocaust and the establishment of Israel as the Jewish national home in 1948 Zionism became hegemonic. Often unable to deal with traumatic histories of the recent past, young Jews were taught to identify Israel with the future and there was little recognition that the refugee camps had been created through the events of 1948 – rather it was as if they had just always been there while Israel/Palestine was presented as an empty space waiting to be cultivated as the desert was to be turned green. There were different Zionist movements and visions of national coexistence.[9]

Demonization

Ian Kershaw argues that Auschwitz 'warns us where the demonisation of minorities or those labelled "undesirable" can lead in the hands of a ruthless modern state.'[10] He recognizes how Auschwitz has to be understood, not as an aberration, but as Bauman's *Modernity and the Holocaust* argued as part of modernity. But in this way the Holocaust provides a challenge to the intellectual traditions in the West that tended to reorganize in the post-war period as if the Holocaust had not really happened. In contrast to the First World War intellectual traditions were not shattered but Germany came to carry the blame, as if eugenics and the forms of anti-Semitism and racism that it masked had not been central to the eugenics projects of nation states. In their different ways they were determined to weed out weaknesses, so that the state could be strengthened and so compete more effectively.

Though the Holocaust is now remembered it is difficult to recognize that it was barely acknowledged until the mid 1980s. The questioning of ethnocentric intellectual traditions that, in Theodor Adorno's words, have made Auschwitz thinkable, are still developing.[11] We still need to explore connections between the diverse masking of racisms and anti-Semitisms and the inheritances of slavery and colonialisms that were for so long legitimated through dominant Christian traditions. Rather than treat these as separate histories the difficult questions they raise for dominant Western intellectual traditions have gradually taken their place on intellectual agendas.

As Simone Weil recognized in *The Need for Roots* this means interrogating intellectual traditions within the West and the distinctions between the Humanities and the Sciences.[12] She insisted that fascisms needed to be understood not simply as masking class relations or as aberrations within Enlightenment rationalism, but as integral to Western cultures in its relationship to other cultural traditions. We still tend to think of genocide and massacres as 'savage acts' that mark the breakdown of civilization and still have to come to terms with the ways Nazism's extermination policies were developed at the heart of European culture. For whatever reasons, the Holocaust did happen and Jews were murdered in millions. Whether this means they have somehow earned the right to self-determination can be difficult for some to concede, especially where they are suspicious of nationalisms.

We might have wished for history to turn out differently. We have learnt with Walter Benjamin that not even the dead will be safe from the enemy if he wins, and there have been many dead on both sides in the Israel/Palestine conflict.[13] Possibly, it is through honouring the sufferings on both sides and remembering what each side has often chosen to forget, that a path to peace can hopefully be

explored. But if justice is to be achieved there has to be compromise and Israel has
to recognize the power it has in the situation and the injustices of occupation. It
also has to appreciate that criticisms of the government of Israel are not masks for
anti-Semitism, though claiming that Israel has no right to exist or that the Jews
have no right to self-determination can be a mask for anti-Semitism.

But this involves recognizing that the Palestinians have also been asked to pay a
price for the sufferings that were perpetrated in Europe during the Holocaust. But
as Rabbi Michael Melchior has argued:

> But we have to teach Auschwitz in the right way, that when we deal with
> anti-Semitism we are also fighting for dignity for every human being... We
> should have peace with the Palestinians and they should have a state sooner
> rather than later. But to link the (Israeli-Palestinian conflict) with the Holo-
> caust, as is done by all sides in the debate, is also to trivialise the Holocaust.[14]

It can also be to demonize Israel in ways that can mask anti-Semitism.

Can Religions Make Peace?

When we consider the histories of religious wars and remember the Crusades and
the destruction they wrought for Jewish and Islamic communities both in Europe
and the Middle East it seems easier to conclude that religions make war more easily
than they make peace. If religious tolerance emerged in Europe as an ideal it was
painfully wrought through a balance of religious forces. For many who adopt a
militant atheism it becomes difficult to begin to take seriously the question of
whether religions can help to make peace, even if they no longer have the power to
make it on their own. For within the terms of an Enlightenment vision of modernity that has shaped intellectual traditions within the West it can be difficult not to
think that religious belief is always part of the problem that needs to be 'explained'
and can never be part of a solution, especially to the intractable issues of social
justice, military occupation and resistance in Israel/Palestine.

Antonio Gramsci in the *Prison Notebooks* helps us understand that rather than
treat religion as a form of 'irrationality' – as a form of false consciousness that
would somehow disappear when tested against the 'truths' of a scientific Marxism,
itself echoing a modernist idea that faith would inevitably give way to reason – we
have to learn how to engage with religious belief.[15] A sense of time shaped, as
Gramsci engaged with Catholic traditions in the Italian south, a notion that this
world was inevitably a world of suffering and penance that had to be endured
in the present in the hope of an eternal life in the future. This echoes aspects
of Islamic fundamentalisms that preach sacrifice through martyrdom within an
'otherworldly ethic' that offers rewards in a world to come. Religious traditions
have their own forms of martyrdom that need to be carefully engaged with.

Jewish fundamentalisms that lay claim to land as 'given by God' and therefore
needing to be defended at any cost have been dangerous and difficult to contest
within a fragmented religious tradition. In June 2004 there was public concern over

a remark by Rabbi Avigdor Nebentzal, a settlement supporter and rabbi in the Jewish Quarter in the Old City of Jerusalem, that 'according to Jewish law, anyone who turns over territories that are part of the Land of Israel to non-Jews is subject to *din rodef*[16] – the religious rationale cited by Yigal Amir after he killed Prime Minister Rabin. *Din Rodef* (law of the pursuer) calls for the killing of anyone who endangers a Jewish life. Rabbi Nebentzal went on to emphasize that his remark was meant only as a general comment on Jewish law, and that he hoped that 'none of my students carries out such an act of this sort.'[17] Far-right extremists are organizing against the planned withdrawal of settlements from Gaza.

Some of these students and many of the settlers are not born in Israel but have migrated from Brooklyn in the USA or North West London, drawn into a religious fundamentalism through the uncertainties and spiritual poverty of modernity. Late capitalist societies have found it difficult to explore moral traditions that can provide an alternative to consumerism, and given the crises on the left in the face of the fall of the Soviet Union, religion can seem to provide a clarity and sense of direction that can assuage the psychic fears of a postmodern culture. But often the secular terms of intellectual disciplines can make it difficult to engage critically unless we can also appreciate the moral appeal of diverse religious and spiritual traditions. Listen to young Moroccan men talking about the appeals of Islamist ideas as an alternative to the greedy consumerism offered by American capitalism, which will leave them with an abiding sense of lack and poverty because they know that only a small minority could ever emulate the consumer images they absorb through the global media.[18]

But there is also the arrogance of modernity that has sustained the attack on Iraq against the wishes of so many in the West. This was shown in the righteousness of Blair's language at the Lord Mayor's banquet in November 2003 when he was hoping to undercut critics before President Bush's visit. Iraq, he said, was 'the battle of seminal importance for the early twenty-first century. It will define relations between the Muslim world and the west.'[19] As Salim Lone, former director of communications for the UN mission in Iraq, pointed out without wanting to underestimate the impact of the current war and occupation, he was right but a decade late, because:

> It was the first Gulf War in 1991 and the accompanying sanctions and stationing of US troops in Saudi Arabia that had driven deep cleavages between Islam and the West. More important, it had given rise to the age of global terror – beginning with the first World Trade Centre bombing in 1993.[20]

The current war has made the US a reviled power in the Muslim world.

Sufferings of Others

As Salim Lone reminds us, '[m]any had warned of unprecedented Muslim fury if Iraq were attacked' and the most punitive sanctions in modern history that destroyed Iraqi society and killed at least half a million children, was not forgotten when the Americans came again after having betrayed the Marsh Arabs and Kurds who had risen against Saddam Hussein. Lone recognizes that the depth of this anti-US animus is recent since the Muslims and Arabs gravitated towards the US for decades but 'even the most moderate now see the US as bent on crushing Islam.'[21] He recognizes that '[t]he rise of such militancy is driven by US policies and cannot be glossed over with self-serving assertions that 'they' hate western freedoms and are inherently barbaric and uncivilised.'[22] This echoes the civilizing mission of modernity whereby the 'colonized others' who was deemed to be 'closer to nature' could not be reasoned with because the only language they supposedly responded to was the language of power and violence. This is also echoed in Israeli responses to the Palestinian resistance to an unlawful occupation.

Lone also reminds us that 'merely rolling back the aggressive Bush administration policies will not be sufficient to win Muslim trust'[23] and that:

> In the quest for peace, a just solution to the Palestinian crisis remains a vital priority, but we should discount wishful assertions that ending that conflict will make indirect US occupation over Iraq more acceptable. Over the past 14 years Iraq has for millions replaced Palestine as the touchstone of Muslim pain.[24]

But arrogance of modernity also lies in the failure to appreciate the depths of suffering and humiliation that has been endured through the Israeli occupation so that we need to appreciate cultural differences and the memories of traumatic displacements that stretch back to 1948 and the Catastrophe – Nachba – that followed for so many Palestinians.

Rather than Jewish pain and suffering of the Shoah sensitizing to the pain of others, this has often produced insensitivity to the sufferings of others. Guilty at their own powerlessness to intervene to prevent the destruction of European Jewry at the hands of the Nazis, Israelis often took refuge in heroic masculinities that hardened them against recognizing what their policies were doing to others. Often unable to experience vulnerability they feared any signs of 'weakness' and reassured themselves that it was only overwhelming force that 'Arabs'/Palestinians could respond too. The occupation has threatened the moral resources of Judaism and has fostered its own fundamentalism.

Fadi, an Israeli/Palestinian Arab whose voice is heard in the play *The Arab-Israeli Cookbook* by Robin Soans, a verbatim play from the words he collected, says:

> If there's one place in Israel where there's been any hope, it's Haifa…a degree of Jews and Arabs living in harmony…finding a way of peaceful co-existence; and of all the places in Haifa, Maxim's was the most symbolic. It was co-owned by Jews and Arabs…what made it special is what it stood for…it's what me and my friends wanted to be part of…this attempt to buck the trend.

...The force of the blast was enough to blow people's heads off...The bomber was a 29 year old lawyer...a woman. In the previous three months her cousin, her brother and I think her fiancé had all been killed in Israeli army raids. I know the western attitude is, it doesn't matter how long the death-list, she should somehow pull herself together and carry on. But that's the trouble...it's no good looking at this in a western way...For a woman from the Arabic culture, the ties to her male relatives are what gives her her strength, her energy, her status, her reason to live. Here loyalty is absolute. To have one of these ties severed unexpectedly would be tragic for her; two, catastrophic; three...to have three destroyed...I tell you...if she was born like a white sheet of paper, there would be a microdot of it which wasn't now covered in black shit. She would be dehumanised, that's the word – dehumanised – nothing left except an overwhelming need to advent blood and end her own life. Her tragedy was that with only grief and agony left in her heart there could be no other way of resolving it; our tragedy was that she chose as her target the one beacon of hope. But she hasn't killed my optimism...[25]

Sacrifices and Peacemaking

If religions are to help making peace, both traditions have to be prepared to listen to each other. Nations have to be ready to make peace and as Uri Sagi, the former head of military intelligence whom Ehud Barak chose to lead the talks with Syria acknowledged, confirming evidence in former US President Bill Clinton's recent autobiography, '[t]he breakdown in trust that happened after the Sheppardstown talks in January 2000 was awful. Syrian Foreign Minister Farouk al-Shara'a said some terrible things about the credibility of the Israelis, and I have to say, unfortunately, he was right. Barak's failure is unforgivable.'[26]

The moral underpinnings of the Jewish State have to be rediscovered if truth is to be restored and a just peace made possible. Harvey Morris writing in the *Financial Times* magazine entitled 'Remember Zion? How a vision of Utopia became a nightmare' paints a graphic picture of how far modern Israel has moved from its humanitarian roots, 'not least the failure to recognize the rights of the other nation in their midst.'[27] It has also produced intense tensions between Ashkenazi and Sephardi that have been difficult to reconcile within an increasingly polarized society between secular and religious Israelis. Morris writes that Zionism has created 'a new and unique Israeli nation, predominantly Jewish but also distinct from the Jews.'[28]

If we follow scripture, Abraham makes peace in two ways, by dividing land and also through making a peace treaty. Jews, Christians and Muslims regard themselves as children of Abraham but they seem incapable of dividing land or making treaties. Israel refuses to acknowledge the power it has with the occupation and though it continually calls for peace, it has often refused the conditions of a 'just peace'. A poem by the Israeli writer Shin Shalom, born in Poland 1904, swears reconciliation with Ishmael, Abraham's son and Isaac's brother, as well as the recognition of shared roots in the revelation of Sinai and the diverse paths traditions have taken.

Ishmael, my brother,
How long shall we might each other?

My brother from times bygone,
My brother, Hagar's son,
My brother, the wandering one.

One angel was sent to us both,
One angel watched over our growth-
There in the wilderness, death threatening through thirst,
I a sacrifice on the altar, Sarah's first.

Ishmael my brother, hear my plea:
It was the angel who tied thee to me…

Time is running out, put hatred to sleep,
Shoulder to shoulder, let's water our sheep.[29]

Karl-Josef Kuschel in *Abraham*, draws upon Sadat's journey to Jerusalem. This peace mission apparently coincided with the sacred Islamic feast of the sacrifice of Abraham, who 'personified a fixed and unshakable belief in ideals which had great significance for humankind.'[30] Sadat had declared 'I come to you today to shape a new form of life and to bring peace on a firm basis. We all love this land, this land of God; all of us, Muslims, Christians and Jews who worship God. God's teachings and commandments of love, honesty, security and peace.'[31] He was remembering connections that fundamentalist traditions would often chose to forget. As Kuschel wants to argue, without bringing in the religious and spiritual dimensions of humanity:

…there will be no trust to give permanence to treaties desired politically and negotiated legally. Indeed a peace policy built on a religious conviction can shape consciences, seize hearts and move former enemies…'Islam' then ceases to be the enemy of the West and the 'West' the enemy of Muslims, the screen on which anxieties, warlike scenarios and apocalyptic dramas are projected.[32]

He also recognizes that a readiness for peace needs its peace symbols…places where Abraham is recalled which can bring people together in dialogue and prayer.[33]

Abraham died at the age of 175, 'an old man full of years' (Gen. 25 7–11), and was buried in the cave of Machpelah, Hebron, where he had previously purchased a piece of land. And not only his son Isaac but surprisingly also his expelled son Ishmael stood at his grave. With this text (Gen. 25 7–11) there is the picture of the reconciliation of brothers who had been made enemies and who yet were capable of standing side by side beside their father's dead body. This has other resonance for Hebron, as al-Khalil is in the occupied territories. Not only have many died during the two *intifadas* but it was where on 25 February 1994 an Israeli settler, Baruch Goldstein, determined to destroy the possibilities of a peace process, forced his way into the Ibrahim mosque firing at Muslims in prayer with 29 left dead and dozens injured. Places carry their own traumatic memories. Hebron was also the place where on 24 August 1929, 67 pious Jews were killed by Arabs.

In an interview, Ben-Chorin, an Israeli peace activist, recognizes that Ishmael and Isaac did not love each other, '[b]ut by the body of their father in the cave of Machpelah in Hebron they mourned together and became reconciled. It is my hope and my prayer that this reconciliation will be repeated.'[34] It will only come with justice and an end to the occupation, but there have been too many dead bodies on both sides. It has been parents on both sides who have lost children who have come together to insist on peace. This is not simply a feature of the Israel/ Palestine conflict but it has also characterized other conflicts where it has been parents, affected by traumatic loss, including those who lost family after 9/11 in New York and the bombings in Bali and Madrid, who have often insisted that revenge will only mean that other families have to bear the sufferings they have been through. We learn that personal pain is often a source of political resistance and a means for peacemaking, reminding religious traditions of their spiritual commitments to peace. Often it is a maternal voice that has initially challenged masculine legitimations of war and the insistence that it is only through violence that the enemy can be defeated.

A Mother's Pain

There is a scene in Michael Moore's film *Fahrenheit 9/11* when Lila Lipscomb talks with an anti-war activist outside the White House in Washington about the death of her 26-year-old son, Michael, in Iraq. A pro-war passer-by does not like what she overhears and announces, 'This is staged!' Ms Lipscomb turns to the woman, her voice shaking with rage, and says: 'My son is not a stage. He was killed in Kabala, April 2. It is not a stage. My son is dead.' Then she walks away and cries: 'I need my son.' Watching Ms Lipscomb doubled over in pain on the White House lawn, Naomi Klein, writer and anti-globalization activist, was reminded of other mothers who have taken the loss of their children to the seat of power and changed the fate of wars.

I was reminded by the reference to 'the seat of power' to the idea that people have to give an account of themselves when they die at the seat of God's throne and to the biblical story of Solomon where he is called upon to dispense justice when two mothers both claim a newborn baby as their own. Justice is often imagined to lie in dispassionate impartiality that can often seem to involve a distance from emotions that might otherwise affect judgement. Solomon suggests that if neither mother is prepared to admit a false claim, then possibly the baby should be divided in two. One of the mothers cries at the very thought and said she would allow the other woman to have the baby rather than allow this to happen. Solomon recognizes that it is the mother who is speaking and he judges in her favour. She would prefer to give up her baby than to see the baby suffer.

Klein was reminded of the mothers of the Plaza de Mayo who gathered every Thursday in front of the Presidential palace in Buenos Aires to protest against the fate of their children who had been 'disappeared' by the military regime during Argentina's 'Dirty War' of 1976–1983. As Klein recognizes they:

> ...revolutionised human rights activism by transforming maternal grief from a cause for pity into an unstoppable political force. The generals could not attack the mothers openly, so they launched fierce covert operations against their organisation. But the mothers kept walking, playing a significant role in the eventual collapse of the dictatorship.[35]

In *Fahrenheit 9/11* Lila Lipscomb stands alone with her fury but other mothers are also coming forward to voice their moral outrage at the losses they have suffered in the military conflict in Iraq. Nadia McCaffrey, a Californian resident, defied the Bush administration's ban on photographs of flag-draped coffins, arriving at air force bases. Earlier photographs had caused disquiet in the administration and they had sought to ban images citing the right of privacy for the families. They did not negotiate with families about what they wanted but assumed the authority to legislate in their name. McCaffrey invited news cameras to photograph the arrival of her son's casket from Iraq. She was able to do this because his remains were being flown into the Sacramento International airport. 'I don't care what (President Bush) wants,' Ms McCaffrey declared, telling her local newspaper: 'Enough war.'[36]

Just as Patrick McCaffrey's body was coming home to California, another soldier, 19-year old Gordon Gentle, from Glasgow, was killed in Iraq. Upon hearing the news, his mother, Rose Gentle, blamed the government of Tony Blair saying: 'My son was just a bit of meat to them, just a number...This is not our war, my son had died in their war of oil.'[37] At the same time a similar sentiment was being voiced by Michael Berg as he was visiting London to speak at an anti-war rally. Since the beheading of his 26-year-old son, Nicholas, who had been working in Iraq as a contractor, Michael Berg has insisted that 'Nicholas Berg died for the sins of George Bush and Donald Rumsfeld.'[38] Asked by an Australian journalist whether such bold statements were 'making the war seem fruitless', Mr Berg responded: 'The only fruit of war is death and grief and sorrow. There is no other fruit.'[39]

As families lose their fear and speak out with great clarity and power, this presents a dangerous challenge to the Bush administration, which as Klein recognizes, 'likes to claim a monopoly on "moral clarity". Victims of war and their families aren't supposed to interpret their losses for themselves.'[40] As Klein appreciates:

Parents and spouses are supposed to accept their tremendous losses with stoic patriotism, never asking whether a death could have been avoided, never questioning how their loved ones are used to justify more killing. At Patrick McCaffrey's funeral last week, Paul Harris, the chaplain of the 579th Engineer Battalion, informed the mourners: "What Patrick was doing was good and right and noble…There are thousands, no millions, of Iraqis who are grateful for his sacrifice."[41]

But Nadia McCaffrey knows better and she insists upon being able to speak for herself. As Klein recognizes, she 'is insisting on carrying her son's own feelings of deep disappointment from beyond the grave. "He was so ashamed by the prisoner abuse scandal," Ms McCaffrey told *The Independent*, "he said we had no business in Iraq and should not be there."'[42] Freed from military censors who prevent soldiers from speaking their minds when alive, Lila Lipscomb has also shared her son's doubts about his work in Iraq. She has given voice to what he was not allowed to say demonstrating the limits of democracy within the army where obedience is so often interpreted as a duty of silence. In *Fahrenheit 9/11*, she reads a letter from Michael mailed home, '[w]hat in the world is wrong with George, trying to be like his dad, Bush. He got us out here for nothing whatsoever. I'm so furious right now, Mama.'

These are not just alternative narratives that construct their own visions of truth, but show a need of for an ethics of truth that can insist on its right to speak directly to power. Fury is an entirely appropriate response yet the American right is forever trying to pathologize anger as something menacing and abnormal, as Klein explains, 'dismissing war opponents as hateful and, in the latest slur, "wild-eyed".'[43] But as she acknowledges this is much harder to do when victims of war begin to speak for themselves and claim their own voices. People find it harder to question a mother or father who has just lost their son or daughter, or the fury of a soldier who knows that he is being asked to kill, and to die, needlessly. First it was the September 11 Families for Peaceful Tomorrows which spoke out against any attempts to use the deaths of their family members in the World Trade Centre to justify further killings. Military Families Speak Out has sent delegations of veterans and parents of soldiers to Iraq, while Nadia McCaffrey is planning to form an organization of mothers who have lost children in Iraq.

Since the Greek tragedies have been staged, mothers have expressed their pain in public in ways that have powerfully moved hearts and minds. As Simon Goldhill, professor of Greek at Cambridge points out in relation to his *Love, Sex and Tragedy*:

Greek tragedy collects everybody together in one place and, on stage, presents them with really difficult problems. The audience is persuaded that there are no easy solutions, that they themselves must do some tough thinking…In assuming they know, they politically lose sight of intellectual humility. That's where the dangers of amnesia come in, of forgetting the world is a complex place. If you live at a superficial level, you will find superficial answers to your life.[44]

Goldhill also reminds us that:

> Democracy has become a brand name of what we do. People have forgotten that, for centuries, England was a monarchy that rejected and despised democracy. When we turn back to Greece we must take note of the direct engagement of the citizens in the democratic process. Now, we appoint people to represent us.[45]

Parents who are speaking out of their suffering and refusing to be silenced are searching for a more direct democratic voice. It is clear in Britain that Tony Blair is paying a heavy price for taking the country to war when so many people were ready to march in the streets against it. Somehow he felt that he had a duty to do what he felt to be right, regardless of what so many people in a democracy felt. There was an arrogance that he could not even recognize in himself and people have not forgiven or forgotten. Blair showed no genuine humility, though he presented himself as ready to listen. People felt that the decision to go to war in support of the Bush administration had already been made so that it was a matter of somehow persuading the public to go along with it.

There was no way of questioning the wisdom of the decision to go to war but a sustained arrogance that has still meant, after the Butler report into the intelligence on which the decision was made and the Hutton inquiry into the circumstances surrounding the death of Dr Kelly, a government scientific advisor, that Blair still refuses to apologize for taking the country to war on an understanding that there were Weapons of Mass Destruction (WMD) ready to target Europe in 45 minutes. The fact that these claims have been disproved so that the arguments for not allowing the United Nations (UN) weapons inspectors more time has been under-mined, has not led to any apologies. Rather, Blair has insisted that the war was still justified to remove an evil dictator. Against all the evidence Blair insists upon the righteousness of the cause, even though this was not the ground on which so many soldiers were to risk their lives. Unlike the United States where 'regime change' had been mentioned as a war aim it had been explicitly denied by Blair. There is a widespread feeling in Britain that Blair can no longer be trusted and that however he chooses to present the results of the Butler report, the evidence has been made clear. He had acted irresponsibly and showed a lack of judgement. It is not a matter of whether he lied or deliberately invoked false intelligence, but that he was concerned to convince people about a decision he had already taken.

Destructions

Once wars and ethnic conflicts begin they have a momentum of their own and it can be difficult to break the cycles of violence, of attack and counter-attack. The hatred of the other that often covers the fear of the other becomes so entrenched, that it is difficult to imagine how peacemaking can succeed. Often it is only when the fires of conflict seem to have exhausted themselves and people recognize that they cannot achieve their goals through violence alone, that they can listen to the claims being made by others. Through the power of the global media people around the world are positioned as witnesses of horrors that a previous generation would only have been able to hear or read about later, when the conflict had moved on. It was the attention of the world's media and the continual resistance of the Palestinians against occupation that forced the Israeli government to consider withdrawing from the settlements in Gaza in August 2005. The settlement movement was forced to concede. On both sides memories were still fresh of the destructions that had been carried out in the name of security. Images of pain wrought by destruction were met by memories of the terrible loss of lives caused by suicide bombings in Israel.

Amid the rubble of dozens of homes that the Israeli army continued to deny demolishing, the wreckage of the tiny, but only zoo in the Gaza strip took on potent symbolism for many of the newly homeless. 'People are more important than animals,' said the zoo's co-owner Mohammed Ahmed Juma, whose house was also demolished in the operation to hunt down Palestinian fighters and weapons-smuggling tunnels running under the border from Egypt:

> But the zoo is the only place in Rafah that children could escape the tense atmosphere. There were slides and games for children. We had a small swimming pool. I know it's hard to believe, looking at it now, but it was beautiful. Why should they destroy that? Because they want to destroy everything about us.[46]

More than 40 people have been killed in the assault, about a third of them civilians according to Chris McGreal writing for *The Guardian*. About 45 buildings were razed by the army in the area, some of them two or three storeys high and housing several families.

> "The blade of the bulldozer hit the room we were sitting in," said Mrs Monsour. "I waved my white headscarf at the soldiers as we pleaded with them to let us go. We were running between the tanks and the shooting and counting the children as we were went to make sure they were all still with us. This is revenge, absolute revenge, for the seven Israeli soldiers killed in Rafah."[47]

But this is not accepted by the Israeli army whose spokeswoman, identified as Eli, told McGreal, '[w]e did not destroy any houses in al-Brazil. There was damage to buildings from fighting. The terrorists activate explosive devices under the road or next to the buildings. These bombs that destroy tanks can easily destroy a house.'[48] But as McGreal has it:

...aside from the accounts of Palestinians who fled their homes, the destruction is not consistent with individual explosions. On al-Imam road, nearly 20 houses in a row were wrecked. There was no sign of a massive explosion, such as a crater in the road or damage to houses standing next to the wrecked buildings.[49]

McGreal also reports that on Tuesday 18 May 2004 the military had dismissed accusations that an Israeli sniper shot two children in the head, claiming they were blown up by a Palestinian bomb. But the bodies of both children were later shown to each have only a single bullet wound to the head. As Chris McGreal reported from Rafah:

> The tiny hole buried under Asma Mughayar's thick black hair. Just above her right ear, is an illusion, according to the Israeli army. So is her family's insistence that Asma, 16, and her young brother Ahmed, were both shot through the head by an Israeli soldier as they fed their pigeons and collected the laundry from the roof of their home in Rafah refugee camp.[50]

But their corpses tell a different story, as do the bodies of other children brought to Rafah's hospital and makeshift mortuaries. Dr Ahmed Abu Nkaria, who pronounced the Mughayar children dead, insists on proving the manner of their killing to McGreal:

> The Israeli propaganda is that they were killed in a work accident – a euphemism for bomb-makers blowing themselves up – these are the kind of lies they tell all the time. They say all the dead are fighters. They say they do not deliberately kill children, but a quarter of the dead from the first day of shooting are children. The evidence is here in the morgue.[51]

Asma's body lies in the hospital mortuary unburied, like all the other dead from Tel al-Sultan, because their relatives are trapped in their homes by a curfew.

Saber Abu Libda, 13, was shot dead by Israeli soldiers after he had left his home in Tel al-Sultan in the morning to find water for his family. Dr Nkaria's finger probes a tiny hole in the small child's back which masks the devastation done to his heart as the bullet shot through it. 'No one can say this child was a fighter. Look at the size of him and look where they shot him – in the back, not coming to attack someone,' the doctor says.[52]

On Wednesday 19 May 2004 the army said armed men made up the majority of ten people killed when an Israeli tank fired into a peaceful demonstration during the ongoing assault on Rafah refugee camp. The army had described the incident as 'very grave', claiming it had only fired warning shots and said there was no intention to harm civilians. 'We were marching down shouting "We need help" as a message to the world, and "No to occupation",' said Hussam Mustafa, a civil engineer, '[t]here was a missile and then people started running back and then there

was another missile right into the crowd.'[53] As McGreal reports, '[i]n fact half of
the victims were children and television footage showed no weapons among the
demonstrators.'[54] More than 40 people were wounded in the demonstration and
the Israeli army has killed 33 Palestinians in Rafah, some of the highest casualties
of the present *Intifada*. 'These are not bullet wounds, they are much worse,' said Dr
Ayad Rubi at Rafah hospital, '…[m]issiles cause so many wounds, to the head, to
the chest, all over.'[55]

The army also initially denied that soldiers deliberately wrecked the zoo. As
McGreal reports:

> The destruction was comprehensive. The fountain and its tiles were a jumble
> of rubble in one corner. There was no sign of the swimming pool… The
> army's explanation evolved through the day. At first it said it had not
> destroyed the zoo, then it said a tank may have accidentally reversed into it.
> By the end of yesterday, the military said its soldiers had been forced to
> drive through the zoo because an alternative route was booby-trapped by
> Palestinian explosives.

> Finally a spokesman said the soldiers had released the animals from their
> cages in a compassionate gesture to prevent them being harmed.[56]

The *New York Times* in its editorial of 20 May 2004 recognizes that, 'Israel
indisputably faces a threat from Hamas cells within Gaza, but it is hard to see how
these sorts of attacks on Palestinians will do anything other an serve as a recruiting
campaign for Hamas.' It also argues that Israel's persistence with its policy 'of
demolishing hundreds of Palestinian homes' looks like 'a heavy-handed form of
collective punishment.' This has 'brought horrifying scenes of death as an Israeli
tank and helicopter opened fire on a group of Palestinian demonstrators, in the
Rafah refugee camp.'[57] Alongside it quotes a revealing editorial from *Ha'aretz* also
from 20 May 2004 reflecting on the same tragic events saying:

> The damage done to Israel's image in the world is immense… The Israeli
> Defence Force (IDF) has always inculcated its soldiers with the belief that
> innocent people must not be hurt… The commanders of the army
> understood, that without a moral basis for its actions, even the best equipped
> army cannot win. These moral values, however, have been badly eroded in
> the long years of occupation and with the action in Rafah, they have suffered
> yet another blow…[58]

Fatima Sharif Hassan fled the Block O neighbourhood of Rafah refugee camp a
week ago as Israel's giant mechanical wreckers tore at the home she shared with
her son and his family. As Chris McGreal reports:

The great grandmother, 75, sought refuge in another section of the camp, al-Brazil, where her daughter lived. Mrs Hassan felt certain it was far enough away from the volatile Israeli security strip and Egyptian border to be safe from the bulldozers.

But yesterday Mrs Hassan who is crippled and suffers from diabetes, had to be hauled through a hole in the wall shortly before the building was brought crashing down. [59]

"We heard the Israeli bulldozers starting to demolish the house over us," she said. "We only escaped because the men knocked a hole in the wall and carried me between the buildings. We lost everything. I lost my false teeth. I lost my money. The neighbours had to give me this scarf to cover my head."[60]

As McGreal reports:

After the destruction of nearly 200 homes in Block O and other parts of Rafah last week, the Israeli government vigorously denied that the goal of its sweep through the camp was to break armed resistance through the widespread demolition of Palestinian homes – even though the army chief of staff said as much on Sunday before a public change of heart… The army says it only destroys the houses of 'known terrorists' or where the buildings are used for as cover for fighting by groups such as Hamas or Islamic Jihad.[61]

According to Jonathan Steele if Israel withdraws from Rafah it will not be because Ariel Sharon is listening to Washington but 'it is more likely to be out of fear that more Israeli soldiers will die. Thirteen have been killed by the Palestinians' armed resistance in the Gaza strip over the last three weeks.'[62] Steele thinks the latest actions in Gaza have been:

…motivated by revenge, cynicism and desperation. As such, they have destroyed the political and moral capital that Sharon briefly acquired when he announced his unilateral plan to close the Israeli settlements in Gaza.

Determined not to let the Palestinians or the world view the withdrawal as a defeat, he chose to wreak as much havoc as he could before the settlements were dismantled. He ordered the murder of Sheik Ahmed Yassin, the leader of Hamas, as well as that of his successor, Abdel Aziz Rantissi, using air strikes which inevitably also killed and wounded bystanders.[63]

Steele recognized that:

Sharon was also trying to use the Gaza withdrawal as a bargaining chip to win international acceptance for his hopes to retain large chunks of the West Bank. George Bush eagerly obliged him in Washington last month with his fulsome endorsement of the notion that up to half of West Bank settlers would be entitled to stay.[64]

Memories

The sights of Rafah are too difficult to bear, writes Meron Benvenisti for the tragedy takes him back to the grim events of 1948 – trails of refugees alongside carts laden with bedding and the meagre contents of their homes; children dragging suitcases larger than themselves; women draped in black, kneeling in mourning on piles of rubble. Writing in the Israeli newspaper *Ha'aretz* he shares that:

> ...in the memories of some of us, whose number is dwindling, arise similar scenes that have been part of our lives, as a sort of refrain that stabs at the heart and gnaws at the conscience, time after time, for over half a century – the procession of refugees from Lod to Ramallah in the heat of Julky 1948; the convoys of residents of Yalu and Beit Nuba, Emmaus and Qalquilya, in June 1967; the refugees of Jericho climbing on the ruins of the Allenby bridge after the six-day war.[65]

Benvenisti is reminded that 'the attackers adopt the same tactics, spread rumours and fire warning shots; and when the residents flee out of fear, the attackers claim that they are not responsible for the flight, but then destroy the homes for, "after all, they are empty and deserted".'[66] Attempting to frame a lesson, he recognizes that:

> Laundered language and sterile military terms camouflage a primitive desire for vengeance and uninhibited militancy. Slogans, such as 'combat heritage', 'righteousness of our path', and 'the most moral army in the world', immunise the soldiers and their commanders from the humanitarian tragedy they are creating.

> The political echelon, supposed to guide the army according to ethical criteria, reveals even cruder tendencies than the army. All they are interested in is Israel's 'image' and condemning the 'hostile media'.[67]

In a reflecting piece, Benvenisti wonders whether:

> If after half a century their enterprise still faces existential threat, this can only mean that they condemned it to eternal enmity, and there is no community that can for years on end survive a violent war for its existence.

And if this is merely a pretext (and operation Rainbow in Rafah was an instinctive reaction that evolved into second nature), we must reflect deeply and sadly on our responsibility for the enterprise that at its start embodied so many exalted ideals.

Is there some 'original sin' that lies at the foundation of the Zionist enterprise? Those who initiated the Rafah operation, and those who executed it, should know that one of the outcomes of their actions will inevitably be the raising of questions about this heresy.[68]

A historical observation about the history of Zionism and the different ways it has been related to on the left might help frame such necessary questions or at least help us appreciate changing contexts in which such questions are raised. Colin Shindler reflecting on British Jews' uneasy relationship with *The Guardian* newspaper observes:

The old left, under Aneurin Bevan, which had fought Fascism alongside the Jews, passionately championed Zionism. The new left, distant from the Holocaust and unaware or unconcerned with the moral and other reasons for the rise of Israel, elevated decolonisation to the top of its agenda in the 1960s. The Palestinians fitted more easily alongside the struggles in Vietnam and Southern Africa than did the Israelis.

Zionism became an inconvenient anomaly, Israel an historical accident… The unease that British Jews currently feel is not about rampant anti-Semitism on the high street, but of a drip-drip de-legitimization of the state of Israel, with the attendant fear that this will be followed by a de-legitimization of the people as a whole.[69]

This is against a background in which, according to *Guardian* writer Martin Woollacott, 'the European media has already shifted from a line which attempts to save Israel from itself to one that calls out to save the world from Israel.'[70] As Shindler comments, '[t]his ominous proposition suggests that the fantasy days are only just beginning.'[71]

Learnings

Michael Berg whose son was murdered in Iraq talks about '[m]y son, Nick, was my teacher and my hero… He quit the Boy Scouts of America because they wanted to teach him to fire a handgun. Nick, too, poured into me the strength I needed, and still need, to tell the world about him.'[72] He goes on to say that he blames the men who murdered him 'no more or less than the Bush administration.' He declares:

George Bush never looked into my son's eyes. George Bush doesn't know my son, and he is the worse for it. George Bush, though a father himself, cannot feel my pain, or that of my family, or the world that grieves for Nick, because he is a policymaker and he doesn't have to bear the consequences of his acts. George Bush can see neither the heart of Nick nor that of the American people, let alone that of the Iraqi people his policies are killing daily.[73]

Berg recalls:

Donald Rumsfeld said that he took responsibility for the sexual abuse of Iraqi prisoners. How could he take the responsibility when there was no consequence? Nick took the consequences. Even more so than those murderers who took my son's life, I can't stand those who sit and make policies to end lives and break the lives of the still living.[74]

In this way, as a father, he was voicing what he had learnt and the questions that it leaves us with. He recalls:

Nick Berg was in Iraq to help the people without any expectation of personal gain. He was only one man, but through his death he has become many. The truly unselfish spirit of giving your all to do what you know in your own heart is right even when you know it make be dangerous... My son's work still goes on. Where there was one peacemaker before, I now see and have heard from thousands of peacemakers.[75]

Reflecting back to the crucial attack on the Twin Towers on 9/11 Berg asks a vital question to the American people:

So what were we to do when we in America were attacked on September 11, that infamous day? I saw we should have done then what we never did before: stop speaking to the people we labelled out enemies and start listening to them. Stop giving preconditions to our peaceful coexistence on this small planet, and start honouring and respecting every human's need to live free and autonomously, to truly respect the sovereignty of every state. To stop making up rules by which others must live and then separate rules for ourselves.[76]

If we are to learn to act on our beliefs, so following Nick's example to his father:

We need to let the evildoers on both sides of the Atlantic know that we are fed up with war. We are fed up with the killing and bombing and maiming of innocent people. We are fed up with the lies. Yes, we are fed up with the suicide bombers, and with the failure of the Israelis and Palestinians to find a way to stop killing each other. We are fed up with negotiations and peace conferences that are entered into on both sides with preset conditions that preclude the outcome of peace. We want world peace now.[77]

Retired high school teacher from West Chester, Pennsylvania, Michael Berg said in an interview with the *Jewish Chronicle* that his son had 'wanted to be recognized as a Jew working in Iraq. He was a person without boundaries. He accepted all peoples. He studied very carefully every culture he came into contact with, and learnt the Arabic language.'[78] He said his son was also keen to work in Iraq because of his close relationship with an Iraqi-Muslim uncle. His Judaism had been important to him though he had come to it 'on his own.'[79] In London for a Stop the War rally he asserted that US President George W. Bush was shielded from the consequences of a war in which he has 'essentially raped Iraq. He hasn't to this day contacted me, and I don't know of any Iraqis he's contacted either.'[80]

4

RELIGION AS A SOURCE OF CONFLICT IN THE POST-SOVIET STATES

John Anderson

The so-called resurgence of political religion over the last two decades has pro-voked a variety of responses from academics, journalists and politicians. For some it represents a hopeful development, enabling the marginalized of this world to stake a claim against the neo-liberal and individualistic ideological hegemony of the Western states;[1] for others it marks a return to a darker past in which religious differences promoted conflict within and between states. Suddenly religion, which the Westphalian settlement and Enlightenment ideology had pushed into the priv-ate sphere, was once again making claims on the public sphere where its impact could only be divisive. Images of the Crusades and the wars of religion came to the fore as communities divided by religion in Bosnia, South Asia and the Middle East fought over land and symbols sanctified by their religious significance. Of course, many could argue that these were not religious conflicts as such, but conflicts about power and resources where religion as a mark of difference could be mani-pulated by political entrepreneurs seeking to mobilize support for their causes. Nonetheless, the more visible evidence of religious rhetoric and symbols make it hard to exclude religion from the equation, even whilst one needs to be aware of the other factors at play in any conflict situation. Moreover, in some contexts the religious dimension is clearly a more powerful force in motivating action in so far as it places the conflict in the context of cosmic struggles between good and evil and, through the promise of heavenly rewards for the actor (and sometimes a guarantee of earthly rewards for the family), may increase the willingness to sacrifice for the cause.[2]

This chapter offers a few sketches of the ways in which religion has fed into conflict situations in the post-Soviet states. Arguably religion per se has not been a major cause of conflict in the former Soviet Union, though it has flavoured several conflict situations in Russia, the Caucasus and Central Asia. For ease of analysis we have tried to separate out conflict situations coloured by religion from those that might be argued to be caused by religion, though the line of separation is somewhat artificial. At the same time we have sought to make a distinction between micro-level and macro-level conflict situations (see Table 1).

Table 1: Types of Religious Conflict

	Religion colouring conflict (or having potential to cause division in society)	Religion as an actual or potential 'cause' of conflict
Micro	Debates about identity and belonging	Religious pluralism; proselytism
Macro	Tajik civil war; Chechnya; Nagorno-Karabagh	Activities of Hizb ut-Tahrir and the Islamic Movement of Uzbekistan (IMU)

Most analysis focuses on the latter, where religious-oriented conflict leads to actual violence within or between states. But there is also a lesser level of conflict where disputes tend to have local or communal implications, and where religious differences animate political debate or stir up local tensions without posing a fundamental challenge to domestic, regional or global order. Though these types are less significant for the international community, they can be very significant for those involved, in creating dissension within families and communities that potentially can be exploited by political actors for their own ends. We will make passing reference to the first of these and concentrate on one or two examples from the other three, though overall, this should be viewed as a rather over-simplified survey chapter which points to some of the key issues and conflicts but cannot possibly do them justice in such a short space of time, for each conflict clearly deserves a monograph in its own right. We end with a brief discussion of the role of religion in resolving conflict within the former USSR. Unfortunately, however, this latter section will be brief because religious actors have made a very limited contribution to reconciliation in conflict situations, perhaps thus confirming the belief of those who view religion as inherently divisive.

A. Conflict Coloured by Religion

Micro-level conflict – religion and belonging in new states

As fifteen states emerged out of the Soviet collapse each faced the issue of how to define belonging within the new order, in particular deciding how to reconcile incl- usive notions of citizenship with the demands of creating a new sense of national belonging. Such problems were particularly acute in states such as Kyrgyzstan, Ukr- aine, Latvia and Estonia with sizeable minorities, and in Kazakhstan where the titu- lar people made up less than half the population. The situation was further comp- licated by the fact that often differences in ethnicity within a state were reinforced by difference in religious tradition. At the heart of early debates lay the question of belonging and identity – how to create a single sense of belonging in multi-ethnic states and, at least in some parts of the former USSR, how to restore national tradi- tions in ways that did not drive out a skilled work force in which the significant ethnic 'other' tended to predominate. In practice this issue gave rise to less conflict than some had feared, as all the states bar Latvia and Estonia adopted inclusive citizenship laws, and in the 'southern' states the most articulate and skilled sections of the Slavic population 'returned' to their traditional homelands. If on the 'civic' front the point at issue remained the extent to which members of non-titular nationality would enjoy full rights and adequate prospects in the new states, on the religious front the question was whether there would be any attempt to create new political orders on the basis of religious beliefs. In particular the question was rais- ed whether the Central Asian states with their Muslim tradition would opt for an Islamic state.

In practice this never became a serious issue, as all the post-Soviet states and their essentially non-religious leaders opted to create secular states based upon a separation of religion from the state. During constitutional discussions in Kyrgyz- stan during early 1993 President Akaev raised the question of whether the pream- ble to the document should make some reference to the importance of religious values in general but this proposal fell in the final drafting process.[3] Even in Uzbekistan and, at least initially, in Tajikistan where Islam had a greater hold on popular culture, there were no serious efforts to make adherence to Islam a feature of the state order or a mark of full citizenship. Ironically, it was in the much more secularized Russia that there was some public debate about the relationship be- tween being Orthodox and being truly Russian, a debate that had a long historical pedigree. During the early 1990s this point was raised most explicitly by the late Metropolitan Ioann of St Petersburg and Ladoga, a reactionary anti-Semite who explicitly linked religious and national identity and blamed all Russia's misfortunes on 'outsiders' who denied the true faith. Whilst he made no explicit calls for citiz- enship to be dependent upon Orthodoxy, his calls for restrictions on the rights of non-Orthodox communities came close to linking citizenship to religious adher- ence.[4] In all of these cases what could have served as the basis of conflict failed to do so because the relevant state authorities, perhaps shaped by their Soviet up- bringing, opted for inclusive notions of citizenship and belonging, though such discussion certainly contributed to feelings of insecurity amongst minority ethnic and religious communities. Yet though these debates lost their intensity after the first years of independence, they have periodically resurfaced in a number of states, for example in Central Asia where, as we shall see, some groups still call rather insistently for the creation of an Islamic state and in Russia where 2003–2004 witnessed heated discussions about the appropriateness of introducing a course on 'the foundations of Orthodox culture' into the state school curriculum.[5]

Macro-level conflict – Nagorno-Karabagh, the Tajik civil war and Chechnya

In all three of these cases there has been a tendency to view conflict as arising out of the religious differences between the warring parties, though in none of them was religion the primary cause of the dispute. In the first, the issues revolved primarily around the question of which of two parties (Armenia and Azerbaijan) had legitimate claims to sovereignty over disputed territory. Here the immediate roots of the conflict lie in events of the Mikael Gorbachev years where increasing political freedom allowed Armenians in the disputed territory of Nagorno-Karabagh to seek independence from Azerbaijan and eventually merge with Armenia. This political campaign descended into a period of violence which left the territory as an autonomous region, since which time there has endured a lengthy stalemate that successive negotiators have failed to resolve. Yet, though the two sides adhere to different religious traditions – Islam and Armenian Apostolic – leading parties to the conflict have rarely utilized religious rhetoric in explaining their differences and I will not explore this dispute further here. In the case of the Tajik civil war, discussed below, the roots of the conflict lay in regional competition over who should govern the country and how it should be governed, whilst in our third case, what was essentially a secessionist conflict acquired a religious dimension over time as the Chechen authorities sought to increase their legitimacy and as external actors became involved in the conflict.[6]

The Tajik conflict emerged out of the collapse of the USSR and the emergence of an independent state. Following a contested presidential election at the end of 1991 a coalition of opposition forces refused to accept the result which placed former Tajik Communist Party boss Rakhmon Nabiev back in power. A series of street demonstrations and counter-demonstrations ensued in the capital Dushanbe until in May 1992 Nabiev agreed to the formation of a coalition government. But this led to further problems as powerful regional elites refused to accept the new deal and by the end of the year the coalition government had been overthrown and a new regime emerged headed by Imomali Rakhmonov, a former collective-farm chairman from the southern Kulyab region. In consequence opposition leaders went into exile, thousands of refugees fled to neighbouring Afghanistan and from 1993–97 a civil war ensued during which the active opposition was increasingly dominated by Islamic groups with varying, and sometimes competing, visions of how a new Tajikistan might look. In practice these visions proved irrelevant in so far as the opposition was unable to overthrow the Russian-backed regime in

Dushanbe, though in 1997 a peace deal was finally negotiated which led to the creation of a new coalition arrangement that included some representatives of the opposition.

Initially the conflict in Tajikistan tended to be explained in ideological terms, as a coalition of religious, nationalist and democratic forces emboldened by the Gorbachev reforms sought to overthrow the old communist order. Yet those representing the latter were less concerned with ideology than preserving the personal and regional hegemonies built up over previous decades. Under this system the elites of the economically prosperous Leninabad region (now renamed Khojent) had dominated the political order, leaving the other regions very much subordinate – as peripheries within the periphery (Tajikistan was the poorest of the Soviet states). In turn opposition forces tended to have regional bases – the intellectual dominated nationalist party Rastokhez in the capital Dushanbe, the Democratic Party in the Kurgan-Tyube regions, Lali-Badakshon representing the Ismaili community in Gorno-Badakhshon, and the Islamic Renaissance Party, particularly strong in the Garm district.

Islam in Tajikistan had faced seventy years of hostility from the Soviet state, with particularly violent persecution from the late 1920s till the early 1940s, and considerable administrative pressure under Khrushchev. Nonetheless, by the 1970s the authorities had de facto recognized that the long-term eradication of religion was likely to be a lengthy process, and in practice regional elites tended to give low priority to anti-religious policies. Most Tajiks continued to observe customary practices relating to the major rites of passage and in parts of the country small groups were increasingly influenced by the Islamic revival taking place in other parts of the Muslim world. Gorbachev's reforms allowed greater latitude for both official and unofficial religious activity, as mosques opened and Muslim intellectuals became acquainted with ideas being developed elsewhere. In mid-1990 an Islamic Renaissance Party (IRP) was created in the USSR and its most significant branch proved to be that operating in Tajikistan. Its leaders described the party's aims as primarily religious, concerned with regenerating the faith of a people whose knowledge of their religion had been severely attenuated by the Soviet experience. Attempts to create an Islamic state were firmly eschewed by IRP leaders,[7] though some would later suggest that the people re-educated in the spirit of Islam might choose this option. This moderate position was also adopted by the head of the official Muslim administration Kazi Abkhar Turadzhonzoda who called on his clergy to remain strictly neutral in political matters. As the demonstrations in Dushanbe developed during the spring of 1992 the IRP became increasingly prominent as a result of its growing ability to mobilize the often impoverished constituencies it represented and its ability to tap into authentic communal identities – as opposed to the rather artificial and intellectual dominated programmes of other opposition groups.

As the conflict turned from civil unrest to civil war the voice of the Islamists became louder, especially as the development of links with the *mujaheddin* in refugee and training camps in Afghanistan reinforced the notion of Islam as providing a voice to the dispossessed in their struggle with oppression. But as with the Afghan *mujaheddin*, the persistence of a state of war led to the emergence of warlordism as individual commanders took to trading in weapons and drugs, in the process perhaps forgetting their original commitment to Islamic ideals. Nonetheless, as the outlines of a peace deal began to emerge in 1997 considerable dispute raged around the role of religious-based parties in any future government and over their influence on key areas of policy. In particular the IRP was incensed when the Rakhmonov sought to introduce a constitution that banned the creation of religious-based political parties. Further tensions emerged in 2004 over the refusal to allow women to wear the *hijab* for internal identity documents, despite being allowed to do so for international passports. As a result of this policy, in a few of the more conservative parts of the country up to 90 per cent of women were reportedly not carrying ID cards, despite the legal requirement to do so.[8]

The key point of this rather sketchy analysis of the Tajik situation has been to suggest that whilst religion helped to colour and shape the evolution of the conflict, it was not the primary cause. This lay originally in elite differences over how to handle the transition process and regional disputes over control of economic and political resources in the newly independent state. Yet at the same time religion helped to provide a focus for some groups and provided a mobilizing force for at least one of the competing groups. This is not to say that the religious commitment was false or should not be taken seriously, but to stress that it was not the primary factor creating a conflict situation. It is also perhaps worth noting that since the signing of the peace treaty differences have emerged within the Islamic community, with the IRP's participation in the government rejected by some within its own constituency who have in consequence turned to more radical groups. These include the largely peaceful Hizb ut-Tahrir with its commitment to the creation of an Islamic caliphate (see below) but also to groups willing to use violence to achieve their aim of creating an Islamic state. At the same time there is evidence to suggest that, whilst the social hold of Islam has strengthened in recent years, the appeal of Islamic politics has declined.[9]

It is very difficult to see the contemporary Russian-Chechen conflict as essentially religious, though the conflict between Russia and the 'mountain peoples'[10] in the nineteenth century had a strong religious flavour, with Shamil and other leaders clearly fighting under the banner of Islam against the Orthodox Russians. Over succeeding years, and especially during the Soviet period, both Chechen ethnicity and religious traditions faced major problems, as anti-religious policies enjoyed some success in 'privatizing' religious experience and repressive policies – including the 1944 deportation of the whole Chechen nation – sought to destroy the linkage between ethnicity and territory. In subsequent years Chechens gradually returned to their homeland and, as Gorbachev's programme unfolded (or unravelled), Chechens followed the example of other nations in seeking greater autonomy. This culminated at the end of 1990 with a formal proclamation of sovereignty and Chechen independence from the USSR by a national conference meeting in Grozny. Following the August 1991 coup attempt in Moscow Chechens voted for independence and, despite a brief attempt by Boris Yeltsin to restore central authority, drifted into a state of quasi-autonomy over the next three years. During this period the social influence of religion grew as mosques were opened – or in many cases actually existing ones were given legal recognition – Islamic leaders given more prominence, and religious rituals more publicly observed.

> For all this, the roots of the conflict were not religious. The early proclamations of the Chechen authorities and President Dudaev made few references to Islam, instead focusing on the need to revitalise the national tradition in the newly independent republic. At the same time the language of resistance to Russian attempts to re-assert its influence utilised the language of national resistance to colonial oppression. Most sources agree that only as Moscow's pressure began to mount during 1994 did Dudaev turn to Islam for legitimisation, and only in November 1994 did the republic become an Islamic state in which shari'a law was to be implemented.[11]

Following the Russian invasion in December 1994 there were further attempts to promote political Islam in order to shore up support for the opposition to Moscow, and an increasing number of *Sharia* courts emerged in the regions controlled by those fighting the invaders. Moreover, for the first time there were appeals for support from the wider Muslim world that very slowly brought results in attracting several foreign fighters with experience of training and fighting in Afghanistan – though these were to be a mixed blessing for the Chechen opposition. At the same time religious missionaries sought to promote the more puritanical vision of Islam sometimes associated with the Wahhabi tradition, though in a region where Sufism and syncretic practices were the norm such preachers were not always well-received. In the period following the ceasefire of August 1996 the Chechens were able to elect their own president, Aslan Maskhadov, but it quickly became apparent that he was unable to exercise effective authority over a republic, 'where law and order collapsed and kidnappings and extortion became widespread' and where Islam allegedly 'defined the splits among the Chechen leadership.'[12] Here militant Islamists such as Shamil Basaev and the 'Arab' Khattab encouraged local Chechen fighters and a growing, if often exaggerated, number of foreign fighters to wage an uncompromising war against both Russian invaders and their local collaborators. Though commentators such as Anatol Lieven[13] have suggested that Basaev and several of his collaborators are as keen on war for its own sake as for the pursuit of religious ideals, there was little doubt that a jihadist rhetoric served to encourage participation in the struggle, though it may have alienated many within the Chechen population who were the victims of war. Yet it was these figures who initiated the incursion into neighbouring Daghestan which served as the pretext for then Prime Minister Vladimir Putin to launch a second Chechen war that was to bring further tribulation to this war-torn area but which also was to see the war extended well into Russian territory. Post-9/11 the Russian authorities were able to reinforce the focus on the 'extremist' religious dimension of the conflict by linking their campaign to the US led 'war on terror' and associating the Chechen rebels with Al Qaeda and its radical message.

The key point here is that the parties to the conflict did adhere to differing religious traditions which certainly coloured the ways in which the conflict developed, especially after the first war (1994–96) when the Chechen leadership often encouraged appeals to Islamic solidarity when seeking foreign support for their cause and when a handful of foreign religious activists joined the struggle and gave it a more radical edge. Equally it is probably true that for many Chechens the centuries old Russian campaign to subdue them may sometimes have had the air of a religious crusade – a perspective perhaps reinforced by reports of individual Orthodox clerics speaking in terms of going to war with Chechnya as a religious duty. Indeed, the Russian Orthodox Church struggled to come up with a consistent position, making general calls for peace, protesting when its clergy were kidnapped, beaten or killed, and offering rather generalized condemnations of human rights abuses committed by either side, whilst generally defending the position of the Russian state as having a duty to ensure the country's territorial integrity. Along with President Putin the Church has also sought to distance itself from any suggestion that Islam is to blame for the conflict or that this is a religious war.[14] And in September 2004 the President told a group of leading clerics that recent terrorist attacks represented an attempt 'to split society and incite one faith against another' and urged all religious confessions to struggle against terrorism.[15] All this suggests that whilst for some participants on both sides this is a conflict that has a much stronger religious component than when it first emerged at the beginning of the 1990s, it is not a conflict that was caused by religion.

B. Conflict Caused by Religion

As suggested earlier, the distinction between conflicts coloured by religion and those caused by religion remains an artificial one, for in all our cases one can find individuals or groups inspired by religion, but also actors appealing to religion as a means of mobilizing political support. Nonetheless, we could argue that the issues of religious pluralism throughout the former USSR and the alleged rise of political Islam in Central Asia have, to varying degrees, more directly contributed to conflict situations.

Micro-level conflict – coping with religious pluralism

With the collapse of Communism most of the post-communist states opted to remove state control of religion and the emergent default position assumed a free market in religious ideas. This had two consequences, enabling local religious communities greater freedom to extend their activities beyond the narrow parameters permitted by the Soviet state, and allowing the entry of external actors keen to propagate their own visions of religious truth. Loud and prominent evangelistic campaigns by a variety of evangelical and charismatic groups or by 'new age movements' attracted media attention and aroused fears amongst 'traditional' religious communities about 'unfair competition', leading to growing demands for restrictions to be imposed on these 'sects'. Whilst such campaigns often had their roots in fear of religious competition, they sometimes acquired popular resonance – as the new media focused on extreme cases of family disruption to label any unknown group as a 'cult' – and political resonance as politicians tied debates about religion to debates about identity. As in the West such campaigns were often one-sided, exaggerating the impact and activities of both foreign and domestic groups, and were used to preserve the hegemony of traditionally dominant religious groups, but in many of the post-Soviet states they led to the creation of restrictive legislation that often breached international agreements on religious freedom.[16]

In Russia the campaign to restrict the rights of minorities began in the Russian Orthodox Church but later drew in a broad coalition of issue-seeking politicians, hack journalists, nationalist intellectuals, security officials searching for a new role (or a continuation of their old role) and concerned parents who had seen their children 'lost' to 'new' religious groups. For the Orthodox Church the old order had led to the destruction of their independence, but under the last two decades of the Soviet order they had enjoyed the odd status of *primus inter pares* amongst the harassed religious communities. With the creation of a free market there emerged not only different trends within their own community, some critical of past compromises, but a multiplicity of other religious groups many of whom made no bones about their intent to proselytize throughout Russia. For the Orthodox leadership Russians were simply Orthodox and other groups had no right to encroach on their territory (except in the service of the religious needs of ethnic minorities), though in fact Roman Catholics, Lutherans, Baptists and some other protestant groups had histories in Russia that pre-dated the 1917 revolution and, in the case of the first two, went back centuries. Other groups were indeed 'new' to the late and post-Soviet period, though few were as well-funded as suggested by their critics and the vast majority of 'sects' were indigenous in their origins and development. Nonetheless, from 1992 onwards the Orthodox Church and its supporters waged a campaign to create a new law on religion and, after several false starts, new legislation emerged in 1997 which in many ways marked a step back from the laws on religious freedom that had been approved under Gorbachev. This is not the place to explore the outworkings of this law, but simply to note that by stigmatizing certain groups the potential for religious conflict was created. Spokesmen for the Orthodox Church sometimes stated that by their very activities such groups created dissension within a disoriented society in need of a period of stability,[17] but in most cases religious minorities simply wanted the freedom to practice and promote their faith. And in practice, though the rhetoric of the new law was about preventing extreme actions of 'totalitarian cults' – always better done through criminal law – the groups most affected by its implementation were often groups with at least some historic roots in the country. Yet by 2004 there was some evidence to suggest that the general level of harassment was declining in many parts of the country as the Ministry of Justice sought to promote a more permissive regulatory regime, though the very federal nature of the system meant that policy was frequently enforced inconsistently, and groups such as the Jehovah's Witnesses and Mormons tended to face continued problems in practising their faith.

In Russia, despite the presence of an extensive range of 'new religious movements' the predominant issue revolved around which broadly-Christian groups would influence the Russian population. In Central Asia the question was complicated and intensified by the fact that Christian groups were proselytizing amongst traditionally Islamic communities and radical Muslim groups were emerging who promoted a far more rigorous and puritanical Islamic vision. During the Soviet era Baptists, Pentecostals, Adventists and others had by and large confined their activity to the Slavic and European populations, but with greater freedom came more missionary activity as they sought to promote their message to the indigenous populations. For example, in several towns and settlements in Kyrgyzstan services would increasingly be held in Russian and Kyrgyz, and literature in the latter language began to be produced and distributed. In addition several of the foreign missionary organizations that became active in the republic adopted what were often seen as aggressive tactics by publicly denigrating national customs and traditions. Increasing publicity was given to some of the tensions that arose when ethnic Kyrgyz converted to Christianity, as in the village of Iskra in the northern Chui region where problems arose over the burial of an ethnic Kyrgyz who had become a Baptist – traditionally Kyrgyz and Slavs were buried in different cemeteries so the problem arose of whether this person could be buried with his relatives given his conversion to a 'European' religion. In some cases conversions led to exclusion and isolation for the individual, rejection by families or spouses, or physical violence as local communities attacked minority religious groups.[18]

Though conflict of this sort is less obvious to the wider world because it has not fundamentally challenged state authority, or has done so very indirectly, at the local level both state policy and public attitudes, rooted in a partially Soviet-created suspicion of 'otherness', do create divisions within society that impact upon the lives of local communities.

Macro-level conflict – 'fundamentalism' and the State in Central Asia

The most direct religious contributions to political conflict would appear to be in Central Asia where several movements have emerged that are ostensibly committed to the overthrow of existing regimes and their replacement by religiously-based governments. Here religion appears to have been the primary motivating factor for some actors in conflict situations, rather than becoming an issue in conflicts that developed for other reasons. Of particular interest here are political disputes emerging as a result of the activities of the Islamic Movement of Uzbekistan (IMU) and Hizb ut-Tahrir, with the former deliberately provoking violent confrontations with state authorities and the latter's seemingly peaceful activities arousing a harsh response from the Uzbek regime in particular. Yet even here ambiguities remain, particularly with regard to the IMU which has often seemed more committed to the overthrow of the Karimov regime in Tashkent than the promotion of an Islamic state.

The IMU sprang out of developments in the Fergana Valley region of Uzbekistan as the Soviet Union collapsed. At the end of 1991 in the town of Namangan
and its surrounding districts political authority was seized by a group of Islamic
militants led by Tohir Yuldashev, a local mullah who had been trained in the religious underground, and by Jumaboi Khojaev (later to become known as Namangani) who had served briefly in Afghanistan during the Soviet occupation. Very
quickly they imposed *Sharia* law and set up vigilante groups who meted out rough
justice to those offending against their vision of the law. This brief interlude was
brought to a rapid end in the spring of 1992 and the two leaders fled to Tajikistan
where Namangani got caught up in the civil war, and then after 1997, they fled to
Afghanistan and developed links with the Taliban and, reportedly, with Osama bin
Laden. Here Yuldashev developed a network of *medressahs* to provide young Uzbek
refugees with the rudiments of an Islamic education whilst Namangani developed
his military networks. From 1999–2001 they engaged in a series of small scale
incursions into southern Kyrgzystan and Uzbekistan, but none of these posed a
serious challenge to regional authorities and there is little evidence that they
enjoyed much popular support.[19] Following 9/11 and the US attack on Afghanistan it was reported that Namangani had been killed and much of his network
decimated, though by 2004 it was reportedly active again under the leadership of
Yuldashev and was blamed (along with other groups) by the Uzbek regime for the
fighting and explosions that took place in Uzbekistan during March 2004.

According to Ahmed Rashid, the IMU was different to some other religious
groups, including the Tajik IRP, in having 'no respect for official Islam, no patience
with tradition, and no fear of the political regime, which they over-optimistically
considered to be on the verge of disintegration and collapse.'[20] Problems arose,
however, when this did not happen and the IMU had to brace itself for a much
longer struggle both in combating the regime and winning the support of the
Uzbek population. Perhaps inevitably the military units created by Namangani in
exile quickly got sucked into the warlord pattern that had emerged in the Afghan
and Tajik conflicts, with individual leaders perhaps diluting their religious commitment as they engaged in the weapons and drugs trade in order to finance their campaigns. Most accounts suggest that Namangani was first and foremost a guerrilla
leader, though the ineptitude of the raids into the Fergana Valley during 1999–2001
does not suggest a brilliant military tactician. Moreover, the IMU found that it had
limited support within Uzbekistan itself beyond the home territories of its leaders.
Indeed, here as elsewhere in Central Asia, some resented these young activists who
presumed to understand Islam better than anyone else, who denigrated traditional
customs, and whose activities brought state repression for many other religious
activists who simply wanted to pursue their faith more devoutly. This in turn led to
recruitment problems, despite the potential large pool of unemployed and disillusioned young men available. At least some sources suggest that those recruited often
had little idea of what they were getting involved in, with one fighter reporting that
his IMU career started because he was a devout believer seeking further knowledge
of Islam. Having been sent by his teacher to study in Tashkent, his group was effe-

ctively diverted en route and told they were going to fight for Islam in Tajikistan. Here he joined a camp where the new recruits studied Islam and were given weapons training, until bored by the process he fled home.[21] How representative this story is remains unclear, but one has the impression that many of those recruited into the ranks of the IMU had a strong commitment but limited knowledge of Islam, and that the latter tended to focus on the injustices suffered by Muslims around the world rather than on the positive benefits of Islamic rule. Nonetheless, there can be little doubt that for some the initial impetus to involvement in the organization and the willingness to take up arms in a seemingly one-sided struggle was essentially a commitment to the idea that religion was the solution to the problems of their society.

Hizb ut-Tahrir is probably exceptional in that it is in effect a revolutionary political party whose ideology is based upon a particular reading of Islam. As a worldwide organization it aims to create a global caliphate said to be modelled on that of the classical period, but in recent years has seen the Central Asian region as a potential flashpoint where this revolution might be started. It only started to organize in Central Asia during the mid-1990s and since then has developed its activity through much of the region, though with particular strengths in the Fergana Valley region of Uzbekistan, Tajikistan and Kyrgyzstan where Islam has traditionally held greater sway. Organizationally its owes much to revolutionary parties with a cell structure in which groups of 5–7 people dedicate themselves to study and propagation of literature, and in which only the group leader has contacts with the next hierarchical link. At the centre of the message is criticism of existing domestic and international powers, whether for their enmity towards Islam or betrayal of true Islam, and promotion of *Sharia* law as the solution to society's problems – though they do not offer a concrete political and economic programme. In essence the first task is the removal of secular leadership, with the development of detailed policies left until after this has been achieved.[22] Though they stand for the promotion of Islam, they remained hostile to many strands emerging from within the Muslim tradition, demonstrating particular hostility towards Shiites, Sufis, Ahmadiyas, Ismailis and Bahais. Some spokesmen stress that in an Islamic state people of the book would enjoy religious freedom within their own homes, but other religions would be banned and all would have to live by *Sharia* law outside the confines of the home. There is also an anti-Semitic edge to much of their literature with pamphlets found in Uzbekistan describing President Islam Karimov as a 'Jewish kaffir' and America as dominated by Jews.[23] Despite this radical agenda they formally remain committed to peaceful means of struggle, to the path of persuasion rather than violence, though regional governments continue to link them with violent assaults on officials and several bombings in Uzbekistan.

What is very clear is that this is a group with a much larger constituency than the IMU or any other radical group in Central Asia. The regional press carries frequent reports on the arrests and trials of members and anything from 5–10,000 are said to be imprisoned in Uzbekistan alone. Despite this continuing arrests suggest a considerable network of active members, alongside many more passive supporters.

For some commentators the growth of this organization stems from the economic marginalization of many following the collapse of communism and the absence of political representation for those seeking to change the situation. Yet though poverty may provide some recruits, as with other 'fundamentalist' movements the leading activists do not all come from the most marginalized sectors of the population but include scientifically and technically trained graduates, and skilled factory workers. There is also a sense that repression endows the group with a certain mystique that actually aids recruitment rather than inhibits it, leading the Kyrgyz ombudsman on human rights Tursunbai bakir-uulu to suggest that it might be better to legalize the movement and bring it into the sphere of public discourse – though this might be problematic in that the group seems uninterested in discussion and most of the region's states do not have an open political space. More recently there has been some suggestion that members of the organization, and possibly some within its local leadership, have toyed with ending the peaceful commitment in the face of ongoing repression by the Uzbek and other Central Asian governments. There certainly appear to have been some discussions about collaboration with the IMU and several authors report the emergence of splinter groups who believe that non-violent tactics cannot unseat the secular regimes and that therefore violence may be essential.[24] But however the movement develops, their can be no doubt that from the perspective of Hizb ut-Tahrir this is a religious conflict, a view reciprocated by regional governments who see their struggle against the movement in terms of a battle against 'religious extremism' – as well as, post-9/11, a battle against 'international terrorism'.

Religion and Reconciliation

Turning to the reconciliation side one has to recognize that the contribution of religious communities has generally been disappointing in the former Soviet Union. This side of religious thinking and practice remained undeveloped in the Soviet period, when such religious activity, as was permitted, was confined to celebration of the liturgy or formal prayer service. Nonetheless, there are a few instances of religious attempts to mediate conflicts or offer different ways of looking at conflict situations which I shall simply note here. Firstly, during the stand-off that followed Boris Yeltsin's constitutionally dubious decision to dissolve his parliament at the end of the September 1993 and just prior to the bloody resolution of that conflict in early October, the Russian Orthodox Church attempted to find a compromise solution. Cutting short a visit to the USA, Patriarch Aleksii offered to mediate between the two sides. Together with two senior hierarchs he met with Yeltsin, then with representatives of parliament and the Constitutional Court, with talks focusing on disarming those remaining in the parliament prior to formal discussions taking place. Whilst these discussions went on, the Patriarchate also sent a priest to the White House to meet the spiritual needs of the resisting parliamentarians. On 2 October 1993 Metropolitan Kirill appeared on television calling for all concerned to avoid bloodshed and stressing the need for Russians to be united and avoid civil strife. But on the night of 3 October, when talks between the two sides were going on in the Danilovsky monastery, armed groups supporting the parliament clashed with the police and in the early hours of the morning Yeltsin forcibly ended parliament's activities with tanks.[25]

My other examples come, perhaps surprisingly, from Azerbaijan. The first represents a practical attempt to promote religious pluralism in the republic, and the second a more theoretical response by an Azeri scholar and translator of the *Qur'an* to the rise of the radical Islamist groups within Central Asia and the Caucasus that we discussed earlier. The first stems from the attempts of the Azeri authorities to close down a Baku mosque, where, perhaps unusually in the post-Soviet context, Muslim and Protestant activists joined together to protest restrictions on religious freedom. The story dates back to the presidential election of October 2003 when Imam Ilgar Ibragimoglu, prayer leader of the Juma mosque in Baku supported an opposition candidate. Alongside Azer Ramizoglu, the *imam* had for some time been a thorn in the side of the authorities through his support for human rights groups and involvement in Devamm, the Centre for the Protection of Freedom of Conscience and Religion. Though accused by the authorities of promoting Wahhabism and being linked to Al Qaeda, this organization appears to have promoted religious freedom for all religious communities, as suggested by the reciprocal support given to the *imam* by Baptist leaders in Azerbaijan.[26] Arrested and then given a five year suspended sentence, the *imam* returned to the mosque he had run for the previous 12 years but on 30 June 2003 the mosque was raided by the police and a new *imam* loyal to the official religious administration installed in his place despite the protests of several hundred demonstrators.[27]

The other Azeri case relates to a paper published by Azeri scholar Nariman Gasimoglu, who heads the Religion and Democracy Group in Baku, which argued that contrary to the view of officials the best means of resolving conflict and preventing religious extremism in the Caucasus and Central Asia was to promote religious freedom. By banning Islamist groups and denying the people representation, leaders such as Islam Karimov in Uzbekistan were giving such movements an aura or martyrdom which made them attractive to the young and marginalized in society. Groups like Hizb ut-Tahrir may propose deeply reactionary agendas, but driving them underground and persecuting anyone who takes their religion seriously is only likely to aid radical groups. So, put crudely, the solution is liberalization and democratization, so that their ideas can be engaged with and combated in the public sphere. In a word religious freedom (for all, not just Muslims) will help democracy but will also serve as the best means to combat religious extremism and reduce the levels of conflict in these societies.

In many respects these cases offer tenuous evidence of religious contributions to resolving conflict situations. In the first the Russian Orthodox contribution to resolving conflict was largely marginalized by the unwillingness of either side to compromise, and the fact that some within the Orthodox Church sympathized with those remaining in the parliament building. By and large, however, in conflict situations where the Russian Orthodox Church might be thought to have an interest it has, as an institution and despite the work of a few individuals, tended to

be complicit – for example, failing to condemn serious Russian excesses in Chechnya except in the vaguest terms – or supine – for example, doing virtually nothing
to defend Russians from discrimination in Central Asia. In the Azeri case the conflict at issue revolved around the question of religious pluralism, but was remark-
able in countering the general trend of the 1990s which has seen some religious
groups seek restrictions on the rights of others.

Conclusion

As Scott Appleby suggests, the contribution of religious ideas and organizations to
public life is often deeply ambivalent, capable of contributing to both violence and
reconciliation.[28] The former Soviet Union, unfortunately, provides more examples
of the ways in which religion can feed into political conflict or be used by those
seeking to mobilize political support for their own agendas even when the original
causes of political disputes have little to do with religion. As we have seen, in
Chechnya and to some extent in Tajikistan, these conflicts often relate to questions
of who should inherit political power in a situation of imperial collapse. In the
latter case one party to the conflict did have a religious agenda, but again it was
interlaced with questions of regional influence; in the former case, leading Chechen
politicians sought to mobilize a pre-existing but also an 'imagined Islam' when their
own legitimacy needed reinforcement because of political failure. The situation in
Central Asia was more complex, because at least in the case of Hizb ut-Tahrir we
see groups whose public involvement is fuelled primarily by a rather simplistic
Islamic vision and who prior to 9/11 were depicted by local regimes as movements
of 'religious extremism'. Here religion, or to be more precise the absence of religion from public life, is the core motivating factor, though even here there may be
those who see the utility of religion for achieving power. Even then we cannot
simply dismiss the religious angle as some form of 'false ideology', for the very fact
of using religious discourse affects – some would say infects – those involved in
conflict situations, providing both motivation, solace and reward. Whilst religion
may not be the major source of political conflict in this region, all too often its
presence can be detected lurking in the background, influencing some actors, being
promoted or demonized by others, and looked to as a source of comfort in the
face of violence and human insecurity. Whether those religious actors present in
these regions can step beyond rebuilding communities shattered by anti-religious
persecution, to building a new, more inclusive and conciliatory role for religion
remains to be seen.

5

ACCOMMODATION, COMPETITION AND CONFLICT: SECTARIAN IDENTITY IN PAKISTAN

Saleem Khan

Most research on community conflicts in South Asia is concerned with conflicts between members of different religious traditions. For instance, there exists a massive body of literature on the various inter-communal conflicts between Hindus and Muslims in India, and Sinhala Buddhists and Hindu Tamils in Sri Lanka. Less has been done on community conflicts within a single religious tradition or between sects.

This chapter focuses on the formation, development, and political consequences of sectarianism and the possible reconciliation in Pakistan between the Sunnis who, as in most Muslim countries are in majority, and the Shias, a much smaller but relatively powerful minority. It is also concerned with the interconnected ongoing struggle between the various modernist, fundamentalist and Sufi tendencies within the broader category of Sunni Islam. The simultaneous intra-Sunni conflict both impacts and is influenced by the Shia-Sunni conflict. The Shia-Sunni divide in Islam shares some aspects of the Catholic-Protestant separation in Christianity, as Shia Islam does have a recognized clerical hierarchy. The intra-Sunni subdivisions roughly correspond to the established-church/free-churches (non-conformist) splits in Protestantism. Pakistan is probably the country which has the most diverse collection of Muslim sects, subsects and political parties, and in which sectarianism is implicitly or explicitly a part of the political discourse. Pakistan is also a country which has been under military rule for considerable periods of its troubled history. As a result, it has also experienced violent regional and linguistic based separatist movements which have seriously challenged the military, partly because the majority of the army, like most of the rest of the establishment, is recruited from the dominant province of Pakistan, the Punjab.

Islam has therefore been used by the state as a source of social cohesion. During the last phrases of the Cold War, the then military dictator of Pakistan, President Zia ul Haq (d.1988) popularly known as the 'military mullah', justified the Islamization of Pakistan by saying 'Pakistan is like Israel. Take out Judaism from Israel and it will collapse like a house of cards. Take Islam out of Pakistan and make it a secular state, and it would collapse.'[1] However, as there are many interpretations of Islam in Pakistan, the state, by imposing a particular one on society, greatly undermines its own approach towards national unity.

Over the last quarter of a century, relatively mild animosities have flared up into organized political violence between Muslim sects and subsects. Not only rival sectarian party members but religious scholars (*ulema*), doctors, lawyers, politicians, government officials, police cadets, foreign diplomats and even the premier Shia Shrine of Imam Reza in Mashhad, Iran have been targeted by Pakistani militants.[2] Mosques, *imambaras*, and businesses belonging to rival sect members have been regularly bombed. In the seven year period from 1990 to 1997, official figures reported some 600 lives were lost with 1997, the fiftieth anniversary of the birth of Pakistan, being the most violent. Independent organizations and academics dispute these figures as being greatly underestimated and some even claim that the real death toll could be actually up to ten times what the government acknowledges. The Shia minority has suffered more from Sunni extremist attacks than the latter has received in retaliation.

The Shia

The division between Shias and Sunnis has its origins in the violent leadership disputes that followed the death of the holy Prophet Muhammad. Sunnis believe that the Prophet had not left any clear instructions regarding his succession. In contrast, Shia Muslims believe the Prophet had designated his closest kinsman Hazrat Ali, who was his cousin and son-in-law, as the undisputed head of the entire Muslim community (*umma*). So, Shias continue to argue that the Muslim community's early leadership should have been restricted to the sacred line of Ali and most of them also support the claims of Ali together with all of his eleven direct descendents, who are collectively known as the *imams*.

Most of the *imams* were assassinated by their political opponents. The last and twelfth *imam* is believed by Shias to have gone into hiding and they expect his return as the messiah (*medhi*). The Twelve Imams are thus ascribed a very high religious status by Shias as they are believed to be divinely inspired scholars and saints, ranking below only the Prophet himself in the Shia religious hierarchy.

The *imams*, according to Shia doctrine, have certain attributes that according to other Muslims only prophets possess. The *imams* being sinless are also governed by the Shia concept of infallibility (*isma*). Sunnis praise the *imams* but the fundamentalists among them consider that the Shia doctrine of *isma* is too extreme, while the Sufis among them have extended the *isma* doctrine to embrace their own saints.[3] This shows that some Sunnis are closer to Shias on certain aspects of theology than they are to other Sunnis.

Shias themselves have over time split into numerous smaller subsects each holding a different view on the number and lineage of the *imams*. Some like the Nizari Ismailis or Khojas, found especially in certain regions of Pakistan and neighbouring countries, follow a living *imam*, the Aga Khan. The largest grouping within the Shia sect of Islam is referred as the Twelver or Imami Shias who are the focus of this chapter, and who represent some 10 to 15 per cent of the world's billion Muslims. So the term Shia by itself in this chapter really refers to the Twelver or Imami Shia.

Most Sunnis, although sharing with the Shias a high level of respect for the Prophet's descendents, differ from the Shias, as Sunnis take a more open view of the political and spiritual authority of the early Muslim *umma* by not restricting it to just those descended from the Prophet's immediate family (Ahl al-Bayt) – Ali, Fatima, Hassan and Husain. Gradually these two sects, originally separating on the lines of religious authority, developed some further differences regarding beliefs, festivals, sacred law, rituals and practices. The most heavily contested issue was the ritual cursing (*tabarra*) by the Shias of some of the Prophet's contemporaries (*sahaba*) who the Sunnis revere, during the holy month of Muharram. Shias believe that *sahaba*, many of whom belonged to the Prophet's own tribe, the Quresh, had gravely sinned as they usurped the leadership rights of the Imams. Where Shias are in a minority as they are in Pakistan, they have sometimes come into violent conflict with Sunnis over the performance of *tabarra*. Ayatollah Ruhollah Khomeini had discouraged Shias from performing this ritual cursing; despite being a senior Shia cleric he wanted to build bridges between Islamists of different sectarian backgrounds, perhaps to form an anti-Western alliance. Khomeini's famous or infamous *fatwa* against Salman Rushdie can also be seen as an attempt on his part to emerge from the confines of Shi'ism and to reach out to a wider audience in the Islamic World.

Revolutionary Iran is the only country where the Shias are in the majority. They have been religiously and politically dominant there since the early sixteenth century, the period from which Iran was gradually transformed from being a Sunni majority country to one with a Shia majority under the Safavids, who themselves were once Sunni Sufis before they become Shia monarchs.

Neighbouring Pakistan has probably the world's second largest Shia population after Iran, as some Sunnis in what is now the Pakistan Punjab had converted from Sunni Islam to Shia Islam during the nineteenth century under the guidance of certain Sufi orders.[4] This appears somewhat surprising considering that the Punjab has never been under a Shia dynasty, unlike the adjoining regions such as Kashmir and Sind.

The exact percentage of the Pakistani population in Muslim sectarian terms is difficult to establish as there are no official figures published. The government only

acknowledges that there is a Shia minority and also that there are religious differences which are present among the Sunni majority. The only government statistics
available regarding religious affiliation is based on the binary divide between Muslims and non-Muslims which shows the latter category including as little as 3.5 per
cent of the entire population of Pakistan.

The major non-Muslim communities in Pakistan are Christians, Hindus and the
Ahmedis who have been entered under protest into the non-Muslim category since
Zulifikar Ali Bhutto's religious reforms of 1974. The Ahmedis, also known as Qad-
ianis, believe that the Prophet Muhammad was not the last of the prophets. This
belief has periodically brought Ahmedis into intense conflict with both Sunnis and
Shias, despite Ahmedis themselves strictly observing the major rituals of Sunni
Islam from which they had separated during the nineteenth century.

Some sectarian Sunnis had, with the help of their Shia rivals, successfully urged
Bhutto to change the status of the Ahmedi community. These Sunnis had temporarily set aside their long-standing disputes with their counterparts in the Shia community, so the Ahmedi community was targeted by what appeared to be a united
front of Shia and Sunni *ulema*. Shias were reluctantly accommodated by Sunnis
during the anti-Ahmedi campaign but their rivalries and differences remained
intact. Since 1974 when the Ahmedis had their status as Muslims revoked by the
state, these Sunni fundamentalists have wanted to extend the argument regarding
the precise definition of who is or is not a Muslim from the tiny Ahmedi community to the much larger Shia community.

Sectarian Sunnis also tend to greatly underestimate Shias, and portray them as
an unrepresentative elite community at the apex of a pyramid-like social structure
enslaving the Sunni masses. For their part, Shia sectarian organizations grossly in-
flate their numbers so to emphasize their relative strength and the growing appeal
of their faith to new converts from the Sunni Muslims. So estimates can be found
that range widely, from as little as 2 per cent to as high as 35 per cent of Pakistan's
Muslim population.[5] Most scholars believe that the range of 15 to 25 per cent is
more realistic, so even taking 20 per cent as a median means that there are around
30 million Shias in Pakistan, far exceeding the figure for third-placed Iraq, which
probably has less than 15 million Shias.

The late 1970s saw a massive upheaval in the geopolitics of the West Asian
region, such as the ousting of the pro-West Muhammad Reza Shah regime in Iran
by the radical Shia cleric Ayatollah Ruhollah Khomeini, and the ill-fated Soviet involvement in Afghanistan. These developments caused Saudi Arabian and American interests to quickly and sharply coincide as they hoped to create a Sunni fundamentalist wall that could impede the spread of radical politics, both secular and
religious, in that region. One method used by the Saudis which continues even now
is the funding of Sunni fundamentalist *madrasas* in Pakistan, especially in the provinces that border Iran and Afghanistan.

The Saudi Legacy

Saudi Arabia, a country with a far longer and more violent history of sectarian conflict than Pakistan, is the cradle of not only Islam itself but of the eighteenth-century Sunni Wahhabi movement. This probably has the most fundamentalist interpretation of Islam partly because it is influenced by the Hanbali legal school, the strictest of the four Sunni legal schools which each have dominance in specific regions of the Muslim World. Wahhabism is a highly rigid ideology which shows little tolerance towards alternative Sunni interpretations of Islam such as the three non-Hanbali legal schools or of Sufism.

Wahhabis are especially intolerant of Shi'ism. Wahhabis depict other schools or sects of Islam as being products of inter-religious syncretism or inheriting pre-Islamic traditions. All alternative versions of Islam are regarded as being dangerous to society by the Saudi Kingdom as they are deemed to be sources for discord (*fitna*) within the *umma*, threatening its unity and diluting its belief. Some Wahhabis will go so far as even considering non-Wahhabi Muslims as being non-Muslims.

If a parallel can be drawn with Islam and Christianity in terms of historical time lines, it could be argued that Muslim society as a newer society needs more time to mature and is in certain aspects at a stage where Christianity was during the late medieval period. For the Protestant reformer Martin Luther, the Roman Catholic establishment was the main enemy and he believed that Islam could never be defeated until Roman Catholicism as the enemy within Christendom met a similar gruesome fate. Sectarian bias was also present in the Catholic Church where Protestantism was grouped with Islam, even on occasion denounced as being the more repugnant.[6] This mindset is almost replicated in the Saudi Arabian establishment which on occasion finds interaction with non-Muslims like the Americans a more attractive option then with fellow non-Wahhabi 'deviant' Muslims.

The Saudi-American axis was greatly enhanced by the willingness of the military regime of Muhammad Zia ul Haq in Pakistan to join it by helping to train and equip the most fundamentalist factions of the Afghan Sunni *mujaheddin* resistance in return for massive funding, which during its peak during the Reagan years ran into billions of dollars per year.[7] President Zia himself had come from a family with Sunni fundamentalist leanings as his relatives were represented in the hierarchy of fundamentalist organizations like the Jammat-e-Islami which initially strongly supported his military administration.

Although his views were not as extreme as those of his Saudi-Wahhabi backers, Zia's relationship with the Saudis became temporarily strained when he refused Saudi requests that every Pakistani soldier stationed on Saudi soil should be a Sunni. The Saudis wanted to bar Pakistani Shias who may latently sympathize with the Saudi Kingdom's persecuted Shia minority. However, Zia preferred senior military appointments to be offered to Sunni officers who shared his religious background.

The Military, Islam and Islamists

Zia had come into power in 1977 by overthrowing the elected Shia Prime Minister Zulfikar Ali Bhutto (d.1979). However, the power struggle between the Sunni Zia and the Shia Bhutto should not be portrayed in simple sectarian terms as that of a Shia against a Sunni. During the peak of Bhutto's power in the early 1970s, his left-wing politics alarmed some of the Shia landed, business and religious elites. These entered into an alliance with the anti-Bhutto camp which contained in its ranks many Sunnis of similar class and interests as well as fundamentalists, such as the then Saudi-funded Jammat-e-Islami.[8]

In order to provide badly needed legitimacy for an unpopular military regime and Saudi finance, Islam was invoked by Zia and Pakistan progressed further towards the path of Islamization which was not the intention of its founding father, the Shia but secular-oriented Muhammad Ali Jinnah (d.1948). Jinnah had envisaged Pakistan as a geographical space where Muslims being the majority would be free from real or alleged Hindu domination, rather a religious state gove-rned primarily by Islamic religious law (*Sharia*). The other military strongman in Pakistan's history, regarded by some as the antithesis of Zia, was President Muh-ammad Ayub Khan (d.1974). Ayub Khan had clashed with the Jammat-e-Islami in the early 1960s, especially over their strong opposition to his modernist reforms regarding Muslim family law. However, most of the leading Sufi sheikhs gave Ayub Khan their full support in his struggle against the Jammat-e-Islami, which shows that the secular-sacred dichotomy is not always clear-cut in Pakistan.

The Jammat-e-Islami in the subsequent election endorsed Fatima Jinnah, the sister of Pakistan's founding father, as the opposition candidate in her unsuccessful campaign against Ayub Khan. The Jammat-e-Islami had broken one of its pledges, that it would never support a woman for high office on theological grounds, but the Jammat-e-Islami believed that it could impede Fatima Jinnah from making any further modernist reforms. The Jammat-e-Islami justified its unusual actions as being the lesser of two evils.

The U-turn on this gender-cum-political issue on the Jammat-e-Islami's part shows that some fundamentalists are more pragmatic than the term 'fundamen-talist' would suggest. So, some scholars prefer to describe the more pragmatic or realists of the fundamentalists as 'Islamists', and use the term 'fundamentalist' for those with more utopian or uncompromising inclinations. Where this divide actu-ally begins is problematic to determine and so the terms 'Islamist' and 'fundamen-talist' are sometimes used in both senses in this study.

This was the only time in Pakistan's history when the Sunni religious estab-lishment has been divided with one section supporting quasi-secular elites. The Jammat-e-Islami like many other Islamists and unlike most of the Sufi sheikhs had opposed the creation of Pakistan in 1947. The Jammat-e-Islami feared that a state dominated by secular-modernist Muslim elites with the backing of Sufis was more of a threat to Islamists than a Hindu dominated united India. This shows that the Jammat-e-Islami was more concerned with internal differences between Muslims than external rivalry between Hindus and Muslims.

The Jammat-e-Islami's initial opposition to Pakistan's creation has always been a hindrance to it gaining popular appeal, and a weapon used against it by its oppo-nents. The recent conflicts in Afghanistan and Kashmir helped to some extent redeem the Jammat-e-Islami's image, especially regarding its commitment to Pakistani nationalism, as the Jammat-e-Islami has pursed a very aggressive policy in both these conflicts. This convergence of national and Islamist agendas challenges the concept that nationalism and fundamentalism are contradictory terms.[9] So what is being defined here as religious nationalism is really a political term which emphasizes the solidarity of a particular religion with a particular nation-state. Such a concept shows little tolerance of diversity within that nation-state.

In 1979, the military regime imposed Islamic legislation regarding taxation and charity endowments uniformly on the entire Muslim population. This state legislation which was based on the Hanafi Sunni interpretation greatly enraged the Shia minority despite the Hanafi school being the least strict of the four legal schools of Sunni Islam and the one dominant among South Asian Sunni Muslims. The founder of the Sunni Hanafi legal school was Abu Hanifa who had once been the student of the sixth Shia *imam* and the most scholarly of the *imams*, Jafar al-Sadiq (d.765). Jafar al-Sadiq gave shape to a specific Shia legal school named after him called the Jafari school (*al-madhhab al-jafari*). Shias are not bound by the four Sunni schools of law or their understanding of the Islamic traditions, as Sunni scholars and religious leaders are considered by Shias as being fallible.[10]

Shias, like other minorities in Pakistan, also tended to be supporters of the Pakistan People's Party (PPP) which has always been dominated by the Shia Bhutto clan. The Iranian Revolution helped to boost confidence in the Shia minority, as some of them successfully organized themselves into a political group called Tehrik Nifazi-Fiqhi Jafaria (the Front for the Defence of the Jafari Law, TNFJ) in order to confront the military government, which was eventually forced to grant Shias exemption from the Sunni laws.

The military government's concessions in the face of massive Shia demonstrations caused Sunni fundamentalists to worry about the increasing strength of their Shia rivals, as the state's reluctant granting of religious autonomy to the Shias implied that Shia law had a status that was equal or near to that of the Hanafi law that governed the majority of Sunnis, both the Deobandis and the Brelwis in Pakistan. For extremist Deobandis this U-turn by the military administration seemed to be damaging to their ultimate aim of having Shias declared non-Muslims.

The Sunni Subsects

So who are these Sunni fundamentalists? Despite massive media attention being focused on them, the Sunni fundamentalists are a minority within Sunni Islam. The great majority of Sunni Muslims in Pakistan belong to the Brelwi subsect which is especially strong in the countryside of the Punjab and Sind where the bulk of the population resides and the feudal social structures are still intact. In this region of Pakistan the social structure is more inclined towards quasi-caste lineages called *biraderis* rather than in most of the North West Frontier Province (NWFP) where tribe, which as a social system is less concerned with hierarchical status, is a more powerful identity and where more rigid forms of Islam like Deobandism (see below) predominate.

The Brelwis

Inclined towards the mystical dimension in Islam or Sufism, Brelwis are, or were, usually more tolerant towards Shias as they revere the Prophet's descendents almost to the same degree as Shias. The Islam of the Brelwis apart from the usual Islamic rituals such as praying and fasting is also based on pilgrimages to Sufi shrines, sometimes made in the hope of experiencing miracles. Some Brelwis become the disciples (*murids*) of holy men (*murshids*) and pay respect to saints both dead and living known locally as *pir sahibs* or Sufi sheikhs. These *pirs* or *murshids* can themselves sometimes be *ulema* but usually they are simply the descendents of the medieval saint whose tomb is the centre of the shrine of which they are the custodians. Often they are also charismatic individuals who have large followings and are sought after as candidates by major political parties.

Most major *pir* lineages are or are connected by marriage to *sayyids*, descendents of the Prophet Muhammad, so they place the Shia *imams* among their early ancestors. In the Sufi hierarchy, the Prophet Muhammad apart from being the last Prophet is also blessed with external knowledge (*zahir*) and internal knowledge (*batin*). He still provides spiritual guidance through the Sufis to others as he is also the first and the supreme Sufi *murshid* for all Sufis. Those who are near to him, such as the Twelve Imams, form the holiest lineage in Sufism and have supremacy over their own descendents, whereas the ones further along the descent lines gradually lose their intimate knowledge of the *batin*. So some of the *pirs*, particularly the *sayyids* amongst them as the highest ranking *biraderi* in society, have incorporated various elements from Shi'ism into their own beliefs and practices, but most *pirs* have remained within the Sunni fold. The religious ceremony that binds Shias with Sunni Sufis is the traditional celebration of the Prophet Muhammad's birthday (*Milad-ur-Nabi*), which most fundamentalist Sunnis consider as a form of idolatrous worship dressed in Islamic terminology.

Some *pirs*, especially those from the Suhrawardi order in the Multan division of the Punjab, went over to Shi'ism and some of their *murids* followed them. So there are Shia *pirs* in addition to Sunni *pirs*. So Sufism covers both Shia and Sunni Islam in Pakistan. Sufism transcends the major sectarian divide in Islam and some will argue further that Sufism transcends the religious divide as non-Muslims are welcome at Sufi shrines. The Brelwi *ulema* because they are primarily *ulema* tend not to be as liberal or flexible as the Sufi sheikhs.

The Brelwis *ulema* despite their theological training are subordinate to the Sufis in the Brelwi hierarchy. The Brelwi *ulema* may be invited or hired by a *pir* to attend ceremonies at a Sufi shrine, conducting special prayers that require higher knowledge of Qur'anic Arabic that the *pir* may lack, but the *ulema* are not the focus of the setting. The *pir* is accorded far more importance, but often even the living *pir* and everyone present at such a gathering are just paying homage to the *pir's* medieval ancestor, who according to Brelwi doctrines intercedes between man and God. This inferior status accorded to the *ulema* in Brelwi Islam is, perhaps, one of the reasons why Brelwi *ulema* are a minority among the *ulema*, even in the rural areas of the Punjab and Sind where the majority of the population is still more inclined to follow a spiritual (*ruhani*) rather than a dogmatic (*shariati*) interpretation of religion that is more associated with urban areas.

The religious year of the Brelwis is dotted with the numerous festivals of saints (*urus*) where, depending on which particular Sufi order is organizing the event, singing, chanting, drumming and even dancing in trance is allowed. Peasants who are Sunnis sometimes will even take part in Shia festivals. Thus there is some convergence between Sunnis and Shias in rural areas. Sunni *ulema* fear that such a porous identity boundary will help to convert Sunnis to Shi'ism especially in areas where landlords are Shias. This fear of the Sunni *ulema* has helped sharpen sectarian identities.[11]

The Al-e Hadith

As mentioned previously, the Wahhabis or Al-e Hadith as they are often referred to in Pakistan, regard Sufism as an un-Islamic innovation (*bida*). Wahhabis are the extreme opposites of the Brelwis in the spectrum of Sunni Islam as they oppose Sufism in all its forms and actively promote the destruction of both Sufi and Shia shrines. They are highly conscious of their sectarian identity and are represented mostly in the urban business or trading professions, thus their small number makes them an ineffective opposition to the far more numerous and powerful Shia minority. This is why the Saudis have, to the dismay of their own sect in Pakistan, decided to give more funding to the Deobandis, who, because of their larger share of Pakistan's population, can be used as a more formidable counterweight to the Shia community.

The Deobandis

The Deobandis are the second largest Sunni subsect in Pakistan and the one to which most of Pakistan's and neighbouring Afghanistan's anti-Shia militants are affiliated and educated by at its numerous *madrasas*. This particular Sunni subsect holds an intermediate position between polar extremes of Brelwism and Wahhabism in the Sunni spectrum. The Deobandis discourage many of the popular festivals and rituals that the Brelwis associate with Sufi shrines but, unlike the Wahhabis, Deobandis do not actively promote the wholesale destruction of shrines. This is probably why the Taliban, itself an extremist Deobandi organization, especially regarding matters relating to gender and entertainment, was more welcomed by Afghan people than some of the *mujaheddin* parties such as the Hekmatyar's Hezb-e-Islami and Abu Sayyaf's Ittehad-e-Islami, both of which demand a Wahhabi influenced society. In a rare instance, the Taliban is at the middle of a religious spectrum or is considered as a compromise movement, a very strange occurrence.

Deobandi Islam is centred on mosques and especially religious schools and colleges, collectively called *madrasas*. Deobandi *madrasas* outnumber Brelwi *madrasas*. It comes as no surprise that Deobandis are the majority of the Sunni *ulema* in Pakistan. The Deobandis with their foreign-funded *madrasas* produce more *ulema* than the Brelwis, despite their smaller share of the population. Traditionally, Deobandis

72 CAN FAITHS MAKE PEACE?

have come from areas in Pakistan such as the NWFP which are known for their religious zeal, often reinforced by strict tribal codes.

The Deobandis are expanding their geographical territory. For example, in the Punjab, a place famous for Sufi shrines, there has been a ninefold increase in the number of Deobandi *madrasas* since 1973 when the then Prime Minister Zulifikar Ali Bhutto declared Pakistan an Islamic Republic.[12] However, not all Pakistani Deobandi *madrasas* are explicitly associated with anti-Shia organizations, which includes the Siphe Sahaha Pakistan (SSP) and Afghanistan's Taliban movement.

The SSP

The SSP (Army of the Companions of the Prophet-Pakistan) was formed during the Zia era in the district of Jhang in the Punjab, which is one of two regions of Pakistan where there is intense debate over which sect is in the majority. The SSP draws much of its strength from the urban areas of Jhang where migrant families from the violent 1947 partition of British India settled. Most of these families were from the peasant society of East Punjab, which was relatively free from the domination of high status landowning castes or tribes, while Jhang's agrarian economy is still dominated by landlords known locally as 'feudals' who own some two thirds of Jhang's land and are usually Shias.

Despite the obvious vertical rivalry between the mostly lower-middle-class SSP and the Shia feudals, most of the SSP's violence is directed against the Shia militant organization Siphe Muhammad Pakistan (SMP or Army of the Prophet Muhammad Pakistan), which recruits from the same socio-economic strata. Many SMP activists like their SSP rivals have seen action in Afghanistan, initially fighting the Soviet-backed communists in different militias, and later on opposing sides: the SSP on the side of fellow sectarian Deobandis, the Taliban and the SMP on the side of the various Iranian-backed Shia Hazara militias that later allied themselves with their former rivals, the Russian backed Sunni dominated Northern Alliance, which finally drove out the Taliban from Kabul with American help.

Even more strange are the circumstances in which the SSP has experienced some success in the political arena. The SSP supported the PPP minority administration in the Punjab during the second and rather chaotic reign of Benazir Bhutto in 1993–1996 despite the Shia affiliation and Shia vote-bank of the Bhutto clan. Two SSP Local Assembly members even became ministers in Pakistan's most important province. In the adjoining NWFP (North West Frontier Province), the PPP political alliance with the Deobandis was used as a counterweight to Pathan nationalist parties.[13] The PPP extended support to the Taliban movement with American approval[14] to bring about much-wanted stability in war-torn Afghanistan, which brought the SSP and other Deobandis organizations closer to the PPP.

As a result, many in the Shia community shifted their political allegiance to the PML (Pakistan Muslim League) of Nawaz Sharif. This shift in voting on the part of the Shias was one of the contributing factors that benefited the PML as Nawaz Sharif returned to office in 1997 ousting the PPP with a huge victory. Nawaz Sharif was once the Deobandi General Zia ul Haques's protégé. However, he soon passed the Anti-Terrorism Act of 1997 which was designed to curb sectarianism which had gained considerable ground during the Benazir Bhutto administration. Nawaz Sharif himself become a target of an unsuccessful assassination attempt by the Lasker Jhangvi (LeJ) a splinter group from the SSP which is even more violent and has alleged links with Al Qaeda.

This intra-Sunni violence represents a dilemma for the anti-Shia Deobandi extremists as they have to maintain their anti-Shia stance yet avoid alienating moderate Sunnis. Some Sunni Islamist organizations, such as the Jammat-e-Islami who view sectarianism as damaging the Islamist anti-secular agenda, have organized the Milli Yikjahati (National Unity) Council where sectarian differences can be discussed with the aim of reconciliation.

The Jammat-e-Islami has also opposed sectarianism as much of its Saudi funding has been diverted to the SSP and the Taliban. The most extremist of the Sunni and Shia sectarian organizations, such as the SSP, LeJ and SMP, strongly oppose such meditating steps as threatening or compromising what they consider as the essentials of their faith.

The War on Terror in the aftermath of the events of 9/11 has, however, achieved some of the objectives of the Milli Yikjahati Council. The massive air bombing which helped to remove the Taliban in Afghanistan created a powerful image of Islam being in danger from the West, which many Islamists of various sectarian affiliations used successfully to enhance their political standing. They joined in a political alliance, the Muttahida Majlis Amal (MMA), based on anti-Americanism which included such diverse and opposing partners as the Brelwi Jammat Ulema Pakistan (JUP), Jammat-e-Islami and the Taliban's parent Deobandi organization the Jammat Ulema Islam (JUI). It even included Shias belonging to the TJP, which had its origins in the opposition to Zia's Islamization of the late 1970s, a process which had the strong support of the JUI and the Jammat-e-Islami.

However, the SSP did not join the MMA which since the October 2002 elections has controlled the NWFP adjoining the sensitive Afghanistan border. The SSP not only opposed the MMA, which included the TJP, the forerunner of its bitter rival the SMP, among its ranks, but also supported General Musharaf, despite him officially banning sectarian organizations, curbing extremist *madrasas* and making a U-turn regarding support for the SSP's sectarian ally, the Taliban, in the face of threats from the United States. Despite the MMA being a strong vocal critic of Musharaf's pro-American stance, it is a junior partner of the Musharaf-backed Muslim League administration in Baluchistan.

Conclusion

The above account shows that sectarian organizations have alliances and counter-alliances with more mainstream religious and supposedly secular-oriented political parties in Pakistan. As such alliances are more inclined to be situational than being based on principles it is hard to say if there will be any real reconciliation between the various sectarian groups in the near future. As Pakistan is still evolving from feudalism to capitalism, it is experiencing problems of an identity crisis as its traditional power structures come under considerable strain. The landlords are losing some of their political clout but the industrialists and bureaucrats have not entirely replaced them and all these categories are becoming increasingly blurred.

All these alignments and realignments leave the religious elites as brokers in a complicated patron-client set-up. Some of them have turned to and away from violent sectarianism in order to enhance their own power-bases depending on whether internal or external enemies can be portrayed as the greater threat. Sectarianism violence threatens civil society yet it is only a symptom of the malfunctioning of the Pakistani state which has used religion to counterweight other forms of identity, an approach that has instead brought into existence a society now fragmented on sectarian as well as regional, tribal and linguistic lines.

6

SYMBOLISM, VIOLENCE AND THE DESTRUCTION OF RELIGIOUS COMMUNITIES IN THE RUSSIAN AND OTTOMAN EMPIRES c.1870–1923

Cathie Carmichael

The geographer Dean S. Rugg remarked upon the way that different regimes and historical epochs had shaped the landscape in Eastern Europe, moving from 'landscapes of multinationalism' in the nineteenth century to 'landscapes of nationalism'[1] in the following period. In both Eastern Europe and the Near East, this process was not without great human suffering and we may interpret these also as landscapes of contestation, tension, violence and finally of destruction.[2] In his journey in Eastern Anatolia in 1930–31, Gerald Reitlinger noted Armenian and Orthodox churches that had been boarded up in Kars and 'burnt and gutted houses…[in] the high street of dead Kulb.'[3] Some regions and towns of the former Ottoman and Russian Empires never regained their previous stature and ethnic and religious communities disappeared altogether, in the wake of the genocides committed during the First and Second World Wars in many of the places that had previously experienced inter-ethnic violence.

The final years of the Ottoman and Russian Empires were characterized by deep systemic instability, which manifested itself in increasing violence against religious minorities in both states and in the successor states in the Balkans. Religious communities were subjected to various attempts to remove or 'cleanse' them, a term itself, which has clear Judeo-Christian overtones.[4] In the Russian Empire, ultra-nationalist newspapers such as *Novoe vremia*,[5] *Bessarabets*,[6] and the Holy Synod itself were responsible for fanning the flames of violence in many cases. Outbreaks of vicious violence, known by the term pogroms after 1871[7] against Jews (and sometimes other religious minorities such as Armenians[8]) most frequently broke out in Easter week. In the Ottoman Empire, Christians were subjected to violent popular and state directed violence. In the 1870s, Bulgarians were subjected to paramilitary violence from Turkish irregulars during the uprising against Ottoman rule. In the 1890s, several hundred thousand Armenians were killed and for the next thirty years, this community as well as other Christian minorities were subjected to genocidal state policies, which eventually resulted in the almost complete destruction of these ancient groups in Anatolia. Armenians were the victims of government propaganda in the 1890s and again in 1914–5. Missionary Henry Harrison Riggs accused the Turkish authorities of dispensing 'a great deal of fiction to prove that the Armenians were a disloyal element menacing the safety of the Turks.'[9]

Comparisons have been made between the situation of the Jews in the Russian Empire and the Christians of the Ottoman Empire. For Vahakn Dadrian, the Jews and Armenians were vulnerable to persecution at a number of different levels. Constant attacks, without the possibility for retribution 'compounded their condition of vulnerability.'[10] As both were also barred from certain occupations, they achieved in other spheres, which made them vulnerable to their neighbours' envy. In addition, neither group had a 'parent state' before the First World War to represent their interests.[11] Dadrian has also argued that the position of the Armenians was made yet more vulnerable by legal discrimination and 'the fixed and intractable prescriptions of Islamic canon law as expressed mostly in the Koran and codified in the Sheriat... In that system the non-Muslims [were] relegated to a permanently fixed inferior status.'[12] One could also argue that for the Jews in the Russian Empire, whose legal statue was restricted by the Pale of Settlement, there was also a conflation between religious and legal discrimination, which also became 'racial' in the late nineteenth century.[13] We should note here that violent practices as opposed to some kinds of discrimination have very little to do with Qur'anic injunctions or the *Sharia*[14] or for that matter Judaism or Christianity, which as faiths all emphasize the need to restrain, control or even forgive violence. Paraphrasing Walter Cotton, E. Valentine Daniel writes 'men will wrangle for, write for, fight for and die for religion – anything but live it.'[15]

The situation of Muslims in the Balkans in the newly formed national states was also clearly parallel in terms of their vulnerability.[16] In the aftermath of war between Greece and Turkey from 1919–1922, both Greeks and Turks were expelled en masse from Asia Minor and the Balkans, which was supervised under the terms of the Treaty of Lausanne in 1923, but also led to atrocities. The gradual collapse of Ottoman power in the Balkans had led to outbreaks of violence against Muslims, particularly in Bosnia in the 1870s and Macedonia in 1912.

The years 1870–1915 saw a clear deterioration, if not complete obliteration in the situations of all these communities, which we might describe as pre-genocidal.[17] The destruction of the Armenians in 1915 clearly raised the limits of the possible in terms of the complete destruction of ancient communities. Thereafter in Eastern Europe and the former Ottoman world, the situation for certain religious and ethnic groups deteriorated. During the Greek occupation of Smyrna, paramilitaries known as Black Fate (Mavri Mira) terrorized Turkish villagers in the hinterland of the port.[18] In Imperial Russia pogroms increased markedly in the years before the First World War and during General Anton Denikin's occupation of the Ukraine in 1918–19, several thousand Jews were systematically massacred. Some historians have estimated that 120,000 people or about 8 per cent of the Jewish population of the Ukraine were killed by the nationalist 'Whites'.[19] By 1923 and the foundation of the Turkish republic most Christian communities in Anatolia had been expelled or killed. Pogroms against Jews continued until 1920 in the former Russian Empire. It was these same communities who were wiped out in 1941–43 by the forces of the Third Reich. By the end of the Second World War in the former Russian Empire and by 1923 in the Ottoman Empire, we can meaningfully talk about the destruction of entire religious cultures. In 1913, Muslim communities in the Balkans remained in pockets such as Albania, Kosovo, Macedonia, Sandžak and Bosnia. In Bosnia and Kosovo, those Muslims were subjected to further genocidal attacks in the 1940s and 1990s when the term 'ethnic cleansing' came into its current usage.[20] Although Muslim communities have survived in the Balkans, their numbers and the territory in which they live have both been severely curtailed by successive waves of violence.

Although we largely construct the violent actions against such groups as Jews or Armenians taken at this time in political and ethnic terms, most contemporaries regarded this as a religious phenomenon. As he travelled through the Balkans, Harry Thomson remarked, 'I do not think that we western Christians, who have not undergone their fierce trial, appreciate fully the religious heroism these poor peasants have displayed during all the centuries they have been under the domination of the Turks.'[21] The massacre of Armenians in the Church of St Stephen was carried out by Turks described as 'sanguinaires et sacrilèges' ('bloodthirsty and sacrilegious') and their victims described as 'iconastases' ('walls of icons' i.e. reminding him of the images of dead and martyred saints in Byzantine churches).[22] In an interview in il Messaggero in August 1915, the former Italian Consul in Trebizond, Giacomo Gorrini, called for 'la più risoluta riprovazione e la vendetta dell'intera Cristianità'[23] ('forceful condemnation and vengeance by the whole of Christendom') against Turkey for its killing of Armenians. Undoubtedly sympathy for Christians and antipathy towards Muslims (and sometimes Jews) affected reporting of these events in Western Europe and the United States. As early as the 1870s, the atrocities committed against the Bulgarians turned the collapse of the Ottoman power into a moral issue and a clash of civilizations as far as the European public was concerned. In 1876, Thomas Carlyle wrote to The Times calling for 'the immediate and summary expulsion of the Turk from Europe'. He continued, 'the peaceful

Mongol inhabitants would...be left in peace and treated with perfect equity...but the governing Turk with all his Pashas and Bashi Bazouks, should be ordered to disappear from Europe and never to return.'[24] In 1915, the Archbishop of Canterbury argued that the Armenian massacres had 'no parallel' in the history of the world and that 'Christian aid should flow out ungrudgingly,'[25] therefore distinguishing between the fate of the Armenians and that of the Muslims of the Balkans who had been killed in vast numbers only three years earlier or that of the Jewish victims of pogroms.

Sources from this period are highly ambivalent and sometimes sympathetic to those who sought revenge on the perpetrators of religious and ethnically inspired mass murder. The assassin of Talât Paşa by an Armenian called Teilirian, was dubbed by one German newspaper 'an Armenian Tell'[26] after the Swiss national hero. He was spectacularly acquitted by a court in Berlin. After the assassination of the Ukrainian nationalist leader Symon Petliura in Paris in May 1926, his killer Samuel Schwartzbard, announced that he was avenging the pogroms. Schwartzbard, a Bessarabian Jew, was also tried and acquitted in 1927. His case was defended by the well-known barrister Henri Torrès.[27] Some reports were coloured by Orientalist prejudice which could be extended towards almost all cultures east of Trieste at the whim of the particular author.[28] Morgan Philips Price, correspondent for the *Manchester Guardian* and an important witness to some important events of this period noted that his Armenian servant gave him 'full particulars of the torturings, burnings and hangings with the added imagery of the East.'[29]

When it became clear that Christianity was likely to disappear from Anatolia with the burning of Smyrna (Izmir) in September 1922 and the exodus of the remaining Greeks, the situation was generally depicted in rather hagiographic terms in a number of influential accounts. The death of Greek Orthodox Bishop Chrysostom was described by one writer as 'glorieuse, mais tragique'[30] ('glorious but tragic'). George Horton's *Blight of Asia* contains one of the most well-known accounts of the murder:

> The evidence is conclusive that he met his end at the hands of the Ottoman populace... He was spit upon, his beard torn out by the roots, stabbed to death and then dragged about the streets. His only sin was that he was a patriotic and eloquent Greek who believed in the expansion of his race and worked to that end. He was offered a refuge in the French Consulate and an escort by the French marines, but he refused, saying that it was his duty to remain with his flock. He said to me "I am a shepherd and must stay with my flock." He died a martyr and deserves the highest honors in the bestowal of the Greek church and government...Polycarp, the patron saint of Smyrna, was burned to death in the stadium overlooking the town. The Turk roams over the land of the Seven Cities and there is none to say [to] him nay, but the last scene in the final extinction of Christianity was glorified by the heroic death of the last Christian.[31]

Violence at this time manifested itself in a number of forms and violent attacks followed patterns. Symbolic violence included dishonouring, dehumanization and quasi-religious abuse and taunts. When the Greeks killed the Turkish leader Çakir-cali Mehmet Efe in the Smyrna hinterland, his decapitated body was 'hanged from his foot to destroy all myths and rumours about his invincibility.'[32] Charles Ydriate remarked of the violence during the uprising in Bosnia in the 1870s 'aujourd'hui encore les irréguliers ne regardent une victoire comme complète que s'ils ont dés-honoré le cadavre de l'ennemi'[33] ('today the irregulars do not regard a victory as complete if they do not desecrate the corpse of the enemy'). No doubt these act-ions reflect more traditional notions of honour and the body[34] and mutilations signal complete victory over the enemy.

Very often dishonouring was aimed at the chastity of women or what has been called 'symbolic rape of the body of that community'.[35] In Bulgaria in 1878, in the village of Oklanli, Turkish women were raped over several days and then burnt alive. The atrocities were carried out by their Christian neighbours in communities that had lived in the same villages for centuries.[36] Norman Naimark remarks of 1915 that '[e]ven in their miserable state, the Armenian women were exploited, brutalized and raped by the guards.'[37] In Macedonia, as the Muslim populations were expelled in 1922–3, women in the village of Guvezna 'were said to have been gathered together in the *aghora* (market) and publicly ridiculed as they were forced to dance naked at gunpoint.'[38]

Dehumanization of victims by equating them with animals is commonplace in the litany of atrocities. During the Balkan Wars, several hundred Muslim men were marched to an abattoir and killed.[39] Between 1915 and 1923, during the break up of the Ottoman Empire, Armenians and Greeks were tortured with horseshoes.[40] During the Greek occupation of Smyrna in 1919, one of the Turks staff was bayo-neted in the face and thrown in the hold of a Greek cattleship among the cattle.[41]

Arjun Appadurai has argued that 'the maiming and mutilation of ethnicized bodies is a desperate effort to restore the validity of somatic markers of "other-ness" in the face of the uncertainties posed by…changes'[42] and only with death comes 'dead certainty'. Often violence is in excess of what would actually be required to kill or maim an individual. Daniele Conversi stresses that '[e]thnic violence often occurs when there are few cultural markers accessible to different-iate between groups'[43] and in these cases violence can be interpreted as an 'experi-ence of solidarity'[44] which reaffirms old boundaries, creates bitter divisions bet-ween the victims and victimizers, but crucially forges new bonds between the per-petrators. In other words, the very existence of violence as a phenomenon is a sign that acculturation has already taken place and that society is becoming (potentially) more integrated. In the Russian Empire, Jews were leaving the *shtetl* (traditional Jewish village), taking professional positions, moving outside the Pale of Settle-ment, and speaking Russian in the immediate years before the Revolution, which is clearly a paradoxical situation given the increase in violence against Jewish persons during this era. In the Ottoman Empire, likewise, Armenians were experiencing greater social integration in state institutions just prior to the genocide.

Plunder and theft of property have also been seen as an important part of this violence. Edwin Pears believed that 'traditional feeling' by the Muslims of the Ottoman Empire gave them the right to plunder,[45] although we should also remember that '[i]n some settings, "tradition" is effectively used to justify, excuse and direct violence.'[46] Discussing the Balkan Wars of 1912–13, Djordje Stefanović, has argued that '[w]hile the motives of enrichment and "revenge" were probably omnipresent at the level of direct perpetrators (of interethnic violence), it is important to distinguish them from more ideological and long term motivations of the military and the political elite.'[47] Nikita Khrushchev suggested enrichment was one motive for the violence he saw as a child against Jews in his hometown of Yuzovka. He described the Ukrainian villagers and Russian industrial workers as desperately poor, but nevertheless emphasized the wanton rather than just venal nature of the destruction in the pogrom that he witnessed, remembering '[t]he workers…were bragging the next day about how many boots and other trophies they picked up during looting… I saw clock repair shops that had been broken into and feathers were flying across the street where the looters were…shaking the feathers out of the windows of the Jewish houses.'[48] Even the poorest Jews in Kishinev had feather beds[49] and the feathers flying through the air as a symbol of violence and chaos is powerfully evoked in the poem 'be-'Ir La-Haregah' (City of Slaughter) by Hayyim Nahman Bialik.[50]

Extant theory can explain why society can be broken down along religious lines and gives possible motives associated with venality, wanton or sexual power, but we should also perhaps ask whether it is religion itself that makes individuals more violent? John Allcock argued that the Croatian fascists in the 1940s treated their Serb or Muslim victims as 'sacrificial animals…[an] atrocity raised to the level of sacrament'[51] and the re-enactment of quasi-religious rites is another fairly common occurrence in the violence in this earlier period. During pogrom violence, spikes were driven through the hands, legs and into the heads of Jews as 'retribution' for the crucifixion.[52] In his description of the pogromist, Leon Trotsky recalled rhetorically that he can 'smash a chair against a baby's head, rape a little girl while the entire crowd looks on and hammer a nail into a living human body.'[53] In 1922, a Greek priest was blinded, then crucified and had horseshoes nailed to his hands and feet by Turkish soldiers.[54] Bulgarians were accused of crucifying Greeks in the village of Doxato in 1913.[55] Crucifixion occurred during the Balkan Wars in Macedonia, apparently committed by the Turks. Officer Penev reported that a soldier of the tenth Rhodope infantry had been crucified on a poplar tree by means of telegraph wires.[56] In the same year in Filibe in Bulgaria, mosques were turned into latrines[57] in order to desecrate them. According to missionary Helen Harris, Armenians were slashed across the breast in the form of a cross and asked 'where is your Jesus?' in the 1890s.[58]

The peoples of the Book were, of course, used to equating suffering with God, and their holy books are full of violent scenes which can be interpreted in ambiguous ways. Examples include the sacrifice of Isaac by Abraham in Genesis, apocalyptic passages in Ezekiel, or even the Passion. When the German Consul described the killing of an Armenian bishop and about seven hundred Christians in Mardin in 1915, he described their fate as having been 'slaughtered like sheep'.[59] It is unlikely that religion provided more than just the form and shape as human societies have been characterized by violence across space and time.[60] It is certain that faith helped some individuals to reconcile themselves to violence and dislocation. Survivors of the Armenian genocide told of 'moments of epiphany when they had visions of being visited and comforted by a Jesus figure and were thus able to forgive the Turks and be reconciled with their past.'[61] In his description of the killing of Bosnian Muslims in 1915, William Frederick Bailey acknowledged the importance of religious faith at the hour of death.

> [T]hey are endeavoring to keep their faces turned towards the sun; and if they live until it sets, and if Allah lends them aid, they will watch the West turn crimson and the great red orb drop behind the mountains. They like to die at sundown these people. Perhaps they fancy that the light of world will bear their souls in a cloud of glory to the rose gardens of Paradise.[62]

Günther Schlee has argued that the sacrificial element in religious belief be interpreted in terms of both good and evil:

> The view that social identification…is often situational and comprises a dose of opportunism…is commonly accepted… Empirically valid as it may be, nevertheless it is hard to combine with an equally valid finding, namely that social identities can mobilise deep emotions, emotions which accompany horrible or noble acts, or acts which can be horrible and noble at the same time.[63]

Each confessional community perpetrated atrocities, which were in some way linked to their religious identity or discovered ethnic boundary marker. Is the religious symbolism in ethnic violence important and how conscious are the perpetrators of their actions? Although the symbolic element is fairly constant, we don't yet have a systematic analysis of this aspect of inter-ethnic violence.[64] Clearly also once violence is initiated, it also has its own bizarre momentum.

Symbolic violence occurs when individuals draw upon experiences outside of their everyday life. In particular it can occur when individuals have heard of atrocities or past acts of violence, but not actually practised them before. Therefore Milovan Djilas' remark that 'religious and ideological murders do not require any imagination, just efficiency,'[65] seems to be an inversion of what actually takes place.

It has been observed that the killing of one's long term neighbours, with whom one has previously been on good terms, is an act of cognitive dissonance.[66] The element of dissonance seems to an almost universal characteristic of religious and ethnic prejudice within texts and may therefore explain the dissonance of violent practice. The Middle English poem the *Siege of Jerusalem* has been seen as anti-Semitic, despite the fact that 'the poem's writer and readers were unlikely to have met any living Jewish people.'[67] Fyodor Dostoyevsky's novels are filled with anti-Semitic stereotypes, including the notion that Jews were rich, at a time when he lived in St Petersburg alongside Jews who were exceedingly poor.[68] In 1903, just prior to the pogrom in Kishinev, *Bessarabets* published a story that the Jews had invented a way to make wine without grapes (and would thus be able to undercut an important local industry).[69] George Orwell believed that '…one of the marks of anti-Semitism is an ability to believe stories that could not possibly be true,'[70] a remark that we might extend to all religious prejudice.

We might therefore want to distinguish between dishonouring and dehumanization and symbolic violence rooted in religious imagery. Whereas an individual might have practised gender-based humiliation or violence and would have certainly witnessed or partaken in gratuitous cruelty against animals[71] as part of their everyday life experience, directed violence (as opposed to suspicion and prejudice towards another community) might be entirely novel and its litany drawn from half-remembered passages from the *Bible* or *Qur'an*. Religious symbolic violence could be described as a reaction to textual influence *in extremis* and is thus almost entirely ideological in character.

To understand the historical processes described here we should perhaps return to Vahakn Dadrian's notion of the 'vulnerability' of religious communities at a time when states were unstable. Henry Morgenthau was sceptical as to whether it was really religion that was at the bottom of the events he witnessed in Turkey in 1915:

> Undoubtedly religious fanaticism was an impelling motive with the Turkish and Kurdish rabble who slew Armenians as a service to Allah, but the men who really conceived the crime had no such motive. Practically all of them were atheists, with no more respect for Mohammedanism than for Christianity, and with them the one motive was cold-blooded, calculating state policy.[72]

The pogroms, genocide, exodus and expulsion of the period 1870–1923 were a sign of the weakness of the states and their inability to transform into strong polities with civic rather than ethnic or religious notions of citizenship. Atatürk admitted in an interview with the Swiss journalist Emile Hilderbrand in 1926 that the Young Turk triumvirate, who had initiated the Armenian genocide in 1915 had weakened the state:

> These leftovers from the former Young Turk Party…should have been made to account for the lives of millions of our Christian subjects who were ruthlessly driven en masse, from their homes and massacred… [T]his element, who forced our country into the Great War against the will of the people,…caused the shedding of rivers of blood of the Turkish youth to satisfy the criminal ambition of Enver Pasha.[73]

Intriguingly, Sergei Witte, perhaps the most talented minister of state in late Imperial Russia, also realized that the radicalization of the Jewish population was undesirable in a strong polity.[74] In his memoirs he recalled:

[h]ow he once told Alexander III that if one admitted the impossibility of drowning all the Russian Jews in the Black Sea - as one must, according to Witte's obvious, though tacit assumption, then one must recognize their rights to live and create conditions which will enable them to carry on a human existence.[75]

In states where religious communities have lived side by side for centuries, where culture and the division of labour is often based on religion, where religion has infrastructural value,[76] then the destruction of religious communities represents an almost fatal blow. In response to the question posed by the editors of this volume: 'Can faiths make peace?', then the answer must surely be that they must. The alternative to peace is on display across the shattered and 'cleansed' landscapes of Eastern Europe and Asia Minor.

7

WAR, RELIGION AND HONOUR

Paul Robinson

A fundamental aspect of war is honour. Perceptions of honour cause wars, influence the way people behave during wars, and affect the ending of wars. Often, honour has a religious basis, and draws its strength from religious teaching. When war, honour, and religion fuse, the results can be particularly devastating. This chapter examines the meaning of honour, the relevance of honour in modern conflict, and the combination of honour and religion as one cause of war. It will then use a case study of religious influences on medieval chivalry to draw general conclusions about the relationship between war, honour, and religion, and to discuss one particular trap which people need to avoid if they do not wish to provide religious sanction for violence.

Honour and War in the Modern Era

Exactly why people do go to war is a question which has been vexing commentators for hundreds of years. The ancient Greek historian Thucydides suggested that there were three prime motives: 'security, honour, and self-interest'.[1] Others have given similar lists: Nicolo Machiavelli cited property, blood, and honour as the main causes of conflict; Thomas Hobbes, gain, safety, and reputation; and Jean-Jacques Rousseau, strength, wealth, and prestige.[2]

Of these, honour may be the most important. Donald Kagan comments that, '[t]he reader may be surprised by how small a role…considerations of practical utility and material gain, and even ambition for power itself, play in bringing on wars and how often some aspect of honor is decisive.'[3] Similarly, Johann Huizinga noted that:

> History and sociology tend to exaggerate the part played in the origin of wars, ancient or modern, by immediate material interests and the lust for power. Though statesmen who plan the war may themselves regard it as a question of power-politics, in the great majority of cases the real motives are to be found less in the 'necessities' of economic expansion, etc., than in pride and vainglory, the desire for prestige and all the pomps of superiority. The great wars of aggression from antiquity down to our own times all find a far more essential explanation in the idea of glory, which everybody understands, than in any rational and intellectualist theory of economic forces and political dynamisms.[4]

There is a tendency to regard honour as 'obsolete,'[5] something which affected behaviour in past centuries, but in the modern world is largely irrelevant. In reality, though, honour is as influential as it ever was. It is mainly the *language* of honour which has disappeared,[6] with the result that modern people have difficulty expressing it.[7] As William Ian Miller notes in a study of humiliation and honour:

> Like ancient heroes, we care about honor, about how we stack up against all those with whom we are competing for approbation. …Honor is not dead with us. It has hidden its face, moved to the back regions of consciousness, been kicked out of most public discourse…But in spite of its back-alley existence, honor still looms large in many areas of our social life, especially in those, I would bet, that occupy most of our psychic energy.[8]

Sidney Axinn rightly says, 'no society seems able to give up some application of honor,'[9] and Michael Ignatieff correctly notes that codes of honour 'seem to exist in all cultures, and their common features are among the oldest artefacts of human morality.'[10] All societies wish to promote certain forms of behaviour, and will therefore reward, or honour, those who excel. Indeed, without honour as an incentive, the drive to excel would be greatly reduced. A society without honour would be likely to stagnate. Honour, therefore, will never be 'obsolete' and will always play a major role in determining human behaviour.

This is as true in war as in any other activity. Honour and war continue to enjoy a symbiotic relationship, just as they have for thousands of years. When the British went to war to recover the Falkland Islands in 1982, the material value of the Islands was negligible, and in material terms the costs of regaining them disproportionate. But national honour demanded a response to Argentine aggression. Similarly, many other modern conflicts have questions of honour at their heart. Barry O'Neill notes that international politics are still guided by issues of honour, and that 'it is simply the name that has changed,'[11] with politicians nowadays preferring terms such as 'credibility' when justifying military action. Thus American governments claimed that their military involvement in Central America in the 1980s was necessary to maintain America's prestige. 'Our credibility worldwide is engaged', stated the Kissinger Commission in 1984.[12] 'If Central America were to fall...our credibility would collapse', stated Ronald Reagan in 1983.[13] In 1999, NATO leaders warned that the 'credibility of the alliance' was at stake when it confronted Yugoslavia, and in 2002, President George W. Bush warned Western states that 'their credibility is at stake' when deciding whether to support the United States in its invasion of Iraq.[14] Government spokesmen in the USA and Great Britain spoke regularly of the 'humiliation' Saddam Hussein had inflicted on the international community by defying its will. After Saddam agreed to allow weapons inspectors into Iraq, British Foreign Secretary, Jack Straw commented that '[w]e have only reached this stage, after years of vacillation and humiliation, because of the threat of force.'[15] The implication was that Iraq had dishonoured the West, and that only the use of force would restore the latter's honour. War, it seems, is still very much a matter of honour.

The Meaning of Honour

Before analysing how honour interacts with religion in war, it is necessary to understand the various meanings of honour. The term 'honour' is open to numerous interpretations and the concept is riddled with contradictions. However, the very confusion this causes makes it all the more important that we find some sort of working definition.

One of the foremost scholars of the subject, Julian Pitt-Rivers, defined honour as variously: 'a moral concept', 'precedence', 'a personal attribute', 'social status', and a 'sentiment, a manifestation of that sentiment in conduct, and the evaluation of this conduct in others, that is to say, reputation'.[16] Alternatively, one can look at honour as: a right; a code of behaviour; recognition of, or a mark or reward for excellence; or a spur to excellence. It can be seen as an internalized sentiment or as a mark of external recognition. It can be individual or collective; absolute or relative; hierarchical or egalitarian; horizontal or vertical; ascribed or acquired. Also important are the concepts of shame and guilt, the former often being seen as either the opposite, or at least the companion of honour, and the latter being seen as in some way opposed to shame and honour.

What all these ideas have in common is that they are in some respect related to questions of personal and collective worth or value. Simply put, according to Hans van Wees, '[h]onour, in general, is the abstract, immaterial "value" that one has in one's own and other's eyes.'[17] This last phrase immediately raises an important aspect of honour, which is that it is both internal *and* external to the individual. As Peristiany notes, '[h]onor is the value of a person in his or her own eyes (that is one's claim to worth), *plus* that person's value in the eyes of his or her social group. Honor is a claim to worth along with the social acknowledgment of that worth.'[18]

A person's sense of honour makes him act in a certain way because firstly he himself believes that it is the right thing to do, and that behaving in such a way makes him a person of worth, and secondly he wishes to validate his worth by gaining the approval of others. In the former sense, honour is similar to ideas such as conscience or integrity; in the latter, it is closer to reputation, name, face, prestige, and so on.

Every society wishes to encourage certain forms of behaviour. It therefore attempts to indoctrinate specific values into individuals, in the hope that they will internalize them and act spontaneously in accordance with them. At the same time, it will reward those who perform in a suitable fashion, and punish those who do not. Honour in the external sense is, therefore, as Aristotle said 'the reward for virtue.'[19]

Problems arise, though, because many people inevitably, value the rewards more than the virtues which they are supposed to represent. Possession of honours implies that you are a person of worth, raises self-esteem, and improves self-image. People will, therefore, resort to short-cuts and underhand methods to gain the rewards without necessarily practising the virtues. Honour systems, which are meant to encourage virtuous behaviour, can paradoxically have the opposite effect.

Another problem is that external honour in theory rewards internal excellence. But only so many can excel. Although all can be virtuous, not all can be outstanding. Honour therefore becomes associated with precedence and rank, in conflict with virtue. In competition for precedence, a person's position is under continual threat from others, and they have to be sensitive to attacks on their honour, and to respond to them. If you allow an assault on your honour to go unchallenged, you in effect cede precedence to the person who has attacked you. Your reputation suffers, and your internal sense of worth declines also. For this reason, one can also view honour as a right, the right to respect. In the absence of easily enforceable laws, honour systems serve to protect peoples' rights, by deterring them from attacking others, as they know that such an attack will call forth a violent response. This is why violent honour systems, which include sensitivity to insult, duelling, and so on, thrive when central government is weak, and have declined where legal systems are strong. It also explains why honour remains an important element in international conflict, because there is no international equivalent to national government enforcing law and order.

Internal and external honour often conflict with one another. What one thinks is right may not be what society wishes to reward. The demands of conscience and reputation are not always the same. However, the two cannot exist without each other. Internal conscience and social opinion are in constant dialogue with one another, and one determines one's identity through reference to both.[20] At the end of the day, though, it is the internal judgement that matters. One is concerned with what others think of one, because their judgement affects one's own judgement of self. Honour is ultimately inward-looking; its primary concern is with evaluations of the self.

This explains why people are so keen to pursue honour, are so sensitive to attacks on their honour, and are even willing to fight and die in defence of it. For most people, feeling good about themselves is a matter of extraordinary importance. As philosopher John Rawls has pointed out, 'the most important primary good is self-respect.'[21] If a man loses his honour he loses his self. Risking life for honour is not necessarily irrational. When fighting involves simply the prospect of loss of physical existence, and dishonour involves the certainty of loss of self, fighting may seem preferable.

Honour and Religion as Causes of War

This analysis indicates that honour causes wars by encouraging competition and glory-seeking, and by encouraging people to respond to assaults on their rights and their dignity. Since competition is likely to involve such assaults, and since competition inevitably pushes people down as well as up, the people who sense they are being forced down will fight back to protect their honour. At the international level, similar competition between nations for precedence causes war. So too does the sense, which nations may feel, that their nation is being dishonoured in some way. Ethnic conflicts, for instance, can be seen as the result of the sense of humiliation one group feels it has suffered at the hands of another. As philosopher Paul Gilbert says of modern wars of secession:

> A "signe of undervalue...in their Nation" is an even more potent cause for people to go to war than it was in Hobbes's day... For to deny statehood to one putative nation when others have it may seem to undervalue it and hence to deprecate its glory. ...All such depreciation is understandably resented. Political independence is intended both to remove the victims from its influence and award them the recognition that depreciation denies. Arguably the majority of new wars are caused by 'Glory'.[22]

In addition, honour implies action. As the twelfth century romance writer Chrétien de Troyes noted, '[n]o one gains a reputation by idleness.'[23] For it is impossible to show excellence, and thus win honour, by doing nothing. In this respect, it is interesting to note the manner in which proponents of war challenge those who wish to maintain peace with wanting to do nothing. 'We can't keep on doing nothing' was a constant refrain prior to the invasion of Iraq in 2003.

Of course, there is no requirement that action be violent, at least in theory. If honour derives from virtue, there can be virtue in things other than violence. That said, historically honour systems have elevated violence. For if one wishes to gain precedence over others, the one sure means of doing so and of making them recognize one's superiority is force. And if one wishes to respond to insult, there may be little other recourse available. In addition, given the violent nature of man's past, societies have placed a great value on those virtues which enable fighters to protect their society – physical strength, courage, skill in arms, and so forth. Society honours those who display these virtues in order to protect it, but by doing so it creates a situation in which the virtues of war-fighting become honourable in and of themselves. Men wishing to gain honour have to find some means of displaying their strength, courage, and skill, and thus seek war.

Although modern monotheistic religions such as Christianity in theory regard the pursuit of earthly reputation as mere vainglory, in practice honour and religion go together extremely well. For as we have seen, honour is primarily a question of self-evaluation and identity, and it is linked to understandings of virtue. The latter are in part religiously-derived, so honourable behaviour is, at least to some extent, religiously-determined. In addition, religion is to many people not so much a question of belief as of personal identity. Religious disputes thus affect the same emotion as matters of honour – the individual's sense of self.

As a result, when religion and honour mix, the potential for violence often increases. Ancient Greeks sometimes saw wars as stemming from the gods' own pursuit of honour. The Trojan War was supposedly the product of the insulted honour of Athena and Hera who resented the fact that Paris had given the golden apple to Aphrodite. The two insulted goddesses provoked war between Troy and Greece in order to have their revenge, and sabotaged every effort to restore peace. The Greeks honoured their gods by placing trophies to them at the sites of their victories, and by hanging captured armour in their temples. Clearly, though, a temple full of enemy equipment testified not so much to the grace of the gods, as to the prowess of the city's men. Man was in effect appropriating religion to elevate himself and his warlike tendencies.

The link between honour, war and religion has continued into the modern era. An interesting example in this respect is the American Civil War. Although slavery lay at the heart of the divisions between North and South, it was the highly sensitive Southern sense of honour which brought the conflict to violence. As Bertram Wyatt-Brown says, '[t]he threat to slavery's legitimacy in the Union prompted the sectional crisis, but it was Southern honor that pulled the trigger.'[24] For Southerners interpreted the attacks on slavery, and Northerners' efforts to restrict it, as attacks not on their politics so much as on their persons. They believed that Northerners were implying that they were morally inferior because they supported slavery. This was an intolerable insult. The election of Abraham Lincoln was one insult too many, and Southerners decided to revenge themselves on those who they felt had demeaned them, by lashing out violently against them.[25]

Southern honour had a religious element. There was something of a religious revival before the Civil War, a revival which accelerated once the war began. Evangelical Christianity provided a force which bound the South together, and because of its focus on personal salvation, rather than on the reshaping of society, it found few difficulties in justifying slavery. Secessionists therefore, 'uttered their calls for action in language borrowing from and mixing together evangelical rhetoric and traditions of honor.'[26] According to Edward Crowther, '[o]ver time, many religious and secular ideals…had fused to produce a hybrid and distinctly southern value, a holy honor that drew on evangelical and martial traditions for its sustenance and animated and, for white southerners, justified southern behavior.'[27]

Holy honour was thus a source of war. We can see the same process today in the so-called War on Terror. The language of Islamic terrorists involves the same combination of honour and religion. The weakness of the Islamic world compared to the West, and its relative lack of precedence, are a source of shame; Al Qaeda seeks to restore Arab honour by proving its strength. Thus the training video which Al Qaeda made in Afghanistan contained the phrase: 'We defy with our *Koran*. With blood, we wipe out our dishonour and shame.'[28] Elsewhere, Osama bin Laden said:

> We believe that we are men, Muslim men who must have the honour of defending [Mecca]. We do not want American women soldiers defending [it] … The rulers in that region have been deprived of their manhood. And they think that the people are women. By God, Muslim women refuse to be defended by these American and Jewish prostitutes.[29]

Along the same lines, Al Qaeda spokesman Suleiman Abu Gheith, issued a statement explaining why the organization was fighting the USA, saying:

> Tyranny only leaves humiliation. Perhaps they also thought that this [oppressive] atmosphere is sufficient to kill a man's virility, shatter his will, and uproot his honour. These people erred twice: once when they ignored [the consequences of] treating man with contempt, and again when they were unaware of man's ability to triumph. This goes for every man – let alone when the man in question is of those who believe in Allah, in Islam as a religion, and in Muhammed as Prophet and Messenger, and anyone who knows his religion is unwilling to allow him to be inferior and refuses to allow him to be humiliated.[30]

This deadly combination of religion and honour is not unique. Similar combinations have occurred throughout history. When warriors appropriate religion to rein-force violent honour systems, bloodshed is almost inevitable.

Case Study – Medieval Chivalry

A case study of medieval chivalry provides further insights. Religion and honour in the Middle Ages had a very close, explicit relationship. The Catholic Church in that era consciously attempted to reform the behaviour of knights and to limit the excesses of war by introducing religious ideas into the martial code of honour. The effort, sadly, was largely a failure. In certain respects the campaign even proved counter-productive, because the Church's activities in effect bestowed honour on knighthood as a whole, sanctifying the profession of arms and so encouraging knights to seek earthly glory in war. The lesson would appear to be that churches should approach this matter with extreme caution. Honouring certain types of behaviour in war, in an effort to encourage better behaviour, tends merely to give religious sanction to war in general.

To the medieval church, pursuit of earthly honour for its own sake was vainglory. Honour belonged primarily to God, not to man. St Augustine wrote that, '[i]f men do good, it is not because of them, but due to God's grace.'[31] Thomas Aquinas similarly noted that, '[m]an is not the source of his own excellence; rather it is a divine gift within him, so in this sense the recognition is owed chiefly to God and not to the man.'[32] However, Aquinas was also aware that the desire for recognition encouraged some men towards good deeds and away from evil. It could, therefore, play a positive role in promoting good behaviour. So long as people do not seek recognition for excellences they do not possess and 'without acknowledgement to God', Aquinas wrote, '[t]here is nothing wrong in seeking a deserved reward.'[33]

In this nuanced way, the Church gave sanction to the pursuit of external honour. As is so often the case, though, subtle nuances tend to pass ordinary people by. From the point of view of knights, the key point was that pursuit of deserved honour was justified. Then, since any honour one received was due to the grace of God, it soon followed that if one won honour it must have divine sanction. Thus the very fact that one had gained precedence was proof that one deserved it. Honour and Christian belief thus merged, producing a martial version of holy honour. As the great fourteenth-century knight, Geoffroi de Charny, noted, 'on your own you achieve nothing except what God grants you. And does not God confer great honour when He allows you of His mercy to defeat your enemies without harm to yourself?'[34] The logic is very clear in a reported statement by Aimery de St Maur, Master of the Temple in England, to the former regent of England, William Marshal, on his death-bed:

In the world you have had more honour than any other knight for prowess, wisdom, and loyalty. When God granted this grace to this extent, you may be sure He wished to have you at the end. You depart from the age with honour. You have been a gentleman and you die one.[35]

This was despite the fact that the Marshal had, as Sidney Painter says, 'passed his life in industrious homicide in tourney and battle.'[36]

The Church gradually went even further than merely endorsing the pursuit of honour. It also elevated and honoured the whole institution of knighthood, again in an effort to control its behaviour. In so doing it was not trying to honour everything knights did, or their profession in general, but that was the outcome.

This policy evolved over several centuries. From early in its history, the Christian church had recognized that the waging of war might sometimes be justifiable, but it tried to avoid glorifying it. Church leaders, while permitting men to fight, recommended that those who had spilt blood should undergo a period of penitence, having to fast for 40 days or forego communion for three years.[37]

By the late tenth century, however, attitudes had begun to change. Disorder in the Western world created a desire to discipline military forces, halt their regular assaults on the civil population, and channel their efforts into restoring order and enforcing justice. The Peace of God movement of the late tenth century did not aim to eliminate the use of force, so much as to turn force into a tool of legal authority to establish order.[38] This changed the status of knights. Whereas once the Church had viewed them as a bane to society, their profession now acquired the theoretical purpose of protecting others, and so became legitimate and honourable. Rather than condemning knighthood, the Church sought to condemn only supp-

osed abuses of knightly conduct, while going out of its way to praise and endorse
what it considered the positive aspects of the profession. Thus Bernard of Clairvaux denounced vainglory saying that 'what engenders such war and raises such
strife among you is nothing more than unreasoned anger, or lust for profitless
glory, or want of some worldly good. Surely it is not prudent to kill or die for
causes such as these'. But, he continued:

> Christ's knight deals out death in safety…and suffers death in even greater
> safety. He benefits himself when he suffers death and benefits Christ when
> he deals out death. Clearly, when he kills an evil-doer he is not a homicide,
> but, if you will allow me the term, a malicide.[39]

The Church sought to direct knightly efforts into positive directions first by preaching that knights must serve God, and second by Christianizing some of the ritual which surrounded knighthood. From the middle of the twelfth century, clergy-
men such as John of Salisbury argued for 'the inclusion of some form of religious
ceremony among those by which a man was made a knight'.[40] In due course, this
happened. In its simplest form, the act of knighting consisted solely of another
knight girding a sword and belt onto the new knight. Eventually, though, a whole
religious ritual developed, which attempted to give a religious gloss to knighthood,
and thereby, it was hoped, persuade knights of their religious obligations. In its
most elaborate form, the initiation ceremony into knighthood required the initiate
to purify himself in a bath (thus the British 'Order of the Bath'), confess his sins,
go to church, stay up all night praying, and then attend mass in the morning, at
which point he was to prostrate himself before the altar and swear to 'keep the
honour of chivalry with all his power.'[41] The priest was then supposed to give a
sermon reminding the new knight of the articles of the Catholic faith and the
obligations of knighthood. Finally, the initiate would kneel before the altar where a
knight would gird him and complete the ceremony.[42]

The Church honoured knighthood in other ways. Just as the ancient Greek temples were festooned with armour captured in battle, so medieval churches began to
be adorned with shields, banners, and trophies of war. The Flemings, for instance,
hung in the church of Notre Dame of Courtrai 500 pairs of spurs taken from the
French in 1302.[43] The Church, according to Malcolm Vale, 'supported and indeed
encouraged the practice of making gifts in money, weapons, heraldic achievements
and military equipment to burial places,'[44] which is why some churches in England
still house coats of armour. Funeral ceremonies in church often included war-
horses, presentations of armour and equipment, and even fully armed men. So, at
the funeral of the great French knight, Bernard du Guesclin:

> There were no fewer than eight warhorses in the church, all bearing du
> Guesclin's arms and emblems… Four shields, four banners, four swords and
> four helms of war and peace were carried by nobles, knights and esquires to
> the altar. The swords were reversed and handed to the clergy.[45]

In all this, the Church was not attempting to glorify war-fighting per se, let alone all acts of war. It continued to condemn excesses and its aim was to direct action into positive channels. If knights could be persuaded that theirs was a holy order, it was hoped that they would feel bound to act in an appropriate fashion.

On top of this, the Church sought to divert knights' attentions away from Europe to foreign lands, by encouraging them to go on Crusade. This last move, though, brought another change in the Church's attitude to warfare and to knighthood in general, and created a situation in which Christianity endowed the waging of war with a glow of holy honour it had previously not possessed. For with the advent of crusading, knights became the protectors of the worldwide Church. As Ramon Lull, himself a clergyman, wrote:

> The offyce of a knyght is to mayntene and deffende the holy feyth catholyque... In lyke wyse as our lord god hath chosen the clerkes for to mayntene holy faith catholike with scripture... In lyke wyse god of glory hath chosen knyghtes by cause of force of arms they vaynquysshe the mescreautes whiche daily laboure for to destroye holy chirche and such knyghtes god holdeth them for his frendes honoured in this world.[46]

Throughout, the problem was that the increasing sacralization of knighthood gave honour to knights in general, not just, as the Church hoped, to the good ones. As Richard Kaeuper and Elspeth Kennedy point out:

> The careful, specific, and highly discriminatory clerical praise of knights from earlier centuries was intended to guide and control knightly behaviour rather than to praise the general company of knights indiscriminately; but knights tended to apply such praise to all knights... In short, knights generalized and laicized a clerical message which in its original form always balanced praise for good behaviour among an elite few with sulphurous denunciation of the vile behaviour of knights in general.[47]

The result was that a process designed to limit war did the opposite. As Peter of Blois complained:

> Once soldiers bound themselves by oath that they would stand up for the state, that they would not flee from the battle-line and that they would give up their lives for the public interest. Now the young knights receive their swords from the altar and thereby they profess that they are sons of the Church and that they have taken up the sword for the honour of the priesthood, the protection of the poor, for the punishment of malefactors, and for the liberation of the homeland. But matters are very different; for immediately they have been girt with the belt of knighthood they at once rise up against the anointed of the Lord and rage violently against the patrimony of

the Crucified. They despoil and rob the subject poor of Christ, and miserably oppress the wretched without mercy.[48]

The Church had made war-fighting and honour religiously compatible, and destigmatized war, '[t]he Christianization of the warrior's function…resulted in a way in the sacralization of war, a reinforcement of the prestige of soldiers and of the profession of arms.'[49] In the twelfth-century *Chanson d'Aspremont*, Archbishop Turpin tells the Pope, '[i]t is our duty to cherish all brave knights. For when we clerics sit down to eat each night, or in God's service sing matins at first light, these men are fighting for our lands with their lives', to which the Pope replies, '[b]rave Christian knights…by striking blows with blades of steel unchecked, your sins will be absolved and your souls blessed.'[50] Saving one's soul now went hand in hand with gaining honour on earth through fighting.

Thus, for all the Church's good intentions, '[t]he concepts of Christian morality and the precepts of the Church concerning *jus in bello* were singularly unsuccessful in restraining the conduct of warriors.'[51] Christianity became a central plank of chivalric culture. But chivalry, could not, as Maurice Keen notes, 'be a force effective in limiting the horrors of war: by prompting men to seek wars and praising those who did so, its tendency, for all its idealism and because of it, was rather to help to make those horrors endemic.'[52]

General Conclusions

The case study of the Church's relationship with medieval honour sounds a clear warning. The Church hoped that by giving honour to those who fought in the manner that the Church approved, it could channel violent tendencies into a positive direction, restricting the use of force to the protection of the Church, the weak and the poor, and the restoration of order and justice. The problem was that the Church thereby redefined the profession of soldiers as an honourable one, for a soldier was no longer someone fighting for himself, but in theory someone fighting on behalf of others. This had the perverse effect of encouraging men to seek opportunities to use violence to prove their worth and gain honour.

One may perceive similar problems with the concept of the 'just war' in general. By laying down criteria for a 'just war', religious leaders have hoped to ensure that others will fight only when those criteria are met, and that war will become less common, and will be fought only in a fashion which promotes good in the world. However, the very act of labelling wars as 'just' enables men who wish to fight to do so with a gloss of sanctity, which may well serve to encourage them to act with even greater excess than would otherwise have been the case.[53]

Human beings will always seek honour. No society can dispense with the concept, and because it relates so closely to self-identity, people will always take it extremely seriously. Honour is not obsolete, and will continue to play an extremely important role in human life. However, while honour will always be there, the virtues which society honours are subject to change. Traditionally, martial values have taken precedence. To a large extent this is still the case. The modern adulation of

Winston Churchill is indicative of a continued tendency to admire strength and a will to fight. Supporters of the recent war in Iraq praised Prime Minister Tony Blair for his 'courage' and denounced opponents of the war as 'appeasers'. Fighting is still seen as honourable in a way that peacemaking is not. But just because this has mostly been the case in the past, it does not necessarily always have to be so in the future. Churches have a role to play in this. If they attempt to control war by honouring certain types of military activity while condemning others, they are likely only to end up honouring military activity in general, for the subtleties of their message will be lost. If they want peace, therefore, they would do better to honour peacemaking. It is interesting to note that under Pope John Paul II the Catholic Church moved somewhat away from just war theory towards an ethic of peace-making.[54] This seems to be a sensible approach. In the Sermon on the Mount, Jesus did not say, 'Blessed are those who fight to protect others', or 'Blessed are those who fight in a decent way', but 'Blessed are the peacemakers.'[55] People will do what wins them honour. Honour the peacemakers more, and peacemaking may become more common.

8

CATHOLICISM AND CITIZENSHIP: RELIGION IN THE FRENCH REVOLUTON

Nicholas Atkin and Frank Tallett

Render therefore unto Caesar the things which are Caesar's;
and unto God the things that are God's.
(Matthew 22:21)

The powers that be are ordained by God. Whosoever therefore resisteth
the power resisteth the ordinance of God.
(Romans 13:1-2)

These two biblical injunctions might lead one to suppose there would be no con-flict between religion and politics either because there is a separation between the two, as implied by the words of Christ himself in St Matthew, or because Christians will necessarily be obedient to the secular powers, as suggested by St Paul's letter to the Church at Rome. Such a supposition comes more easily to contemporaries since church-state relations have been largely harmonious within Western Europe since the end of the Second World War, notwithstanding the occasional jousting over issues of personal morality, for instance divorce, abortion and gay rights. A longer perspective on history, of course, tells a different story in which the reality of church-state relations has frequently been one of conflict and tension. Even during the Middle Ages, when Western Europe defined itself as Christendom by virtue of its adherence to Catholicism, struggles over the relative extent of lay and clerical authority led to notable clashes, such as the eleventh-century and twelfth-century confrontations between popes and Holy Roman Emperors over the investiture of bishops, which at one point saw Henry V standing barefoot in the snow to beg pardon from His Holiness, though the Emperors later had their revenge.[1] Within the early modern period, too, there are abundant instances of conflicts between pious rulers, Gallican churches and the papacy;[2] for instance the willingness of eighteenth-century monarchs to sequester ecclesiastical property and close down religious orders.[3]

Of all European countries, it is arguably France that has witnessed the most severe tensions within religion and politics, notably during the modern epoch. With the exception of the Vichy government (1940–1944), successive regimes since the Third Republic (1870–1940) have endeavoured to realize the Revolutionary dream of 'a one and indivisible republic', in which citizenship rests on the acceptance of the ideals of liberty, equality and fraternity.[4] Assimilation was the desired goal, and so long as religious and ethnic groups were content to practice their faith and cultural traditions in an unobtrusive manner, and adhere to the norms of French citizenship, then they were welcome. For the most part, the Protestant minority, Jews, and immigrants from southern and eastern Europe have been largely content to accept this tacit bargain.[5] Catholics have undergone a more chequered experience. State fears about their supranational loyalties, together with their supposedly regressive political and economic outlook, led to periodic bursts of anticlerical, and specifically anti-Catholic, vendettas. During the 1880s, as the Republic put down firm roots, clerical influence within elementary schools was gradually eroded; within public life, cemeteries were taken out of ecclesiastical control; and liberalization of the divorce laws indicated firmly that the state was not going to allow the definition of citizenship to be at the behest of the Church.[6] At the turn of the century, in the wake of the Dreyfus Affair, it was the turn of the religious orders, thought to be 'foreign, unpatriotic and corporatist', and deemed unnatural in their vows of chastity and poverty, to feel the weight of republican displeasure, many religious houses being forced to close down and suspend their activities.[7] In 1905, all notions of partnership between Church and state were ended with the Law of Separation which abrogated the Napoleonic Concordat of 1801.[8]

Once the state was triumphant, anticlerical outbursts became relatively few and far between: the abortive attempt on the part of the secular Cartel des Gauches cabinet of 1924 to extend the laic laws to the newly recovered provinces of Alsace and Lorraine; the anger at the time of the Liberation, shared by a good Catholic such as Georges Bidault, at the collusion of the Catholic hierarchy with the Pétain government;[9] and the failed Savary bill of 1982 which attempted to bring Catholic secondary schools under the tutelage of the Ministry of Education and, in the process, reduce state subsidies to private education, an initiative which resulted in the largest street protest seen in Paris since the events of May 1968.[10] Significantly, in the past twenty years, with more or less full Catholic acceptance of republican structures, a process which had tentative beginnings in the *Ralliement* of the 1890s,

it has been Maghrebi immigrants, comprising the bulk of incomers, who have become the focus of concern. The colour of their skin, their language, their 'strange
habits', their geographical concentration in impoverished urban areas which often
have become ghettoized, their relative poverty, and most crucially their Muslim
faith, have all served to emphasize their distinctiveness and mark them out as outsiders. It is in this context that governments of both left and right have severely
imposed the laws on neutrality. Ostentatious religious symbols have thus been
strictly prohibited, in this instance the wearing of the headscarf or *foulard* within
public buildings, most obviously schools which Republicans literally regard as the
classroom of citizenship.[11]

To understand the frequency and vehemence of these clashes, one needs to return to the Revolution of 1789 which was a *ligne fondatrice* in respect of religion. It
separated an era in which there was a mutually dependent relationship between
Church and state, notwithstanding occasional difficulties over finance, appointments and Jansenism, and a modern epoch in which the goodwill of the state
towards religion could no longer be taken for granted.[12] As we have noted above,
that goodwill was in desperate short supply after the consolidation of the Third
Republic which endeavoured to construct a community of citizens with a common
identity that owed everything to their acceptance of a set of ideological norms and
values based upon the revolutionary tripos of liberty, equality and fraternity, values
which would be introduced to the very young in the schoolroom. The French
revolutionaries of the 1790s, from whom the later Republicans drew inspiration,
had attempted something similar in their search to create the 'true Republican
man', but there were two significant differences. First, in the dechristianizing campaign of 1793–94, they sought to destroy the Catholic faith entirely; second, and
perhaps paradoxically, they had always sought to underpin revolutionary values
with a state-sponsored religion.[13] It was the catastrophic failure of these initiatives
that taught successive Republican regimes not to repeat the mistakes of the revolutionary decade, but to move towards a position of neutrality in religious matters.
Nor was the lesson lost on twentieth-century Communist, and purportedly, atheist
regimes which were generally happy to persecute Christians but which stepped
back from outlawing religion altogether, the exception being Enver Hoxha's Albania whose constitutions of 1967 and 1976 denied individuals the right to practice
their faith in private.[14]

This chapter sets out to explain the origins and course of this breach between
Catholicism and the state, and how in particular notions of citizenship and belonging were integral to this cleavage. At this juncture, it should be stressed that in 1789
there was little inkling of the maelstrom that was to follow. Catholicism permeated
every aspect of life under the old regime, and the relationship between Church and
state was one of close mutual dependence. The existence of an established church
under the old regime proffered significant benefits to both sides. The state preserved the doctrinal exclusivity of Catholicism by giving it a monopoly of public
worship, by enforcing compulsory attendance of mass at Easter, by prosecuting
blasphemers and heretics, by imposing censorship laws and by regulating public

morality to the best of its ability. Moreover, the state guaranteed the Church's income by enforcing payment of the tithe which had precedence over seigneurial and royal taxes; and it accorded clerics some representation in the machinery of government, from provincial estates to the royal court. For its part, the Church preached submission to the temporal authority, used the pulpit as a medium of government propaganda and communication, collected statistical information via parish registers, and above all handled the charitable and educational services which the state itself was deeply reluctant to undertake. As indicated earlier, this symbiotic relationship did not prevent disagreements which, on occasion, could be volatile, often centring around the Church's unyielding defence of its privileges most notably in the fiscal domain where it refused point blank to pay tax, prefer- ring instead to offer the so-called *don gratuit*, or free gift, a negotiated payment which in no way corresponded to the Church's wealth or the state's financial requi- rements.[15] In this regard, it helped that the French Church was perhaps the best organized in Europe, possessing an Assembly of the Clergy which acted as a mouthpiece for ecclesiastical concerns and a puissant defender of institutional privilege.

Aside from these squalls over money, which disturbed the otherwise tranquil relationship between Church and state, there were other tensions in the eighteenth century which shed light on subsequent events during the Revolution: the un- willingness of the reformed clergy to tolerate mere mass conformity among the laity and its attempt to weed out superstitious and abusive practices resulting in some slippage in levels of popular observance; the emerging dichotomy between upper and lower clergy over the unequal division of power and remuneration; exaggerated accounts of the extent of clerical wealth; and the failure of the Church, left to its own devices, to reform itself, as evidenced by the limited outcome of the 1766 Commission of the Regulars.[16] The Commission reflected a widely-held anti- pathy towards the contemplative regular orders, in particular the males, though there was much more sympathy for the newer women's congregations which esch- ewed the veil and permanent vows leaving them free to undertake a welter of charitable, philanthropic and educational functions within society. There was addi- tionally the long-standing problem of Jansenism. From an essentially theological phenomenon, this evolved into a multi-faceted, politico-ecclesiastical quarrel over the issue of authority and its exercise, Jansenists questioning the despotic use of power both by bishops and by governments.[17] Finally, the Enlightenment posed some serious questions for churchmen. Traditional scholarship has accorded the *philosophes* pride of place as harbingers of the anticlerical storm that would later overwhelm Catholicism yet, of late, a more nuanced view has gained ground. That Voltaire and others were trenchant and outspoken critics of clerical privileges and deficiencies, powerful advocates of religious toleration, and sceptical of revealed dogma, cannot be denied. Yet, if the French Enlightenment was peculiarly aggres- sive towards religion, its impact was blunted by a powerful counter-Enlightenment of the type first outlined by R.R. Palmer and subsequently amplified by Isaiah Berlin, and most recently fleshed out by Derek McMahon.[18] Just as importantly, there was a great deal of consensus between the *philosophes*, educated laymen and churchmen over the intrinsic value of religion, notably its contribution to the good ordering of society and its indispensability as an underpinning of state authority. As John McManners has noted, '[t]he Enlightenment did not endanger the Church in the short term – it was a spectacular firework display on the horizon.'[19] It was the so-called 'low Enlightenment' of the late eighteenth century, which reached out to more readers through the trash novels and pamphlets of the period, than did the high Enlightenment of the salons and *Encyclopédie*, that was peculiarly corrosive of old regime authority, not because it presented a reasoned critique but rather because of its indiscriminate sniping at the bishops, courtiers and royals.[20]

Yet, if there were problems, none of these were fatal to the overwhelming strength of Catholicism. They did not disturb the fundamentally good relations between Church and state, nor do they explain why France was to undergo a revolution whose origins were not directly religious in nature. Once the Revolution had broken out, there would necessarily be implications for Catholicism as most deputies, and indeed the population at large, agreed that the Church stood in need of some reform, like all other institutions of the old regime. It was thus inevitable that there would be some reshaping of ecclesiastical structures by the Constituent Assembly which saw its chief task as being the renewal of France. The specific nature of religious reform was not in any sense predetermined but was, above all, influenced by two things. The first was the revolutionaries' need for money to solve the dire financial crisis which had caused the collapse of the old regime monarchy and instigated the summoning of the Estates General. In November 1789, the deputies voted to put Church lands and property at the disposal of the nation. Prior to this, on the 'Night of 4 August', the representatives had voted to abolish the tithe, together with seigneurial dues, which left the Church with no form of regular income.[21] As a quid pro quo, it was agreed to finance the Church out of state taxation, but it was intended that this would be a slimmed down, cost-effective clerical establishment. Second, the constitutional debates of the summer had given rise to the much broader question of where authority derived from. The answer was supplied by the *Declaration of the Rights of Man and the Citizen* which located sovereignty very firmly with the nation which was made up of citizens not subjects. Only those elected by the sovereign nation could therefore exercise office. This principle applied as much to the Church as it did to any other institution.[22]

It was inevitable, then, that the Revolution would impinge upon the Church, and it was not surprising that an early concern was the regular orders. In October 1789, taking of monastic vows was suspended and, in the following February, these were abolished altogether, and religious orders with solemn promises and others which were deemed to perform no useful function were suppressed.[23] Of much greater significance was the Civil Constitution of the Clergy introduced on 12 July 1790. Its provisions may be briefly summarized.[24] Old regime dioceses were abolished and new ones established whose boundaries were co-terminus with the recently erected departments. There was to be one bishop per department thus reducing the overall number of prelates from 136 to 83. Parishes were similarly rationalized and cathedral chapters abolished. The ranks of the clergy were dramatically thinned since only those priests with cure of souls were retained. Henceforth, the clergy would be salaried by the state with most bishops receiving 12,000 *livres* and *curés* (parish priests) between 1,200 and 6,000 *livres*, a serious reduction of income for those at the top of the tree and an enhancement for many at the lower end. Additionally the Constitution provided for a new system of ecclesiastical self-government involving diocesan and metropolitan synods and elected councils to advise the bishops. Most controversially, the legislation introduced the electoral principle into the appointment of clerics who, in the future, would be elected by the same bodies of taxpayers who voted for other state officials, such as mayors, judges and deputies.

It is possible to identify a swathe of influences upon the Civil Constitution. Part of the radical nature of this document sprang from the Assembly's increasing frustration with the two bishops on the Ecclesiastical Committee drafting the legislation, whose obstinacy blocked earlier moderate proposals. Yet if there was frustration with the attitude of the old regime bishops, the Civil Constitution nevertheless embodied a deep-seated desire to bind the Church to the new order in the same way that religion had underpinned the old regime monarchy. There was, however, an important difference. The deputies attached overwhelming importance to the concept of national sovereignty and this implied both that the Church must be part of the state and that clerics must receive their authority from the people, through election, in the same was as any other government official. As Armand-Gaston Camus, a canon law specialist, put it, 'the Church is part of the state; the state is not part of the Church.'[25] At the same while, lower salaries and the scaled-down size of the clerical establishment reflected the Assembly's determination to have a leaner, cost-effective Church now that it was funded by the state. This was further found in the attempt to return Catholicism to a purer condition, much as the Jansenists had urged. As Treilhard, one of the members of the Ecclesiastical Committee, commented, '[y]our decrees do not attack this holy religion: instead they will merely return it to its primitive purity.'[26] The fact that the committee itself had reached its conclusions without seeking advice from Rome was indicative of the general Gallican flavour which permeated the entire Constitution which was designed to assert the autonomy of the French Church, although schism was not in anybody's mind at this stage. It was thought, somewhat naively, that the Pope would fall into line, and bless the legislation, especially when threatened with the loss of his temporal possessions around Avignon. Finally, the legislation embraced enlightened ideals, for instance in the desire for rationality of clerical government and in the concern for social utility of religion.

There was much in the Civil Constitution to appeal to churchmen, particularly the lower clergy for whom it held the promise of better working conditions, higher salaries and a greater say in ecclesiastical affairs. Yet there were also serious difficulties to be overcome. These centred upon the twin issues of authority and consultation. For many churchmen, even those who wished to be good citizens and who took their social functions very seriously, it was not at all evident that their authority derived from the nation: rather it came from God. Clerical election thus touched upon the Church's spiritual as opposed to its purely temporal affairs. Moreover, clerical election opened up the frightening possibility of *curés* being put into office through the votes of non-Catholics. These points were cogently made by the Archbishop of Aix, Mgr Boisgelin, notably in the *Exposition des principes*.[27] Acknowledging the need for reform, he argued that for such far-reaching proposals to be accepted the Church must be consulted through the holding of an assembly. With the benefit of hindsight, it is not at all clear that such a gathering would have swallowed wholesale the Civil Constitution's provisions, so radical was the suggestion of clerical election. In the event, no such meeting was held. A clerical assembly would have acknowledged the Church's corporate status; it would have been a standing affront to the overriding principle of national sovereignty; and it would have served as a platform to disaffected bishops to voice their opinions.[28]

By autumn 1790, debates in the Assembly over the Civil Constitution had become a dialogue of the deaf. Ecclesiastics protested that they wanted to be good citizens under the Revolution as they had been good subjects under the king but they could not accept secular encroachment on spiritual matters. Lay deputies resented clerical claims to independence and could not understand why the obvious benefits of the legislation were being spurned. When it became apparent that the sale of Church lands was being held up by uncertainties over the Constitution, and believing that it was only the bishops who were holding out, the deputies forced the issue, and on 27 November 1790 decreed that all clerics must swear an oath, accepting the new constitution of the French state, still to be finalized, which implicitly comprehended the religious settlement. For his part, a reluctant Louis XVI sanctioned the decree imposing the oath on 26 December 1790, and oath-taking ceremonies commenced the following month.

From the Assembly's standpoint, the results were disappointing: 60 per cent of the *curés*, 51 per cent of the *vicaires*, and a mere 7 of the 136 old regime bishops took the oath, though these statistics mask considerable regional variations. Space does not permit a detailed analysis here of the geographical response of the clergy, but a number of overall factors played a role. These include age, income, seminary training, but as Timothy Tackett's definitive study illustrates, the oath was above all rejected by those clerics who were faithful to a Tridentine model of Catholicism which stressed Church autonomy, the subservience of the laity to the clergy and the 'separateness' of the First Estate.[29] Such priests were commonly found in Brittany, Languedoc and Gascony. The jurors, who swore the oath and who would comprise the newly established Constitutional Church, were located predominantly in the Paris basin, the Dauphiné, Provence and central departments, and regarded themselves as 'citizen-priests' with responsibility for the promotion of public wellbeing. Neither the jurors nor the refractory priests were especially swayed by lay opinion, yet there was a striking correlation between areas of high religious observance and refusal of the oath, and it seems likely that the non-jurors were supported in their refusal by those elements of the laity who accepted a clericalized, Tridentine model of Catholicism.

The reasons for the rejection or acceptance of the oath were less significant in the short term than the fact that divisions over the Civil Constitution created a body of men, the non-jurors, who might be thought hostile to the revolutionary settlement. This view gained credence when a number of them denounced the sacraments of the constitutionals as invalid and inveighed against the revolutionary settlement as a whole. Moreover, many refractories, including a majority of the old regime bishops, now joined the emigration of nobles and other disaffected social groups, swelling the ranks of counter-revolutionaries abroad.[30] The papal response to developments in France also confirmed the schism within the French Church and cemented official Catholic opposition to the Revolution. In a brief, *Quod aliquantum*, issued in March 1791, in response to Boisgelin's *Exposition*, and subsequently published as part of the wider public brief, *Charitas quae* of 17 April, Pius VI condemned the 'unbridled equality and liberty' in the *Declaration of the Rights of Man* and denounced the revolutionary attempts 'to destroy the Catholic religion and with it the obedience to kings.'[31] After this, there was no going back. As Nigel Aston notes, by the start of 1791, '[d]isputes over religion had destroyed the revolutionary consensus of 1789.'[32] Religion found itself in the camp of counter-revolution. This politicization of religion was further enhanced by the behaviour of the king. While he had sanctioned the Civil Constitution and oath, Louis regarded these actions as a betrayal of his royal duties.[33] When he was prevented by an angry crowd from leaving Paris to take mass from a non-juring priest at Easter 1791, this crystallized in his mind the decision that he must flee France, something which he attempted in June that year in the ill-fated Flight to Varennes. While he would eventually accept the political Constitution of 1791, inaugurating the Legislative Assembly, his motives and conduct were henceforth tainted with suspicion.

It was the war, declared in April the following year, which sealed the fate of the king and which resulted in an outright attack on Catholicism. Here is not the place to go into the origins of the war except to say that these were largely domestic, as those on the left attempted to flush out the waverers while those on the right saw the conflict as a means of reasserting monarchical power and authority.[34] Much to the surprise of the 'war party', the French army initially suffered a series of reverses, while within the metropole counter-revolutionary uprisings, which had been simmering since 1791, boiled over, notably in the Vendée, where priests were fingered as the chief culprits. In summer 1793, another threat to the Revolution manifested itself in the Federalist revolts, essentially anti-centralist uprisings concentrated in large provincial cities.[35]

In this climate of military reverses, swelling internal dissent and general paranoia, revolutionaries asked not *what* was to blame, but *who*.[36] In their search for scapegoats, they inevitably fixed upon the non-jurors. In August 1792, the Assembly ordered the deportation of refractory clergy, suppressed all surviving religious communities and prohibited the wearing of ecclesiastical dress except by constitutionals in their own parishes. The following month, the people of Paris took matters into their own hands. Prompted by fears that the capital was about to be overrun by foreign troops, they stormed the prisons of the city and massacred some 1,400 inmates, including 300 clergy and 3 bishops in the belief they were at the heart of a web of counter-revolutionary conspiracy.[37] For its part, the newly elected Convention acted to meet the threats to the Revolution. A Republic was decreed in September 1792 and in the following January, after a brief trial, the king was executed. A series of decrees ensued, designed to centralize government, enhance its effectiveness and eradicate opposition through the use of Terror. A number of specific measures were directed against the refractories. Execution awaited those involved in public disturbances, deported clerics who dared to return to France were promised a similar fate, and the whole process of deportation was fast-tracked. By autumn 1793, some 30,000 priests had fled France, many settling in Britain and Italy.[38]

The Terror, however, was mainly directed at the constitutional Church, and Catholicism more generally, in an offensive usually referred to as the dechristianizing campaign, though properly speaking one ought to refer to a series of campaigns, such was the regional variation and texturing.[39] Doubts about the loyalty and effectiveness of the Constitutional Church had multiplied during 1791–2. Its purpose, as the Church of the Revolution, had been to inculcate an attachment and loyalty to the new regime, yet this it had signally failed to achieve. In those regions blighted by counter-revolution, the peasants remained stubbornly loyal to refractory priests. Nor did it help that, by summer 1793, Constitutionals had become linked with the Girondin faction within the Convention who, in turn, were associated with Federalism. The Constitutional Church had thus failed the regime and its clergy were perceived as a fifth column.

Having erected a state Church, the state now destroyed it by withdrawing financial support and forcing its clergy to resign and, in some cases, to marry. Ironically, wedlock was regarded as the ultimate proof of a priest's repudiation of his clerical status and was testimony to the success of the eighteenth-century Church in making celibacy a defining characteristic of the priesthood.[40] It was not just the clergy who suffered, but the faith itself. It was regarded as the ideology of fanatics who fought indiscriminately for the return of throne and altar; it was a tool used by reactionary elements to dupe the peasantry; it was an alien and corrosive creed which stood in opposition of the true interests of the French nation. To peel away this alleged superstition, churches were stripped of their statues, bells, crosses, silverware, gold plate, and valuables before being closed. Scarcely any remained open by Easter 1794. Other holy places, for instance wayside shrines, crosses and grottoes, were defaced. And all forms of public worship were prohibited.

As well as destroying Catholicism, the Revolution sought to promote a new ideology subsumed in the form of religious cults.[41] Civic festivals, a cult of Reason and eventually a deistic cult of the Supreme Being were proffered in place of Catholicism. The contents of these cults were varied. They might comprise merely an iconoclastic burning of Catholic hymnals and saints' statues; they could involve a celebration of the Revolution's victories such as the Fall of the Bastille, the overthrow of the monarchy or the declaration of the Republic; or they might centre upon the revolutionary martyrs, Marat, Chalier and Lepeletier de Saint Fargeau.

The theme of Nature figured prominently. The cult of Reason offered a platform for orators to develop every kind of materialist, atheist, theistic and deistic point of view. The most sophisticated of the cults was that of the Supreme Being. Initiated by a decree of 7 May 1794, the cult embodied a belief in an afterlife and in a deity who rewarded virtue and punished vice, and it established a regular round of festivals to be performed on the *décadi*, the tenth day of the new week, set up by the revolutionary calendar.[42]

The purpose of the revolutionary cults was manifold. They served in the first instance as substitutes for Catholicism, reflecting the Enlightenment belief that a well-ordered society could not operate without a state-sponsored religion. They had an educational function, being designed to instruct the citizens about the nature of the revolutionary changes that had taken place. This was coupled with the desire to change men so that they became morally worthy of the new republican institutions that had been created for their benefit. The original intention, advocated strongly by Lepeletier, had been to use schooling alongside the cults, as a way of inculcating revolutionary virtues.[43] Finally, the revolutionaries were seeking for new sources of authority to legitimate and guarantee the durability of their achievements. They had rejected monarchical and ecclesiastical authority, the twin underpinnings of the old regime, and in their search for forms of authority they fastened upon Nature, the antique world and Reason, all of which carried connotations of permanence and durability. Dechristianization was thus a vital element in the consolidation of the new social and political framework.

The impact of dechristianization should not be overstated. Much depended on a series of variables: towns generally suffered more than rural areas; the presence of a militant dechristianizing representative *en mission*, or a revolutionary army, was crucial to its implementation and form; and areas of counter-revolution inevitably suffered most. It is also too easy to present it as an irresistible force whereas, in truth, there was much active and passive resistance to the dechristianizers, much of it led by women, which had an unfortunate legacy as it buttressed the republican belief that women, through their supposedly inferior capacity for reason, were susceptible to clerical blandishments.[44] Even the republican calendar, which had been designed to wean people away from the religious round embodied in the Gregorian year, survived only until 1804. What was indisputable was that the Constitutional Church was wrecked, habits of religious observance were either destroyed or fractured, and the clergy had been devalued, leading to both a subsequent decline in observance and a laicization of religious practice.

By 1794, therefore, the Revolution had undergone a series of leaps. Initially in 1789 a movement which commanded genuine mass support, in 1790 the Revolution had sought to bind the Church to the wider programme of renewal. A working partnership between Church and state might have eventuated embracing a number of possible models: an 'established' Church with religious toleration guaranteed by the state or a 'Constitutional' Church, whose patriotic *curés* worked for the overall good of the nation. But if a breach between the Church and state was not inevitable, an ideological rift had arisen, centred upon the issue of authority, largely because of the unwillingness of either side to listen to the other, and buttressed by Pius VI's wholesale condemnation of the Revolution. Even at the start of 1792 it was just possible for a modus vivendi in which the Constitutional Church played a key part in forging French national identity, as its leading spokesman Abbé Grégoire, the Bishop of Blois, still fervently hoped. Such hopes were shattered with the declaration of war. Over the course of a few months in 1792–3, when the radical Montagnards achieved their grip on power, both juring and non-juring clergy found themselves the objects of derision, violence and persecution which would endure until 1794 when a combination of factors – including the fall of Robespierre, the growing number of military victories and the waning of the hard-nosed ideology of the far left revolutionaries – brought an end to the outright attack of dechristianization.

As in so many other areas, it was left to Napoleon to pick up the pieces and to reassemble them in patterns which unashamedly propped up his own authority, most obviously via the 1801 Concordat which effectively made the Church a department of state. If any doubt remained, the accompanying Organic Articles made clear who had the upper hand. The Concordat would remain in place until the Separation of 1905 but contained within it the seeds of successive Church-state conflicts as both sides periodically manoeuvred to pursue their own agendas. Whereas the Concordat had brought a stability of sorts to Church-state relations, it could not hide the fact the revolutionary experience had polarized so many areas of French life and thought, in particular by introducing a new sense of belonging: no longer was Catholicism the badge of identity as under the old regime; instead it might stand opposed to a new concept of citizenship which involved acceptance of the revolutionary ideals. Throughout much of the nineteenth century, this inherent tension was never fully crystallized but with the consolidation of the Third Republic it was inevitable that Republicans would revisit the whole issue of national citizenship and reformulate ideals of belonging initially sketched out in the chaos of the early 1790s. In so doing, they were frequently brutish in their handling of Catholicism, but they never repeated the mistakes of the Jacobins by attempting to eliminate religion altogether.

9

CATHOLIC-JEWISH RELATIONS IN ITALY FROM UNIFICATION TO THE SECOND VATICAN COUNCIL (1870–1965)

Tobias Abse

In this chapter, I will attempt to survey relations between Catholics and Jews in Italy from 1870 – when the Papacy lost its temporal powers in the City of Rome and the Roman Jews were finally freed from their ghetto by the forces of the Italian state – to 1965, when the Second Vatican Council, under the leadership of Pope Paul VI, issued the declaration *Nostra Aetate*, affirming that the Crucifixion of Christ, 'cannot be blamed upon all Jews then living, without distinction, nor upon the Jews of today.'[1] The Catholic Church's eventual repudiation of the traditional accusation of collective Jewish responsibility for deicide can only be seen in historical terms as a belated response to the Holocaust and as the product of the heartfelt desire of Pope John XXIII who, as Angelo Roncalli, Apostolic Delegate to Turkey during the Second World War, had assisted Jews to escape to Palestine, to make amends for the conduct of his predecessor Pius XII. Paradoxically, Pope John's death meant that it was Paul VI who, as Giovanni Montini, had been one of Pius XII's closest collaborators, conveying apparent Vatican approval of Vichy's Jewish Statute during the war, and later assisting the escape of Nazi and Ustashi[2] war criminals to Latin America, who found himself presiding over the Church's spectacular shift in attitude, even if he ensured that the statement's wording adopted a less explicit vocabulary than Pope John would have favoured. Whilst the long-running controversy about Pope Pius XII's attitude towards the Holocaust and in particular towards the SS round-up of the Roman Jews on 16 October 1943, 'Under His Very Windows' as Susan Zuccotti puts it, will inevitably loom large, I want to examine a longer time period, in order to address the more recent claims that earlier anti-Semitism on the part of the Vatican created the pre-conditions for genocide, an argument put forward in a well-researched and nuanced way by David Kertzer, and re-iterated in a more polemical way by Daniel Goldhagen. Some attention will also be paid to the *Hidden Encyclical of Pius XI* as Georges Passelecq and Bernard Suchecky label a hitherto unpublished draft document drawn up by a group of Jesuits as a result of instructions given by Pius XI in May 1938. This serves as an example of the distinctions that need to be drawn between successive Popes and their attitudes towards the Jews. Furthermore, there will also be some reference to the differing attitudes of various bishops and other Italian clergy, meticulously analysed by Zuccotti in her judicious survey of the Italian Church's response to the partially successful attempt to exterminate the Italian Jews.

Recent defences of the Vatican's record in relation to the Jews, such as the 1998 document *We Remember: A Reflection on the Shoah*, have drawn a very sharp distinction between anti-Judaism and anti-Semitism, acknowledging that the Catholic Church might sometimes have been guilty of the former, but denying all responsibility for the latter. In broad terms, these Vatican categories, frequently employed by Catholic theologians since Vatican II, correspond to what more secular historians have called traditional religious anti-Semitism on the one hand and modern political/racial anti-Semitism on the other. It ought to be underlined that until very recently the majority of non-Catholic historians had to a large extent accepted these distinctions; even if they had not seen them as quite as watertight as John Paul II or Cardinal Cassidy claim they are in *We Remember*, historians had assumed that any elements among the clergy, let alone the Catholic laity, who had slipped from the first 'traditional' to the second 'modern' version of anti-Semitism had done so without Vatican approval, generally in response to particular local conditions and popular prejudices in Central and Eastern Europe. Kertzer has changed the terms of the mainstream debate, arguing that 'the notion that the Church fostered only negative "religious" views of the Jews, and not negative images of their harmful social, economic, cultural and political effects – the latter identified with modern anti-Semitism – is clearly belied by the historical record.'[3]

Before I cite some of the evidence presented by Kertzer in support of this contention, it seems essential to give a brief account of the vicissitudes of the Roman Jews since 1798, an account which may help to explain why the nineteenth and early twentieth-century Popes were particularly prone to link Jews with all the forces of modernity that they loathed so intensely. The French revolutionaries arrived in Rome in 1798, seized Pope Pius VI and freed the Roman Jews from the ghetto in which the Papacy had confined them since 1555.[4] In 1800 the next Pope, Pius VII, forced the Jews back into the ghetto on his return to Rome. In 1809 the Napoleonic armies invaded Rome, expelled the Pope and freed the Jews again. In

1815, the returning Pius VII insisted on restoring the ghetto yet again. The mid-century upheaval can be seen as, in many ways, a repetition of these earlier episodes. In 1848, the Roman Republic of Mazzini and Garibaldi freed the Jews in the aftermath of the Pope's flight from his unruly city and in 1849 the returning Pius IX, not content with the restoration of the Roman ghetto, put pressure on other Italian rulers to reverse any liberation of their Jews triggered by the 1848 revolutions. The Piedmontese kingdom, which had finally abolished its own ghettoes in 1848, did not restore them in 1849 and consequently, when the Piedmontese-led Italian state conquered Rome in 1870, it followed the precedent of the French revolutionaries of 1798 and the Italian republicans of 1848, and once again freed the Jews. The Pope made no secret of his displeasure. In August 1871, Pius, speaking to members of a Catholic women's organization, remarked of the Jews 'owing to their obstinacy and their failure to believe, they have become *dogs*. We have today in Rome, unfortunately, too many of these dogs, and we hear them barking in all the streets, and going around molesting people everywhere.'[5] Whilst Pius' hostility to Jews was undoubtedly intense, this was essentially traditional religious anti-Semitism, based on the Jews' refusal to convert. The shift to a more modern, racial and political variety came with his successor, Leo XIII, often wrongly presented as more liberal, or at least less reactionary, than Pius IX. Some of Kertzer's most damning evidence for this shift comes from the pages of *Civiltà Cattolica*. This was a Jesuit bi-weekly, founded in 1850 with the firm backing of Pius IX, which became the most influential Catholic periodical anywhere in the world. Each issue had to be approved by the Pope's Secretary of State and the Popes were often personally involved in dealings with the journal's director. In short, *Civiltà Cattolica* could not contain anything that met with the Pope's disapproval, even if we cannot always demonstrate Papal inspiration. 1880 saw the start of a series of 36 anti-Semitic articles in *Civiltà Cattolica*. The very first of these contained the following passage:

Oh how wrong and deluded are those who think Judaism is just a religion, like Catholicism, Paganism, Protestantism, and not in fact a race, a people and a nation! While it is certain that others can be, for example, Catholic and either Italian, French or English...it is a great error to believe that the same is true of the Jews. For the Jews are not only Jews because of their religion...they are Jews also and especially because of their race.[6]

If this is clear evidence of racial anti-Semitism, a later *Civiltà Cattolica* article from 1893 provides an exposition of modern political anti-Semitism, asserting that:

With religious liberty proclaimed, and citizenship conceded even to the Jews, the Jews took advantage of it...to become our masters. Indeed, today it is the *Stock Market* that has political control, and this is in the hands of the Jews. What governs is *Masonry*, and this too is directed by the Jews. What shapes and re-shapes public opinion is the *Press*, and this also is in large part inspired and subsidised by the Jews.[7]

The shift towards modern racial and political anti-Semitism was accompanied by a revival of the most barbaric aspects of medieval religious anti-Semitism in the form of ritual murder allegations. The extent of Papal backing for the ritual murder slander is frequently underestimated. Space does not permit a detailed discussion of Kertzer's proof of Leo XIII's involvement in the Vatican's dismissal of the Cardinal-Archbishop of Westminster's attempt in 1900 to obtain a Papal statement repudiating allegations of ritual murder by Jews; suffice it to say, the Inquisition concluded 'ritual murder is a historical certainty', and added, '[g]iven all this, the Holy See cannot issue the statement that has been requested, which, while it may please a few dupes in England, would trigger widespread protests and scandal elsewhere.'[8] Whilst there is some evidence that Pius X was less personally and less consistently hostile to the Jews than his predecessor, his general stance of opposing all modernizing trends inside and outside the Church meant that he was completely reliant on the most reactionary elements within the Church, the very sectors to whom anti-Semitism was most attractive, so new allegations of ritual murder were given total endorsement by *Civiltà Cattolica* as late as the Spring of 1914.[9] Pius' successor, Benedict XV, the first Pope to see that the pre-Napoleonic order could never be restored, soon put an end to the anti-Semitic campaign in *Civiltà Cattolica*, and made serious diplomatic efforts to improve relations with Jewish communities abroad as part of an unsuccessful scheme to assure the Vatican a place at the Peace Conference after the First World War.[10]

Benedict seems to have shown some genuine concern about pogroms in Poland during and immediately after the First World War, whatever self-interested diplomatic motives may have originally prompted his concern. Benedict's preoccupation with Poland survived the Vatican's exclusion from the peace talks, and in 1918 he sent Vatican librarian Achille Ratti, later Pope Pius XI, to Poland on a special mission, first as an Apostolic Visitor and later as Papal Nuncio. Ratti was not recalled from Poland until 1921, so the episode was a very important one in the life of a cleric who had spent the past 45 years as a librarian and had no diplomatic experience. Whilst Goldhagen, as ever in the grip of tunnel vision, exaggerates in giving the impression that Ratti's mission to Poland was exclusively concerned with 'working to improve the lot of the Jews,'[11] Benedict certainly expected his envoy to look into the pogroms occurring at the time. Far from demonstrating any sympathy with the persecuted, Ratti's report of early January 1919 concluded that 'one of the most evil and strongest influences that is felt here, perhaps the strongest and the most evil, is that of the Jews,'[12] and one could cite other anti-Semitic comments from other documents about Poland, either drawn up by Ratti himself or, in the case of the final report on his mission, written by a loyal assistant after his departure.[13]

Pius XI's record on the Jewish question is the subject of much debate, even if these controversies pale in the face of those about his immediate successor, Pius

XII. Some tend to present Pius XI as a man who, by the end of his life, was increasingly at odds with the racism and anti-Semitism of Nazi Germany and Fascist Italy. Others, like Kertzer, Zuccotti and above all Goldhagen, are in varying degrees sceptical of this assessment, with Goldhagen labelling him 'a committed anti-Semite,' and dismissing the suppressed Encyclical as 'animated by…soft Nazism.'[14] His defenders prefer implicit or explicit parallels with John XXIII, Michael Phayer claims:

> At the end of his life, Pope Pius XI had taken strong steps to counter racism and rethink Christian-Jewish relations. By asserting that Christians are spiritual Semites, Pius XI hinted at what was to come in the Second Vatican Council's Declaration on the Relationship of the Church to Non-Christian Religions. But the Pope died before he could instil his vision in the draft of the Encyclical…[15]

Gary Wills' introduction to Passelecq and Suchecky's book asserts that 'Pius deserves more honor than he is often given' and claims, on the basis of the unconfirmed testimony of Cardinal Tisserant that, 'it is known that Pius meant, in the very week of his death in 1939, to denounce the anti-Jewish laws in a public address on the 10th anniversary of the Concordat with Mussolini,' even if the authors themselves are rather more circumspect, concluding 'the document in question, *Humani Generis Unitas*, was not, with regard to Jews, the vehicle of a revolutionary turnaround; far from it – at least in the form in which we have it.'[16] Rather than get too obsessed with the 'Hidden Encyclical' or a speech he might have made in the week of his death, it seems reasonable to judge Pius by what he actually did. We cannot consider Pius' response to anti-Semitic legislation in isolation, in the way Goldhagen on the one side and Phayer and Wills on the other tend to do. Pius' record on other matters is not a good one. His general political stance bears absolutely no resemblance to that of John XXIII. In Italy, he overturned Benedict XV's policy of backing the *Partito Popolare*, a broadly centre-left political party, in favour of obtaining concessions from the state by pursuing closer relations with Mussolini and the Fascists, a line that culminated in the Concordat of 1929.[17] Moreover, he supported a similar approach to Hitler and the Nazis, signing a Concordat with the Third Reich on 20 July 1933. Although his subsequent relationship with the dictators proved less idyllic in practice than he probably imagined it would be, his later criticisms of Mussolini and Hitler in the encyclicals *Non Abbiamo Bisogno* in June 1931 and *Mit brennender Sorge*[18] in March 1937, were almost entirely confined to protests about matters that directly affected the Catholic Church and cannot reasonably be described as a general defence of civil liberties or human rights against dictatorship.

Space does not permit a detailed discussion of the evident limits of his general critique of statism and racism.[19] I propose to confine myself to his response to Mussolini's introduction of racial laws to Italy in 1938. The move towards racial laws was foreshadowed in the government-sponsored *Manifesto of the Racial Scientists*, published on 14 July 1938. This gave rise to some signs of Papal disapproval. On 21 July, Pius announced at a public audience that 'Catholic means universal, not racist, nationalistic, separatist,' and on 28 July he emphasized '[h]uman dignity is to be one single great family, the human type, the human race,' and even pointed out, to Mussolini's great annoyance, '[u]nfortunately, Italy has felt the need to go and imitate Germany.'[20] However, Church-State tensions soon eased, and on 14 August the Vatican daily *L'Osservatore Romano* published an article about past Popes' treatment of the Jews in the former Papal States, which seemed to endorse past restrictions on Jews' rights to hold positions in the public service, professions, teaching and even commerce. Whether or not Pius was directly responsible for this expression of anti-Jewish sentiment, which may perhaps have owed more to his Secretary of State, Pacelli, he certainly did not repudiate it, and Mussolini took it as an implicit endorsement of the restrictions he proposed to introduce into Italy in the near future. The first set of racial laws was introduced in early September 1938, excluding Jews from state schools and announcing that all Jews who had immigrated to Italy after 1 January 1919 must leave the country within six months. More comprehensive anti-Jewish decrees followed on 17 November, prohibiting marriage between Italian 'Aryans' and other races, as well as banning Jews from public sector employment, and placing severe restrictions on their employment in the private sector, and their right to own property. Further restrictions were brought in over the next few months. The definitions of 'Jewishness' in this legislation were based on race, not religion.

How did Pius react? His initial reaction to the original education decree on 5 September 1938 in his speech to 120 Belgian pilgrims at an audience on 6 September, suggests he was 'deeply upset'.[21] In the key passage of his 6 September speech he said, apparently spontaneously:

> Listen carefully: Abraham is defined as our patriarch, our ancestor. Anti-Semitism is not compatible with the sublime thought and reality evoked in this text. Anti-Semitism is a hateful movement with which we Christians must have nothing to do... Through Christ and in Christ we are spiritual descendants of Abraham. No, it is not licit for Christians to take part in manifestations of anti-Semitism. We recognise the right of all to defend themselves and to adopt measures to protect themselves against those who threaten their legitimate interests. But anti-Semitism is unacceptable. Spiritually, we are all Semites.[22]

Whilst the reference to 'the right of all to defend themselves' indicates that Ratti had not abandoned all the anti-Jewish prejudices that he had displayed in his Polish reports of 1919–21, and left open the possibility of a real Jewish threat to Christian society, nonetheless, taken as a whole this speech was a whole-hearted repudiation in principle of the Nazi-style racial anti-Semitism now being adopted by the Italian Fascists. Zuccotti believes that Pius' advisors were startled by the forthright tone of this impromptu declaration, since the Pope had never specifically mentioned anti-

Semitism, as opposed to generic racism, in previous speeches, and had seemed to be retreating from a confrontation with Mussolini after his well-aimed sarcastic remarks about Italian imitation of Germany on 28 July, which had roused the Duce to fury, precisely because deep down he knew that, despite all his claims about the originality of Italian racial doctrine, the Pope's remarks were true. Indeed, Zuccotti believes that some of Pius' advisors were 'more than just startled, for the Pope's words were never printed in Italy.'[23] Whilst the Vatican daily, *L'Osservatore Romano,* reported the audience with the Belgians, it totally omitted the Pope's references to Jews from its brief account. However, the Pope himself did not regret his outburst, and sought to have it recorded for posterity. Pius specifically requested Monsignor Picard, the head of Belgian Catholic Radio, who had accompanied the Belgian party on their Roman pilgrimage, to publish the speech in *La Libre Belgique* on 14 September and ensured it appeared in the French Catholic newspaper *La Croix* on 17 September. Zuccotti's suggestion of a cover-up of the 'we are all Semites' speech by leading figures within the Vatican seems plausible, and Pacelli, as Secretary of State, is the prime suspect in any such conspiracy – after all, on 13 February 1939, with Pius XI dead for a mere three days and before the conclave that was to elect him Pope, Pacelli was to reassure Count Pignatti, the Italian Ambassador to the Holy See, about the famous speech that Pius XI never delivered – 'It will remain a dead letter. It will be put in the Secret Archives.'[24]

Even Owen Chadwick, whom both John Cornwell and Jonathan Steinberg have criticized for an excessively benevolent view of Pius XII, explains the surprisingly conciliatory tone of Pius XI's Christmas Eve 1938 speech about the forthcoming tenth anniversary of the Concordat with the suspicion that 'the drafting was beginning now to slip from the hand of the dying Pope into that of his more peaceable Secretary of State, Cardinal Pacelli.'[25] If, as Chadwick believes, after Hitler's May 1938 visit to Rome to meet Mussolini and the King but not the Pope, who withdrew in protest to his summer residence of Castel Gandolfo, Pius XI felt he 'was getting old and knew that he had not much time, and ceased to care about discretion or the worries of his diplomatic staff,'[26] the attempt by the Vatican hierarchy to limit the impact of the 'we are all Semites' speech within Italy, where the diffusion of its message mattered far more than in Belgium or France, demonstrates the vehemence with which his diplomatic staff, led by Pacelli, fought back. Important as the speech was, Pius XI failed to follow it up with further public protests.

The Vatican regarded the Fascist prohibition of marriage between Italian 'Aryans' and 'non-Aryans' as a violation of Article 34 of the 1929 Concordat, giving the Church the right to determine which couples might marry, and Vatican representatives made a series of private appeals to Mussolini in a vain attempt to over-turn the ban. The Vatican was also annoyed that the legislation applied to some categories of converts, arguing that, since every Catholic convert had broken with the Jewish community, 'it would be unjust to send him back amongst those who consider him a deserter and an apostate, and expose him to reprisals.'[27] Zuccotti points out that 'with the exception of the measures against inter-racial marriage and converts to Catholicism, there is no evidence that Vatican spokesmen objected to the principal Italian anti-Jewish laws.'[28]

Whilst the record of Pius XI in relation to the Jews remains in some respects ambiguous, and the claim that he was struck down by his fatal heart attack at the very moment when he was about to act remains tenable, if not altogether convincing, the case against Pius XII seems much more clear-cut.

Whilst the long-standing and fierce controversy about Pacelli's record centres on his utterances and activities during the Second World War, Cornwell's biography of Pius XII – whatever reservations one might have about its intermittent tendency towards sensationalism, exemplified by both its title, 'Hitler's Pope' and its subtitle, 'The Secret History of Pius XII' – has had the indisputable merit of drawing attention to aspects of his earlier life that previous hagiographical accounts ignored. It had long been assumed that the restricted access to the post-1922 Vatican archives would ensure that any uncomfortable revelations about the Popes of the Fascist era could be suppressed for the foreseeable future. However, under scrutiny from serious investigators, the Vatican's pre-1922 archives have been found to contain damning material that proves the anti-Semitism of future Popes. Just as Kertzer has recently uncovered the documentary evidence of Achille Ratti's anti-Semitism during his Polish sojourn referred to above, so John Cornwell has found incontrovertible archival proof of Eugenio Pacelli's anti-Semitic utterances during his term of office as Papal Nuncio in Munich embedded in his own reports to his superior, Secretary of State Cardinal Pietro Gasparri. On 4 September 1917, Pacelli informed Gasparri that the Rabbi of Munich sought the Pope's assistance in unblocking the delivery of a shipment of Italian palm-fronds, already paid for by German Jews, needed to celebrate the Feast of Tabernacles on 1 October, which was being held up in Como as a result of Italian government action. Pacelli explained to Gasparri that 'the Israelitic community are seeking the intervention of the Pope in the hope that he will plead on behalf of the thousands of the German Jews. They are confident of a happy outcome to this request.'[29] Far from being willing to grant the Jews what might seem a rather minor favour, Pacelli engaged in a very devious piece of obstructionism, telling his superior that:

[I]t seemed to me that to go along with this would be to give the Jews special assistance not within the scope of practical, arms-length, purely civil or natural rights common to all human beings, but in a positive and direct way to assist them in the exercise of their Jewish cult. I accordingly replied courteously to the aforementioned Rabbi…that I had sent an urgent request to the Holy Father on the matter, but I foresaw that in consequence of wartime delays in communication it was doubtful whether I should get an answer in time, and that the Holy Father would be delayed in explaining the matter in depth to the Italian government.[30]

This spiteful conduct by Pacelli, which Gasparri retrospectively endorsed and which was in keeping with the dominant Catholic tradition, even if not quite in the spirit of what Kertzer calls Benedict XV's 'new course for papal relations with the Jews,'[31] may seem rather trivial, but as Cornwell underlines:

> the episode belies subsequent claims that he had a great love of the Jews and that his actions were always motivated by their best interests. That he was capable of implicating the Holy See in a diplomatic sleight-of-hand in order to frustrate the possibility of helping the German Jews, even in this minor liturgical matter, suggests that in his early forties he had little sympathy for the Jewish religion.[32]

A rather more dramatic episode that took place in Munich in April 1919 during Bavaria's post-war revolutionary upsurge provides us with a much more vivid illustration of Pacelli's anti-Semitic prejudices. Pacelli had sent his *Uditore* (assistant), Monsignor Schioppa, to complain to Levien, the head of the Munich Soviet, about the revolutionaries' gross violations of diplomatic immunity. Pacelli's subsequent report to Gasparri contained the following passage:

> An army of employees were dashing to and fro, giving orders, waving bits of paper, and in the midst of all this, a gang of young women of dubious appearance, Jews like all the rest of them, hanging around in all the offices with lecherous demeanour and suggestive smiles. The boss of this female rabble was Levien's mistress, a young Russian woman, a Jew and a divorcee, who was in charge. And it was to her that the *nunciature* was obliged to pay homage in order to proceed.

> This Levien is a young man, of about thirty or thirty-five, also Russian and a Jew. Pale, dirty, with drugged eyes, hoarse voice, vulgar, repulsive, with a face that is both intelligent and sly. He deigned to receive the Monsignor Uditore in the corridor, surrounded by an armed escort, one of whom was an armed hunchback, his faithful bodyguard. With a hat on his head and smoking a cigarette, he listened to what Monsignor Schioppa told him, whining repeatedly that he was in a hurry and had more important things to do.[33]

Some might argue that these remarks about the Munich Soviet leaders, whilst going beyond purely religious anti-Semitism and pre-figuring the habitual Nazi rhetoric about Jewish Bolshevism, are not conclusive evidence of overwhelming racial prejudice, given the extreme emotions aroused by the highly polarized political context of 1919. However, it is worth pointing out that Jews were not the only ethnic group that this Nuncio of the Universal Church seemed to detest; Pacelli's attitude towards blacks did not mirror Pius XI's sympathy for the American Jesuits' campaign for racial equality during the era of segregation, a sympathy which had led Pius XI to choose the anti-racist American Jesuit John LaFarge as one of the principal drafters of what became known as the 'Hidden Encyclical' referred to above. In April 1920, in response to numerous requests from German bishops and laymen, 'Pacelli had informed Gasparri that France's black troops were routinely raping German women and children in the Rhineland, and that the influence of the Holy See should be employed to bring pressure on the French government to remove these soldiers forthwith.'[34] The French ambassador to the Holy See vigorously dismissed the allegations as 'odious propaganda' inspired by Berlin. A United States House of Representatives investigation, held in response to numerous racist petitions at a time when trumped-up charges of rape against black men were commonplace all over the southern USA, dismissed the charges. Pacelli was unconvinced by the American report, and on 7 March 1921 wrote to Gasparri again, once more urging the Pope to intervene on behalf of the allegedly molested German women and children.[35] This obsessive racist belief that all black soldiers were potential rapists was deeply embedded in Pacelli's psyche. Nearly a quarter of a century later, on 26 January 1944, during the brutal German occupation of Rome, an occupation marked by many genuine atrocities against women and children, d'Arcy Godolphin Osborne, the British Minister to the Holy See, confined to the Vatican precincts for the duration, reported to the Foreign Office in London:

> The Cardinal Secretary of State sent for me today to say that the Pope hoped that no Allied coloured troops would be among the small number that might be garrisoned in Rome after the Occupation. He hastened to add that the Holy See did not draw the colour line, but it was hoped that it would be possible to meet the request.[36]

Having demonstrated Pius XII's propensity to racism in relation to a non-Jewish ethnic group, it is worth highlighting that as Secretary of State, in contrast to his immediate superior, the dying Pius XI, Pacelli's attitude to the Jews showed no sign of softening in the late 1930s. At the 34th International Eucharistic Congress at Budapest in May 1938, shortly after the appointment of the violent anti-Semite Béla Imrédy as Hungarian Prime Minister, and whilst the Hungarian Parliament was earnestly discussing new proposed anti-Jewish legislation, Pacelli not only failed to criticize growing Hungarian anti-Semitism at a time when Hungary's leader, Admiral Horthy, was moving closer to the Third Reich, but even appeared to encourage it by his choice of words. One passage of his sermon emphasized that:

> As opposed to the foes of Jesus, who cried out to his face, "Crucify him!", we sing him hymns of our loyalty and our love. We act in this fashion not out of bitterness, not out of a sense of superiority, not out of arrogance, towards those whose lips curse him and whose hearts reject him even today.[37]

It is also significant that Pacelli, as Secretary of State, did not use the occasion to protest against Himmler's ban on German Catholics attending the Congress or reporting it in their press.[38] Lest it be suggested that my interpretation overstates Pacelli's lack of enthusiasm for Pius XI's belated distancing of himself from the Axis powers, it is perhaps worth contrasting this Budapest sermon with one given

in Istanbul by Monsignor Angelo Roncalli (later Pope John XXIII) a few months
later. Owen Chadwick informs us:

> On Epiphany (the Feast of the Three Wise Men, 6 January) 1939, the Nuncio
> in Turkey, Monsignor Roncalli, preached a sermon at the French Church of
> the Holy Spirit in Istanbul. He reminded his hearers that the bodies of the
> Three Wise Men lay at Cologne, in the midst of a country which proclaims
> "We do not want Christ or Christianity any more"; and used the reminder to
> say that "the Church does not know the division of humanity into races" and
> to prophesy that humanity would be reconciled on the ideas of charity and
> equality. About this sermon the Italian government protested to the Vatican,
> because a Jewish journal at Istanbul (*Journal d'Orient*) took the chance to apply
> the condemnation to Italian racial policy. The Vatican took no notice of the
> protest.[39]

Roncalli's sermon in Istanbul contrasted markedly with another Epiphany sermon given by Bishop Giovanni Cazzani of Cremona. Cazzani's sermon included
the following passage, printed in the Vatican daily *Osservatore Romano* on 15 January
1939:

> The Church has always regarded living side-by-side with Jews, as long as they
> remain Jews, as dangerous to the faith and tranquillity of Christian people. It
> is for this reason that you find an old and long tradition of ecclesiastical legis-
> lation and discipline, intended to brake and limit the action and influence of
> the Jews in the midst of Christians, and the contact of Christians with them,
> isolating the Jews and not allowing them the exercise of those offices and
> professions in which they could dominate or influence the spirit, the edu-
> cation, the customs of Christians.[40]

Cazzani also emphasized that the Church 'has always done everything, and continues to do everything, to prevent mixed marriages,' by which he meant marriages
between Catholics and unconverted Jews. He continued:

> Also, Catholics obedient to the directives of the Church at present do not
> take on or accept Jewish domestic servants, or put themselves in the service
> of Jews when they must live with a family; and still less do they entrust their
> babies to Jewish wet-nurses or their children to be instructed or educated by
> Jewish teachers. If in our schools until recently, Jewish teachers were not few,
> it was not because of the work of the Church.[41]

Whilst Cazzani did point out that Jewish converts to Catholicism were equal to
all other Catholics, the general tenor of the sermon was to endorse the Fascist racial laws, and its appearance in *L'Osservatore Romano* suggested that somebody near
the top of the Vatican hierarchy, most probably Secretary of State Pacelli rather

than an increasingly frail Pope dying of heart disease and diabetes, shared Cazzani's view and wanted it widely disseminated. Roncalli's courageous stand against the Third Reich and racism was clearly not the predominant line of the Italian Church in the last weeks of Pius XI's papacy.

The increasingly frantic efforts to beatify Pius XII have, unsurprisingly, not been accompanied by any willingness on the Vatican's part to publish any documents about the Holy See's conduct during World War II omitted from the carefully edited selection published between 1965 and 1981. As Zuccotti succinctly remarks:

> Pius XII, the head of the Roman Catholic Church during the Second World War, did not speak out publicly against the destruction of the Jews. This fact is rarely contested, nor can it be. Evidence of a public protest, if it existed, would be easy to produce. It does not exist. The Pope publicly referred to people who were dying because of their national or ethnic origins on just two occasions…in these two wartime speeches, Pius XII never used the words Jew, anti-Semitism or race.[42]

Zuccotti's detailed study of the Vatican's record in relation to the Holocaust in Italy itself confirms the validity of the more general case against Pius XII, since Pius had far more influence over the situation in Italy in general, and Rome in particular, than he had in Europe as a whole, given that the majority of Vatican officials were Italian by birth and many Italian government officials remained practicing Catholics. Between 1939 and 1942, Pius XII's response to the Italian anti-Jewish laws was confined to some futile intercessions on behalf of individual converts. Whilst visits from Vatican representatives to the internment camps in which foreign Jews were held by the Italian government after 1940 did raise morale, they provided very little in the way of practical help, and the Vatican representatives made no major complaints to the Italian government about the poor conditions prevailing in the camps. Whilst the Pope may not have known about every detail of the Nazi extermination programme by mid-1943, as Zuccotti emphasizes, 'what matters is that the Pope and his diplomatic officials knew enough about the Jewish genocide to believe and understand that it was a disaster of immense, unprecedented proportions.'[43] Whilst the Vatican made some rather feeble and belated efforts in favour of Jews in Italian occupied areas of France and Croatia, the protection these Jews enjoyed up to 1943 owed far more to the independent efforts of Italian diplomats and officers, and to the ambiguity of Mussolini's own stance up to 1943, than to anything the Vatican did on their behalf. During the 45 days between Mussolini's first overthrow on 25 July 1943, and the signing of the Armistice on 8 September 1943, the Italian Jews and their supporters attempted to secure a total repeal of the anti-Jewish laws. The Vatican rejected their request for help. All the Vatican proposed to the new government were three relatively minor modifications for the benefit of converts and the children of converts. As Father Tacchi-Ventura emphasized in his 29 August report to the Secretary of State, Cardinal Maglione, 'I took care not to call for the total abrogation of a law which, according to the principles and the traditions of the Catholic Church, certainly has some clauses that should be abolished, but which clearly contains some others that have merit and should be confirmed.'[44]

The single most crucial event in assessing Pius XII's attitude to Italian Jewry is the SS round-up in Rome on 16 October 1943. The first point to be made is that the Pope had advance warning of the round-up from the German diplomats Moll-hausen and Weizsacker, a warning which, although it did not include the exact day, which remained secret, should have been sufficient grounds for a private warning from the Pope to the leaders of the Roman Jewish community.[45] The Pope failed to issue any such warning. On the morning of 16 October, the Pope learned from Princess Pignatelli, who managed to see him without an appointment, that the round-up had started. This led Pius to get Cardinal Maglione to summon Ambassa-dor Weizsacker to a meeting that same day. Maglione's notes of this meeting were finally published by the Vatican in 1975. Whilst the Cardinal pleaded, 'try to save these many innocent people,' when the ambassador responded, '[w]hat would the Holy See do if these things continued?', the Cardinal then answered, '[t]he Holy See would not want to be obliged to express its disapproval' – hardly the precise threat the situation required.[46] Moreover, when the ambassador stressed, '[t]he directives come from the highest level…will Your Eminence leave me free not to report this official conversation?', Maglione left it to the Ambassador's judgement, 'whether or not to mention our conversation, that had been so friendly.'[47] Weizsacker got the Bishop Alois Hudal, Rector of the German Ecclesiastical College, to write a letter to the German Army Commander in Rome, which was forwarded to the German Foreign Office, containing the following passage: 'I earnestly request you to order the immediate cessation of these arrests in Rome and its environs. I fear, if this is not done, the Pope will take a public stand against it,' and he backed it up with a telegram of his own, claiming 'the Curia is dumbfounded, particularly as the action took place under the very windows of the Pope.'[48]

As Zuccotti points out:

> Weizsacker's warning was not heeded. The Jews of Rome were deported the following morning. Nor did the Pope ever utter a real protest. On October 25-26, after most of the deportees were already dead, an article on the front page of *L'Osservatore Romano* lamented in broad and general terms the suffer-ings of all innocents in the war.[49]

A second article on the same page presented the Pope's reaction to that suffer-ing. It contained more self-justification than genuine indignation. The key passage read as follows:

> As is well-known, the August Pontiff, after having tried in vain to prevent the outbreak of the war…has not for one moment ceased employing all the means in His power to alleviate the sufferings that are, in whatever form, the consequence of this cruel conflagration.

With the growth of so much evil, the universally paternal charity of the Supreme Pontiff has become, one could say, even more active; it does not pause before boundaries of nationality, religion or descent.

This manifold and incessant activity of Pius XII has been greatly intensified recently by the increased sufferings of so many unfortunate people.[50]

The word 'race' (*razza*) as distinct from the far vaguer 'descent' (*stirpe*) was never used in this article. The words 'Jews', 'Germans', and 'round-up' were also conspicuously absent from the text. It provided no evidence that the Pope had actually done anything for 'so many unfortunate people.'[51] Nor did it make it clear that 'increased sufferings' meant certain death. Weizsacker wrote to his superiors two days later that:

By all accounts, the Pope, although harassed from various quarters, has not allowed himself to be stampeded into making any demonstrative pronouncement against the removal of the Jews from Rome. Although he must count on the likelihood that this attitude will be held against him by our opponents, and will be exploited by Protestant quarters in the Anglo-Saxon countries for purposes of anti-Catholic propaganda, he has done everything he could, even in this delicate matter, not to injure the relationship between the Vatican and the German Government or the German authorities in Rome. As there will presumably be no further German action to be taken in regard to the Jews here in Rome, this question, with its unpleasant possibilities for German-Vatican relations, may be considered as liquidated.[52]

Weizsacker commented on the second article from *L'Osservatore Romano*, which he forwarded to his superiors, '[n]o objection can be raised to this public statement, the less so as its text...will be understood by only very few people as having special reference to the Jewish Question.'[53] In fact, wilfully obscure as the second article was, in these particular circumstances most Romans reading it in the aftermath of the round-up would have understood *stirpe* to be a reference to the Jews. On the other, more substantial issues, Weiszacker was of course right – the Pope had not given the Nazis any real trouble. After this document became public in 1964, through the original French version of Saul Friedlander's *Pius XII and the Third Reich: a Documentation*,[54] and Robert Katz wrote a detailed study of the whole episode entitled *Black Sabbath: a Journey through a Crime against Humanity* in 1969, the Vatican realized its official exculpation of Pius XII was starting to disintegrate. The Jesuit Vatican historian Father Robert Graham thundered in 1970 about Weiszacker's 'falsification of the Vatican reaction to the tragic arrest of a thousand Roman Jews on October 16, 1943,' and added, '[f]or years it has been believed, on the word of the Ambassador of the Reich, that the Pope did not bat a eyelash or make any protest on that occasion.'[55] Zuccotti is rightly dismissive of Graham's attack on Weiszacker. She argues:

Maglione agreed that the Ambassador need not report to Berlin about their meeting and the mention of a possible protest "if these things continued". Weiszacker was to use the information as he thought best, and he did so. He certainly advised his superiors of the possibility of a Vatican protest in his report on October 17. With his reference to the French bishops, he seems even to have exaggerated that danger beyond what Maglione had actually implied. If Pius XII had wanted to issue a public protest, he was free to do so at any time. If Vatican officials later wanted the world to know of the meeting between Maglione and Weiszacker on October 16, they could have published Maglione's description of it at any time. They did so only in 1975.[56]

The Italian Catholic Church made some far more serious efforts to protect Jews in Rome and elsewhere after the October round-up. Zuccotti demonstrates that, while the Vatican became aware of the hiding of Jews in Roman convents, monasteries, hospitals and schools, it did not instigate it, and on occasions, expelled Jews from Vatican properties in response to raids by the Germans, and Italian Fascist fanatics in search of Jews and other fugitives. Moreover, whilst many high-ranking clergy, including the Archbishops in Turin, Milan, Genoa and Florence, and the Bishop of Trieste, played an important role in protecting Jews, others, like the Patriarch of Venice, showed no such willingness to help. As Zuccotti emphasizes, such local variations indicate that, contrary to later legends, there was no official Papal directive in favour of protecting Jews; had there been, all the clergy would have carried it out, regardless of their own degree of personal sympathy or antipathy towards the Jews.

One example of the activities and utterances of an Italian bishop in a city with a large Jewish community should serve as a counterpoint to the silences and inactivity of Pius XII. The role played by Antonio Santin, who had begun his duties as Bishop of Trieste and Capodistria in early September 1938, was particularly praiseworthy.[57] Trieste had the third largest Jewish community in Italy, after Rome and Milan, and the largest Jewish community in proportion to its general population. Jews constituted at least 1.8 per cent of the urban population of Trieste, compared with about 0.1 per cent of the population of Italy as a whole. The first sign of Santin's willingness to defend the Jews, or at any rate criticize Mussolini's racial policy, can be seen in his reaction to a speech Mussolini gave in the city on 18 September, when he declared, still angry about Pius XI's charge on 28 July that he was imitating German racism, that '[t]hose who claim that we are adhering to imitations, or, worse, suggestions, are poor defectives whom we don't know whether to disdain or pity.'[58] The next day, Santin asked Mussolini in private to whom he had been referring. Mussolini was obliged to deny that he had intended to insult the Pope, and felt compelled to repeat this denial to a crowd in front of Santin's church. Technically, this was a defence of the Pope, not the Jews, but it showed the bishop's strong character and suggested that Mussolini might well have retreated in the face of a direct challenge from the Church about his anti-Jewish measures.

In December, Santin travelled to Rome to speak to the Duce about a number of problems regarding his diocese, including the Jews. According to his own later account of the meeting, the bishop described the Jews as 'unfortunate people,' and informed Mussolini that 'in Italy, there was no Jewish problem.'[59] In 1942, Santin twice petitioned General Mario Roatta, commander of the Second Army in Yugoslavia, not to allow Jews in Italian occupied areas to be handed over to the Croatians or the Germans. Whilst the General had many reasons for opposing the deportation of the Jews, and Santin's pleas were not decisive, it was another indication of the bishop's goodwill. On 28 August 1942, he wrote to Maglione, Pius XII's Secretary of State, about the Jews in the areas of Croatia not under Italian control. Santin explained:

> [Letters of solicitation] have been repeatedly sent to me asking if some step could be taken to ease the fate of Jews already interned or still being interned in Croatia, a fate that is described as tragic and terrifying.

> Here [in Trieste] we have intervened with good effect for those who find themselves in the part of Croatia controlled by the Italian troops. But for those who find themselves [elsewhere] in Croatia, an intervention with that government is required.[60]

Maglione delayed answering the letter until 6 October, and then responded with bureaucratic evasion, writing, 'I want to assure Your Excellency that since the Reverend Father Abbot Marcone, envoy of the Holy See in Croatia, has already intervened in this regard with the competent authorities, I have not failed to ask him again to take appropriate steps in the desired sense.'[61] Marcone's appeals were halfhearted, limited to specific groups such as spouses in mixed marriages, and ultimately proved futile. When, in 1943, the Germans started to round-up the Jews of Trieste on 9 and 29 October, Santin responded vigorously by writing to Vice-Gauleiter Wolsegger on behalf of the Jews, telling the Austrian, '[t]hey are not my faithful, but the charity of Christ and the sense of humanity know no limits…if they are guilty, they should be punished like everyone else. But if they have done nothing as individuals, they should be left in peace.'[62] Three days later, Santin spoke out publicly during a service at the Basilica of San Giusto on the patron saint's feast day in the presence of Nazis and Fascist collaborators, saying:

> San Giusto signifies the heroic love of Christ and love of our fellow-men and women. Thus, charity, goodness, humanity toward all…in the common misfortune, may every hand offer help, not hide a dagger. As Pastor of the diocese, I am asking for this law of humanity in the name of Christ, also for the sons and daughters of that people from whose womb He came as a man and in whose midst He lived and died.[63]

Santin also did as much as he could to draw the fate of Trieste's Jews to the Pope's attention, writing to him on 12 November and travelling to Rome to meet Maglione and the Pope on 29 November 1943. Although he appears not to have received much encouragement in Rome, he continued to attempt to exercise pressure on Wolsegger during 1944. Santin's consistent interventions in favour of both Jews and real or alleged partisans subject to German reprisals in his city during 1943–44 serve as the best proof that Pius' preferred course of action during the German occupation of Rome was not the only one open to him. It is also worth pointing out that the behaviour of Santin, Roncalli and other Italian Catholic clergy cast considerable doubt on the extreme thesis recently advanced by Wiley Feinstein that seeks to suggest that Italian Catholics were collectively as responsible for the deaths of Italian Jews as the German Nazis and their, often anticlerical, hard-line Fascist collaborators of the Italian Social Republic of 1943–45.[64]

In the aftermath of the Second World War, many Italian and foreign Jews expressed grateful thanks to Pius XII for his assistance to Italian Jews during the Holocaust. For example, in 1961 the Chief Rabbi of Rome, Elio Toaff, declared '[m]ore than all others, we had the opportunity of experiencing the great compassionate goodness and magnanimity of the Pope during the unhappy years of the persecution and terror, when it seemed that for us there was no longer an escape.'[65] As Zuccotti points out, '[m]en and women of the Church in Italy certainly deserved to be recognised and thanked, but the Pope had very little to do with their activities.'[66] The motives for this misplaced gratitude vary. Some had an exaggerated notion of the degree of centralized decision-making within the Church, others felt it was important to build bridges rather than needlessly offending Catholics who had helped them by drawing attention to the Pope's own silences. A third, more disreputable group consisted of those whose desire to obtain Vatican recognition for the State of Israel overrode any concern with historical truth, most notoriously the Israeli diplomat Pinchas E. Lapide, whose 1967 book *The Last Three Popes and the Jews*, very frequently cited by Catholic apologists for Pius XII, Zuccotti dismisses as 'replete with egregious mistakes and distortions.'[67]

However, one might argue that, by the time the controversy over Pius XII had started to impact on Italy,[68] as opposed to Germany, where Hochhuth's play *The Representative* originated,[69] the shift in Catholic attitudes towards the Jews marked by the declaration *Nostra Aetate*, as well as the more general liberalization of Italian society in the aftermath of Vatican II, seemed to be of greater relevance to most Italian Jews than re-examining events that had occurred during the period 1938–45, which Italian Jews, most of whom had been well-integrated into Italian society between 1870 and 1938, wanted to put behind them.

10

CONVERSION AND ITS CONSEQUENCES: AFRICANS AND ISLAM IN CAPE TOWN

Rebekah Lee

This chapter considers the process and consequences of conversion among the African population in Cape Town, South Africa. Evidence suggests that the growth of Islam can be seen as a powerful, and relatively recent, manifestation of African ritual life in the urban setting. However, new sites of conflict have emerged, as issues of belonging, identity, and race fuel and are fuelled by these processes.

This chapter offers some introductory remarks on the nature of some of these conflicts, using as its prism conversion narratives collected from approximately 20 African men and women. Focusing on the more intimate terrain of the household and the inner-lives of individuals, this study provides an important micro-level approach to understanding how religious conflicts are created, resolved and understood. Gender emerges as a central arbiter of these conflicts. In addition, I want to suggest that the phenomenon of conversion is a vital component, theoretically and empirically, in scholarship on religious conflict – precisely because it implies transformation, conversion has the capacity to generate and resolve conflicts on a personal, domestic and communal level.

To begin I will provide a very brief history of Islam and the African population. In recent years, Islam has made marked inroads into the African communities of

Cape Town, South Africa, despite Islam's historical association with the majority 'Coloured' population of the region.[1] Various scholars have contested the authenticity of this association through examining the origins of a distinctive Cape Islam. As Robert Shell (1994) and Shamil Jeppie (1989, 2001) have pointed out, Islam in the Cape was shaped not only by its Malay and Indonesian roots, but also by the large number of slaves and indentured servants from India who entered the Cape Colony in the eighteenth and nineteenth centuries, especially from Bengal, and brought with them different doctrinal perspectives and Islamic traditions. Also, as Shell has argued, runaway and recently manumitted African slaves were a significant source of converts to Islam throughout the early history of the Cape. In particular, Islam provided an alternative and much desired new ethnic identity for the some 5,000 so-called 'Prize Negroes' brought to the Cape in the first half of the nineteenth century, after the slaving vessels in which they were held were intercepted by the British Navy. However, there is little beyond a handful of contemporary letters penned by European observers to give any real sense of how Africans themselves in the early colonial period were making sense of the faith.[2]

Indeed, there is little that seems to connect those initial converts to the Muslim African community in twenty-first century Cape Town. A large gap in the historical record exists about what happened to those first African Muslims and their descendents – did they continue in the faith, did they intermarry and become fully integrated into the Malay community? Were there attempts to proselytize indigenous Africans? By whom and how successful were they?

Whether and how Islam existed among the African population from the mid-nineteenth century until the mid-twentieth century in the Cape, and indeed throughout southern Africa, are important questions future scholars need to address.[3] Possibly, Islam died out among the minority African population of the Cape, or else African Muslims became fully absorbed into a larger, and increasingly more self-conscious Coloured Islamic community that had emerged by the late nineteenth century. Vivian Bickford-Smith (1995) and Kevin Greenbank (1999) have shown the ways in which Victorian Cape Town had begun developing the legal framework for residential segregation by the turn of the twentieth century. This new geography, when coupled with the growing importance and imposition of Christianity in the lives of Africans, may have prevented any real foothold for Islam to develop in the small urban African community of the Cape.[4]

We do know that after 1948, when the victory of the National Party ushered in the apartheid era, the state reinforced the identification of Islam with the Coloured population, partly through legislation such as the Group Areas Act (1950) and the Population Registration Act (1950). Urban areas were carved into racialized zones, and those classified as Africans were effectively prevented from visiting mosques that were predominantly in Coloured areas. Oral testimony indicates Africans were actively discouraged by the state from building their own mosques in African areas, land instead being devoted to the construction of Christian churches, which soon became a familiar feature of township landscapes. Christianity became a strong hallmark of township respectability, and was cultivated within the African community through the development not only of Christian institutions but through informal associations that were imbued with Christian ideology: women's rotating credit associations and burial societies were examples of these.[5]

Despite these factors, Islam made some tentative inroads into the urban African population in the Cape from the 1960s, particularly in the established African townships of Langa, Nyanga and Gugulethu. This we know largely from oral testimonies. From the late 1970s through the 1980s, African youth were mobilized through the Langa Muslim Movement and the militant *Al Jihad* movement, the latter directed by the Jihad Centre based in Gugulethu township. In 1981, the first African from the Western Cape was sent on scholarship to study in Kuwait.[6] However, these activities were relatively small-scale and covert. Organizations such as the Jihad Centre were controlled by a non-African Muslim executive, which may have prevented a broad-base of support from developing in African areas. In addition, the executive of the Jihad Centre became more overtly pro-Shia after the Iranian Revolution, which led many African Muslims, who were largely Sunni, to leave the organization.[7] And it appears that the youth who were mobilized in the late 1970s and 1980s in the context of a larger political struggle for the most part did not remain within Islam. The last few decades up until the ending of apartheid in 1994 was thus characterized by a scattered population of African Muslim families and a relatively large number of youth who took part in Islamic movements that were often directed by non-African Muslims. These youth generally fell out of the faith in their later years.

It was only really in the 1990s that a viable and vibrant African Muslim community took shape. In Johannesburg, the *Al Murabitun* movement, essentially a Sufi movement, grew and made its way to Cape Town. The *Murabitun* movement established an African leadership that helped direct the development of Islam in the townships.[8] There was also the development of township-based organizations, such as the Masakhane Muslim Community in Cape Town, which empowered African Muslims across the various townships within the larger Muslim community. Masakhane Muslim Community continues to be the main organizing body and voice of African Muslims, and conducts various outreach efforts and skills training for the community. In 1994, the first mosque was built in Khayelitsha township, and this, in concert with the construction of mosques in recent years in Soweto, in KwaMashu (near Durban) and in New Brighton (in Port Elizabeth) have marked in very visible ways the establishment of Islam in the everyday social and cultural landscape of the African township.[9] In Gugulethu township two new Islamic centres have sprung up since 2001. My recent research suggests these have been relatively successful in attracting new converts to the faith, in particular young African men.

Official figures tend to broadcast the relative weakness of Islam among Africans, the 1996 Census showed approximately 3,400 African Muslims in the greater Cape Town metropolitan area, compared to 440,000 African Christians. However, informal evidence (unofficial censuses conducted by local mosques) and oral testimonies attest to the growing popularity and dynamism of Islam among Africans in recent years, particularly in the post-apartheid period, as related in the above history. Reliable statistics on African conversions to Islam, and African membership in Muslim organizations have yet to be gathered, though this has been acknowledged by Muslim leaders as a pressing need.

Gender, Context and Text in the Conversion Experience

When examining the changing role of Islam within African communities, it is vital to consider both *context* – the underlying social and political circumstances which may affect religious incorporation; and also, *text* – how people make sense of new belief systems, and how they rewrite them into their everyday lives and practices.

Islam has certainly become more influential among urban Africans in the post-apartheid period, and the historical developments sketched above can be understood in part as a product of dramatic shifts in South Africa's political and social geography.[10] By the early 1990s in South Africa, much of the political and social circumstances underlying previous patterns of religious organization had changed. A coercive racialized order was destabilized and then dismantled. Beginning with the lifting of influx control legislation in the late 1980s, and the removal of racially zoned schooling and residential areas in the early 1990s, urban Africans experienced for the first time the possibility of unrestricted mobility. Some Africans, particularly younger Africans, embraced this new opportunity, and moved to multi-racial areas of the city, attended multi-racial schools and began to create and draw on social networks not based solely in the townships. Access to a dizzying array of products, to information technology, and to new media contributed to redrawing Africans' sense of 'place' and belonging. Democratic change removed South Africa from the political isolation it experienced under apartheid, and increasingly enmeshed the country, and its African citizens, in an ongoing dialogue with the rest of the continent.

These globalizing trends encouraged Africans to engage in sometimes dramatic reordering of their spiritual lives. Islam ably reflected, and actively encouraged, the growing mobility of urban Africans. New adherents were introduced to new areas of the city and the country through regularly attending mosque in formerly Coloured neighbourhoods, and attending sponsored workshops on Islam held across the country. These spurred the development of social ties that transcended both narrow locale and race. Islam also fostered links, both physical and ideological, with the rest of the continent. An influx in recent years of Muslims from other African countries – from Malawi, Mozambique, Kenya, and Somalia contributed to a sense that to adopt Islam is to become connected to a larger pan-African identity. Finally, because Muslim proselytization efforts often provided material relief in the short-term through food and donations, and material prospects for the long-term, such as skills training, jobs and scholarships, potential converts felt a sense of broadening economic opportunity as well.[11]

Undoubtedly, the Christian Church has provided, and continues to provide, social cohesion and an enduring sense of identity, particularly for long-established African residents of the city. The numbers affirm the continuing dominance of Christianity in African religious life. However, these statistics may obscure ruptures now evident within the African Christian community and disguise the sense of disillusionment and detachment many feel towards the Church.[12] Furthermore, because of the Church's long presence within African townships, Africans have tended to view Christian organizations and their membership in them through the narrow lens of the locale. In contrast, Islam may be better placed to offer Africans tools to comprehend and negotiate a globalizing, multi-racial, dynamic social and economic environment.[13]

Given the context I have just related, what can 'text' reveal about the incorporation of Islam into African life? Conversion narratives offer a fascinating window on how Africans themselves comprehended their conversion experiences. They also provide a tangible text through which can be seen subtle, though no less significant, processes of 'translation' of a 'foreign' belief into everyday lives and practice (following Sanneh 1993).[14]

I will start with one woman's story:

Rushda, called Nonotise Rose before her conversion to Islam in 1990, lives in an informal settlement in Cape Town. Prior to her conversion she had been an Anglican, though it is clear her involvement with the Anglican church was troubled, in large part because she did not have the money to pay regular church subscriptions: "At church they told me that if I don't pay the money for ticket, then they won't be able to bury [me] because I'm not a committed or dedicated member…I did explain that the fact that I [am not] paying that monthly ticket is because I don't have money, I don't have a job. And it's not like I drink. I don't drink, I don't smoke, I just don't have money. That's why I'm not paying the ticket. It's not like I wouldn't want to be part of the church, I would love to be part of the church but then I can't meet one of the requirements – and it's the essential requirement – because I am poor." She recalled that when her husband died, he was buried under Anglican rites, but the congregation chose to wear black instead of the customary white, which further emphasized that she and her husband had not achieved "full membership" in the Church. She remembered, "[t]hese people that they say they are holy, they are very cruel kinds of people."

When asked how she came to the Islamic faith, Rushda recalled meeting a Muslim woman who "told me about her type of church. This religion that she was talking about, she told me that there you don't have to pay the tickets." Rushda was attracted to the generosity of Muslims: "it's like sometimes when I don't [have] anything, close to nothing and maybe I have this last money and then decided to use it and go to mosque. When I get there I wouldn't even have to ask, people are just donating. I believe in *sala*, a prayer. I would pray to Allah and He would maybe bring another Muslim person to my rescue." Another appealing feature was the simplicity of the burial procedures: "People don't like spending too much on funerals. People don't like to be buried in these expensive coffins."

An important aspect of her testimony was the strong parallel drawn between Islamic and ethnic Xhosa tradition. She stressed, "Islamic is a Xhosa thing... Muslims have traditions, they have customs and they are more or less the same as Xhosas are supposed to do but they are doing it in a more civilized way... Sleeping with a man is unclean and it's just like our ancestors don't want that sight of sex." Rushda noted parallels between Islamic and Xhosa custom in dress codes and male initiation rights as well.

Muslims in the largely Coloured mosque she attended heard about her ambition to go to Mecca, and helped pay for her pilgrimage. Before she left for Mecca, there was one obligation she had to fulfil: "I am very superstitious and when I heard that I was going to go to Mecca, I had to pay respects to the ancestors and then I made some *umqombothi*, the African beer. They [other Muslims] never knew about it, I never told them because they also do their own stuff that I don't know about. So then I can't lose the Xhosa in me, it['s] already here." She went to Mecca on a passport proclaiming her new identity as Rushda. Her South African ID still bears her former name. She uses either document when necessary.

Rushda prays five times a day and attends mosque regularly. She also teaches Arabic to children from her home. "I strongly believe that if we were all Muslims, then the land would be a better place and we would be more civilized and we would have more *ubuntu* [humanity to others]."[15]

There is a lot that can be drawn from this single narrative, but I will focus on only a few points.[16] Firstly, it is vital to stress the gendered nature of conversion. In Cape Town, African conversion to the Muslim faith in the last decade has been led principally by women, at least until very recently.[17] These women tended to reside in less-established areas of the city, which housed the majority of recent migrants from the rural areas of the country. Their marginal social positions, in the context of both traditional structures and Church organization (where elderly women with long residence in the city tended to hold sway), to some extent can account for the degree to which these women acted as receptive 'entry ports' for Islam. As Rushda's own testimony affirmed, many recent converts' experience of Christianity was largely one of acutely felt social ostracism and pressure to meet the exacting financial demands of membership. Women contrasted these with the sense of acceptance and generosity encountered through participation in Islam, in the form of free food, skills training, and scholarships.

However, African women's decision to explore Islam went deeper than any overt social or material appeal. Importantly, these women were able to transfer spiritual allegiances easily. Many respondents pointed to Islamic rituals as closely mirroring Xhosa rituals as a way of identifying with Islam as an African, and not a distinctively Coloured religion. We can hear Rushda's statement that 'Islamic is a Xhosa thing' most pointedly here. In particular, Muslim funeral rites, dress codes and cleansing regimes resonated powerfully with those who sought familiar cultural ground in the unfamiliar terrain of the city. This sense of returning to something already known is a prominent feature of women's stories. One female convert captured this feeling of nostalgia coupled with familiarity when she said, '[a]ll that is done at Islam is what was happening in the olden days.'[18] To convert to the Islamic faith for these women meant a return to a truer African identity, not a move away from it. This narrative of return eased the process of cultural translation Sanneh (1994) noted as being a primary challenge to the spread of Islam among Africans on the continent. Conversion in these women's stories thus becomes 'reversion', a cyclical 'returning to' Islam, which Kareema Quick argues is a truer description of Islamic notions of conversion than Christian ideas of dramatic transformation.[19]

This logic of return resolved any sense of spiritual or psychological disjuncture in their choice to follow the Muslim faith. Interestingly, women were able to view their participation in Islam as a progression and not a radical departure from the Christian faith. Most converts expressed a general understanding that there was little of significance in belief or practice that separated Christianity from Islam. Conversion thus involved more a translation onto an existing ideological frame-work than a fundamental reordering. This 'translation' applied to social networks as well. It appears to a large extent that these women were not ostracized from their immediate communities because of their choice to embrace Islam, though this must be tempered with the knowledge that by large female converts tended to be on the margins of key township social structures in the first place.

It seems that few female converts chose to view the conversion process as one of dramatic or radical change. Women's everyday lives affirmed this choice. In areas where Islam appeared to contradict long-held beliefs, women exhibited a high degree of flexibility, choosing to accommodate multiple (and sometimes compe-ting) viewpoints. Reports of African women attending church and mosque on a regular basis were not uncommon. Rushda herself, devout enough to accomplish the final pillar of the Muslim faith – the pilgrimage – brewed *umqombothi* to pay respect to her ancestors. She chose not to tell her fellow non-African Muslims at mosque about this act. In instances such as these, converts exhibited a resilient sensitivity to their cultural and Christian identities, and engaged in some level of compartmentalizatiȯn in order to balance their competing obligations.

However, women's domestic lives suggest that conversion was not a seamless process in every domain. Most women returned home to non-Muslim partners, which created a schism between their domestic and religious lives, though children tended to become more involved in Islam. One woman explained to me, 'I embraced Allah when I was already married to this man and I could not tell him to leave. That is difficult, it's not easy.'[20] Another woman concurred, '[w]e cannot just dump them.'[21] Women explained that Muslim practices in areas such as food preparation and abstinence from alcohol were particularly irksome to their non-

Muslim male partners, and prevented them from approaching the faith. Another woman commented on the prospect of her husband ever converting, '[w]ith my husband, that feeling has not come and I don't think it will come.'[22] This discordance in their family lives was cited by African Muslim leaders as one of the key reasons why some women were unable to continue in their newfound faith.[23]

For those African men who chose to embrace Islam, internal and domestic conflicts were expressed and took form in different ways. The following findings are largely based on a limited sample of male testimonies collected in April 2004. These testimonies suggest, albeit tentatively, that men have taken a different route to Islam than women. Women's first exposure to Islam tended to be spurred by dissatisfaction with the Church and further motivated by a desire to feed their children, a need addressed by generous donations of food that often accompanied Muslim proselytizing efforts in African areas. As shown above, women who embraced Islam tended to frame their conversion narratives in terms of a cultural return.

In contrast, male conversion experiences were framed in political and theological terms, rather than through any appeal to cultural or material circumstances. If we look at Ismail Ngqoyiyana's testimony as one example:

Ismail came to Cape Town in 1977 from the Transkei. He converted to Islam in 1986. When asked how he came to embrace Islam he stated that when he first arrived in Cape Town, he became very involved in two Christian churches, and had become so zealous that he even preached the Gospel on the streets and in the city's trains. He became disillusioned with Christianity and his teachers, and contested their views of, among several things, the Holy Trinity and the authority of priests. In this period, Ismail met someone named Ali Allulah, with whom he then had extensive discussions on the merits of various religions. Ali gave him a copy of a book called *A Comparative Study of Religions*, which Ismail studied. Ismail recalled, "Out of those religions I discovered that Islam could be most best, it had the type of God I would like to rely on. A God who is not born of man, who doesn't do bad to people, a God who doesn't die, so that was the God I was looking for in my life."

He was clear that his acquaintance with Coloured Muslims, especially at his workplace, did not draw him closer to Islam. He said of them, "Yes some were drinking, some were smoking cigarettes, some were even smoking *dagga* or marijuana. So their behaviour was not right. But I didn't take Islam because of them, I took Islam because of what I read in the book, the book that man gave me. When I read that I discovered that Islam is this but the behaviour of the people is like this, so I had to differentiate between God and people and the religion of God which is pure and the behaviour of the people which is not good."

After his conversion, Ismail continued his Islamic studies. He currently works for the Islamic Dawah Movement, and has been appointed *imam* of the mosque in Khayelitsha township.[24]

To some extent, one can argue that Ismail's conversion experience was somewhat exceptional, given his eventual promotion to *imam* within the African Muslim community and his early conversion to the faith. However, even those African men who converted recently tended to reflect far more than women on the theological shortcomings of Christianity, and the relative clarity of Islamic doctrine. Young men in particular were eager to embrace the intellectual aspects of Islamic teachings. One of the real benefits of Islam, as one young male convert simply stated, 'I am learning every day.'[25] According to Ismael Gqamane, another African *imam*, young men have shown surprising zeal in their desire to further their studies of Islam, and this was something the Muslim community was trying to harness, through stocking Islamic centres with accessible texts to read and through small scholarships to support studies in local Islamic schools. Perhaps Imam Gqamane was seeing his own avid desire to learn reflected in the young men he taught – in the early 1990s he received sponsorship from the Saudi government to study Islamic law in Saudi Arabia, and he completed his university degree there.

Another important theme that threads through men's conversion narratives was that Islam helped provide Africans an autonomous sense of political identity, free of any perceived historical or ideological links with a racist apartheid past. Related to this, Islam provided a ready channel through which a larger pan-African identity could be understood and expressed. That Islam could be an effective articulator of a broader 'Africanness' was reinforced by the influx of Muslim refugees and work-seekers from across sub-Saharan Africa who flocked to South Africa after the transition to democratic rule. Finally, it would be difficult to ignore the post-9/11 climate, which according to Imam Gqamane exacerbated already existing fears of 'Empire America'. Africans came to see Islam as an effective bulwark against the hegemony of America and the West, and this may account for the cult status of leaders such as Moammar Qaddafi, Saddam Hussein and Osama bin Laden among some African Muslims.

Finally, Islam was cast, in ways that echo the Nation of Islam's appeal in black inner city America in the 1960s, as a path through which men in particular could release themselves from crippling cycles of violence, crime, unemployment and a sense of disconnection and victimhood. Prisons were an important zone of first contact with Islam for many African male youth, who learned of Islam through their Coloured inmates.[26] For these mostly young and single converts, Islamic codes and rituals provided a strict regimen, a sense of discipline, a focus on education, and ultimately a way to recover a sense of personhood denied to them. This association with Malcolm X's own conversion experience in prison is perhaps not coincidental. One male convert expressed how he first came to Islam after being inspired by a photograph of Malcolm X on his pilgrimage to Mecca.[27] Works by and about Malcolm X are part of the small library in the Islamic Information

Centre, which is a new centre in Gugulethu that seems to have become a magnet for young African men.

As in the story of Malcolm X, the decision to embrace Islam was transformative. Unlike the women in this study, the men I interviewed saw their conversion as true 'transformations', and not as any 'return' to familiar rituals or beliefs. Their stories tended to stress how 'bad' they used to be, and how much they have changed since embracing Islam. One convert testified that he used to indulge in 'drinking, liking to fight, going out with girls and fighting about these things…I was working for nothing but nobody could tell me what to do. I was rough.'[28] Islam, he claimed 'really changed my life. I refrained from all the bad things and prayed to God to help me in every which way He can.'[29] Another poignant story was from a young man who said he was on his way to Cape Town International Airport to do 'bad stuff', later revealed to mean pick-pocketing and other petty crime, when he heard the call to prayer sounding from one of the mosques. He stopped, entered the mosque and never returned to his old ways.

Interestingly, some male converts chose to leave their households entirely rather than balance, as women, did competing demands and multiple allegiances. I interviewed several men who had decided to live together, either in compounds built behind a mosque or through sharing a house. This created in essence a new domestic arrangement, one which allowed these recent converts to strictly observe Islamic rituals and prevented them from 'backsliding' into former habits, or associating with no longer desirable friends. Leaders in the African Muslim community affirm that though male conversion lags far behind female conversions in terms of numbers, men are more apt to remain within the Islamic faith and observe far more strictly the various rituals associated with it. Imam Gqamane related the story of one man who was interested in embracing Islam but decided to wait until after he completed his circumcision rites.[30] The man did this because he did not want to test his commitment to Islam, nor subject himself to any internal contradictions between his traditional obligations and his new found Islamic ones. This is quite different from Rushda's story of covertly brewing *umqombothi* beer as a way of thanking her ancestors for her trip to Mecca. For this prospective male convert, compartmentalization as Rushda had done was not a desired option.

In conclusion, I want to stress that it is important to look at the gendered nature of conversion, because men's and women's different routes to the faith led to divergent ways in which Islam was both received and practised. I suggest that women tended to face greater challenges domestically to continue a faithful adherence to Islam, and tended to resolve this by straddling sometimes conflicting worlds simultaneously. Some male converts avoided this dilemma by creating new communal arrangements with other male converts. This allowed them to firmly entrench their new Islamic lifestyles into their everyday lives, which in turn reinforced that to become Muslim was a dramatic transformation, and not a return to familiar ground.

11

BUDDHIST MONKS AND POLITICAL ACTIVISM IN SRI LANKA

Mahinda Deegalle

Sri Lanka has preserved a traditional form of Theravada Buddhism and is home to the longest surviving living Buddhist monastic tradition. Since the disappearance of Buddhism from India at the end of the twelfth century, as a consequence of Islamic conquest and other factors,[1] Sri Lanka has been the traditional home of the Theravada. The Theravada legacy stemming from the Mahavihara in Anuradhapura spread to Southeast Asia to become the dominant religious influence in the Buddhist civilizations of modern Burma, Thailand, Cambodia and Laos.[2]

In Sri Lanka, Buddhist monasticism still continues but recently it has faced challenges requiring significant adaptations and modifications in the light of adverse political, social and economic influences from both within and without. However, these adaptations are not unusual for the Sri Lankan Theravada Buddhist tradition. As a living religious community, throughout its long history Sri Lankan Buddhist monasticism has constantly faced challenges requiring modification in aspects of monastic praxis. Political instability at times of foreign invasions, such as that of the Chola King Rajaraja in 993 CE and the occupied rule of Magha (1215–1232), weakened Buddhist life and practices and several times the higher ordination lineage (P. *upasampada*) was imported from abroad.[3] The *bhikkhuni* (nun) ordination lineage completely disappeared from Sri Lanka in the medieval period. When these ups and downs in the long history of Buddhism are considered and reflected upon, there are reasonable grounds for contemporary Sri Lankan Buddhist fears[4] regarding the threats to the very survival of Buddhism in the country. In recent times Buddhists have experienced provocation in the form of gruesome and brutal terrorist acts against religious communities by the Liberation Tigers of Tamil Eelam (LTTE) who wish to establish their own sovereign government called 'Eelam' within Sri Lanka.

In the context of Buddhist monasticism, civil war and current peace negotiations in Sri Lanka, this chapter examines the role of Buddhist monks in contemporary political activism. Recognizing perceived potential internal and external threats to the very survival of Buddhist monasticism, the chapter analyses the challenges as well as the implications of current monastic political activism for Buddhist community life and the people of Sri Lanka.

Rethinking Buddhism in the Context of the Ethnic Conflict

Rather than creating an idealistic and a rosy picture of Buddhists and Buddhist practices in relation to the ethnic conflict in Sri Lanka, I want to question certain assumptions and arguments that some Sri Lankan groups make against peace negotiations with extreme elements in the Tamil community. My purpose is to understand the basis from which nationalistic and extremist views have emerged in modern Sri Lanka, focusing on the events and reactions during the last two decades following the 1983 ethnic riots[5] which marked one of the darkest points in Sri Lankan history.

In the context of the LTTE's terrorism over the last two decades, there have been several attempts to bring peace to Sri Lanka. After the ethnic riots of July 1983, there were several rounds of peace talks. For the first time, with the mediation of India, peace talks were held in the Bhutanese capital Thimpu in 1985. On 29 July 1987, the Indo-Sri Lanka Peace Accord was signed in Colombo by the Indian Prime Minister Rajiv Gandhi (1944–91) and the Sri Lankan President Junius Richard Jayawardene (1906–96). When the LTTE failed to end hostilities and surrender arms to the Indian Peace-Keeping Force (IPKF), a long and violent struggle began between the IPKF and the LTTE. The Janatha Vimukti Peramuna's (JVP) agitation, brutal violence and terror directed against the Sri Lankan government for signing the Indo-Sri Lanka Peace Accord led to further tensions between Sri Lankan President Ranasinghe Premadasa (1924–93) and the Indian government. This culminated in the complete withdrawal of the IPKF by March 1990. It was against this background that the LTTE suicide bombers assassinated both Rajiv Gandhi (1991) and R. Premadasa (1993).

Peace talks were carried out between President Premadasa and the LTTE in 1989 and the next round of talks was held in 1994 with President Chandrika Bandaranaike Kumaratunga (b.1945) but the talks came to an abrupt end in April 1995 when the LTTE attacked a ship in Trincomalle harbour. President Kumaratunga proposed a package of constitutional reforms enabling the devolution of power to the provinces in 1997 but failed to gain the support of the opposition party, the United National Party (UNP), to secure the two-thirds majority in Parliament required for constitutional changes. President Kumaranatunga resumed another set of talks with Norway's mediation in 2000–1. When Prime Minister Ranil Wick-remesinghe (b.1949) won the parliamentary election in December 2001, the initia-tive was revived for talks with the LTTE and a Memorandum of Understanding (MOU) was signed on 22 February 2002 between the Sri Lankan government and the LTTE, with Norwegian mediation, making the ceasefire formal. Between Sep-tember 2002 and April 2003, six rounds of peace talks were held. These were halt-ed in April 2003 when the LTTE withdrew from the talks. Due to growing inter-national pressure, the LTTE was forced to resume participation at peace talks held in Geneva early in 2006, but unfortunately has withdrawn from the second round of talks scheduled in Geneva from 24-25 April 2006.

Though most of the previous attempts to bring about peace have failed in one way or another, at the time of writing there is some hope for the peace agreement brokered by the Norwegians and signed by the Sri Lankan government and the LTTE. Although the agreement is intact, it has been reported that the LTTE has violated it on many occasions[6] – according to some estimates more than 3000 times. A serious blow to the current peace process in Sri Lanka came on 12 August 2005 with the brutal assassination of Sri Lanka's distinguished foreign minister, Lakshman Kadirgamar (1932–2005), a Tamil by birth but a moderate political lead-er of the Sri Lankan government, who had worked tremendously for the success of the peace process. The LTTE is blamed for the assassination. As a result of these political assassinations and other forms of violence committed by the LTTE, the European Union also imposed a travel ban on the rebel delegations of the LTTE on 27 September 2005.

Past efforts at reaching a settlement between the Sri Lankan government and the LTTE have foundered partly due to the failure of the two main national poli-tical parties – the United National Party and the Sri Lanka Freedom Party – to agree on a bipartisan approach to the ethnic conflict. This is because the political standpoint of the two parties has been very much determined by their own political aims rather than the national interest.

Over the years, focusing on various aspects of the peace negotiations, several moderate and extremist groups have opposed any peace negotiations. This chapter will discuss some of the objections raised by Buddhist monks who have become actively involved in politics and protested in public demonstrations in Colombo.

By examining events in recent Sri Lankan history, I want to demonstrate that those who have opposed the peace process at one stage or another have attempted to mask the reality of the current ethnic conflict. It can even be said that some nati-onalist groups such as the Sihala Urumaya (Sinhala Heritage) have intentionally produced arguments designed to make the peace process fail. The Sihala Urumaya was established on 20 April 2000[7] in the hope of protecting 'the Sinhalese against the violence unleashed by Tamil racists and Muslim fundamentalists.'[8] Its former President Thilak Karunaratna (2000–2004), who resigned from the party due to an internal dispute in October 2004, joined the United National Party and was very cautious about Norway's mediation role in the peace negotiations. When I visited him in their headquarters in Colombo with a Buddhist delegation from the Buddhist Federation of Norway, Mr Karunaratna remarked with regard to Norway's mediation in the peace process, '[w]e do not need foreign mediators. We can manage our internal affairs ourselves.' He further remarked:

> The Norwegians have not been impartial.[9] A clear example is the problem with the resettlements of Indian Tamils that Jon Westborg was involved with... There is no reason to grant Eelam. There is no archaeological evidence that Tamils have been the only ethnic group living in the North. Even human rights violations by the LTTE are not recognized as such by the Norwegian Government and other countries. The Tamils even kill their own people! The real problem is the Tamil extremists. Norway and other foreign countries that have intervened have supported the LTTE by allowing them to raise funds.[10]

The serious drawback with the arguments of the nationalist groups is that they deny the real conditions of the current ethnic conflict and so distort the facts. They misrepresent the situation by asserting 'in Sri Lanka, there is no ethnic problem', and insisting that there is no Sinhala and Tamil war. They reject the very use of phrases such as: 'Tamil and Sinhala war'; 'ethnic problem in Sri Lanka'; 'Buddhism and Ethnic Conflict in Sri Lanka'; 'Buddhism and Conflict' in book titles and academic papers.[11] They do not want to accept that over 60,000 people have died within the last two decades as a result of ethnic cleansing. The lay members of the Sihala Urumaya and the monks of the Jathika Hela Urumaya maintain that there is 'no ethnic conflict in Sri Lanka' between the Tamils and Sinhalas. They question how there could be a significant Tamil and Muslim population within the Colombo city limits if there were any ethnic conflict.[12] On the contrary, they insist that what Sri Lanka has experienced in the last two decades is merely a problem of terrorism. In this way, they reduce the whole problem of ethnic conflict and civil war to a question of Tamil terrorism.

By insisting on the role of 'terrorism' and denying the 'ethnic' dimension of the problem, these groups have removed the possibility for genuine peace in Sri Lanka. Sadly, they have also fanned the flames of war. One must ask how they can still claim to be the followers of the Buddha while using the rhetoric of war? The use of Buddhist symbols and the examples of injustices they claim the terrorists have inflicted on Buddhist institutions in support of their arguments for nationalistic and extremist ends is questionable and problematic. However, their arguments also reveal the underlying nature of their fears and reservations with respect to the peace negotiations.

'Fear'[13] and 'distrust' are the primary stumbling blocks for smooth peace negotiations both between Sinhala and Tamil ethnic groups. Hence, the role of the peace negotiator at this juncture should be finding ways to bridge the 'information gap' between the two ethnic groups and minimizing 'fear' and mutual distrust as much as possible and demonstrating that the other party can be trusted in the process and for the purpose of creating peace.

To understand the Sinhala perspective and the frustration of the Sinhala people in relation to the status of Buddhism, let me start with the thoughts of Ven. Mado-luvave Sobhita, a very influential Buddhist monk and a political activist in contemporary Sri Lanka. Ven. Sobhita is a popular Buddhist preacher in Colombo and a graduate of the University of Sri Jayawardanapura. Though retired for some time now, he taught at Sri Subadrarama Pirivena, Nugegoda, during which time his ideas on ethnicity, nation, and politics developed in relation to popular preaching. As a preacher his popularity grew in strength and a large number of young monks and students admired his preaching style. At the commemoration of the death of a student at the University of Peradeniya, who died in the clash between students and police in the early 1980s, Ven. Sobhita was invited to give a sermon to the student body. Sobhita's style of public speaking is very powerful and charismatic and easily bridges the divide between preaching and politics.

In the past, Sobhita has engaged in many political activities related to the ethnic conflict and has expressed the fears and frustrations of Sri Lankan Buddhists in relation to the ethnic problem. As a popular spokesperson for the Sinhala cause, and as someone who has been actively involved in various national issues within the last two decades, his concerns and thoughts are useful in understanding the roots of Sinhala extremist elements in the modern period. The concerns that Sobhita raises should not be lost sight of and can help in facilitating the peace process. His concerns are intimately related to the status of Buddhism in the future Sri Lanka: if the violence that has erupted against Buddhist monks, Buddhist sacred symbols and institutions continues, then the frustrations of Buddhists will also grow and create obstacles for genuine peace.

In 1988, writing to *Vinivida* (Transparency),[14] a monthly journal published by a group of progressive monks named Manava Hitavadi Bhiksu Sanvidhanaya (Bhikku Organization for Humanity), loosely affiliated with the JVP, Sobhita captured the frustration of contemporary Buddhists with the present ethnic conflict. Let us examine Sobhita's statement, which makes plain the roots of the fears among Buddhists. Sobhita identifies specific threats to Buddhist monkhood in Sri Lanka. Over the last two decades, terrorists have continuously targeted Buddhist monks in order to provoke Sinhala communities, having singled out Buddhist monks as the main cause of Tamil grievances.

Several gruesome examples of direct physical attacks on Buddhist monks in the 1980s and 1990s can be mentioned. First, the Arantalawa massacre, which occurred on 2 June 1987.[15] At Arantalawa in Ampara, terrorists butchered a coach-load of young monks – to be exact, thirty-four Buddhist monks and four civilians – who were on a pilgrimage to Kelaniya Temple from the Mahavapi Temple. This massacre still resonates in contemporary discussions and haunts many Buddhist lives. It reminded the Buddhists and the Sinhalese of the horrific consequences of ethnic turmoil and brought home the threats to Buddhist institutions and their members.

Second, there was the brutal killing of a resident Buddhist monk in the forest hermitage at Trikonamadu located in the North Central Province of Sri Lanka. Sobhita describes the brutality of the savage killing in Trikonamadu in graphic terms. The terrorists killed the resident monk and offered his flesh to the Buddha as alms. Instead of the usual vegetarian offerings, human flesh was offered. This act is an inversion of Buddhist ritual practice and constitutes a case of human sacrifice within the temple, a sacrifice of one of the faithful sons of the Buddha. Its purpose was to show Buddhists what lay in store for them in the unfolding ethnic violence and the battle for land. This event testifies graphically to the imminent death and annihilation of Buddhist communities. When Buddhists see these events and hear accounts of violence perpetuated on Buddhist monks, Buddhist institutions and sacred sites, they despair. They ask what they, as adherents of a doctrine of non-violence, can do in the face of such aggression.

Within the last two decades, terrorist attacks have not been limited to the killing of individual Buddhists but have also involved the destruction of Buddhist sites. As a third example, the LTTE destroyed Nagadipa, a sacred Buddhist site associated with the historical Buddha's second journey to Sri Lanka (*Mahavamsa* 1:45–47).[16] They also began to attack prominent sacred Buddhist symbols that had been the object of pious devotion by Sri Lankan Buddhists for centuries.

Fourth, on 14 May 1985, the LTTE attacked the sacred Bodhi tree at Anuradhapura.[17] On that occasion, 120 Buddhist pilgrims died inside the Sri Maha Bodhi premises. For Theravada Buddhists in Sri Lanka, the Bodhi tree was almost synonymous with the historical Buddha; in a sense, in popular devotion, the Bodhi tree was treated almost like a living Buddha; for pious Buddhists, it was not just another dead relic but a living reminder of the historical Buddha's enlightenment. As Sobhita recounts the events, the terrorists bathed that sacred site with blood as opposed to ritual burning of incense, offering flowers, chanting Pali recitations and pouring water at the foot of the Bodhi tree. Here was another case of brutal violence and human sacrifice in a sacred site that was important for Buddhist devotion.

Fifth and last, is the bombing of the Tooth Relic Temple in Kandy on 25 January 1998.[18] Like the Bodhi tree at Anuradhapura, the Tooth Relic at Kandy is another historically important sacred Buddhist object. The historical Buddha's tooth is the most prominent Buddhist relic in Sri Lanka today and continues to have significant symbolic importance in the country's national affairs. Historically, the Tooth Relic continued to have a close affinity with royalty an as object that legitimated the ruler. Both the Bodhi tree and the Tooth Relic are highly venerated, symbolic objects, which are imbued with sacredness. By attacking those sacred objects, terrorists aimed to provoke Buddhists and lead them to commit violence against Tamils.

In the face of these continuous attacks on Buddhist monks, religious sites and sacred objects, Buddhist communities have observed complete non-violence and strict self-restraint. Sobhita and others like him have captured the frustration and desperation of Buddhist communities in these circumstances. Groups who oppose any peaceful negotiations with terrorists can use these violent events to manipulate and mislead the Sinhala public. These wounded, powerful, historical memories can become obstacles to peace.

Buddhist Monks as Agitators

In the last five decades, in dealing with various political issues that concerns the Buddhists and Sinhala communities in relation to land and the rights of the majority community in Sri Lanka, the Buddhist monastic order or *sangha*, in general, has functioned as a pressure group in determining the country's politics. However, in discussing the *sangha's* involvement in Sri Lankan politics, it is important to remember that the Sri Lankan *sangha* is not a monolithic entity; as a religious group, its members hold diverse opinions with regard to political issues and take different stands on national issues. Some are more vocal than others, and while those of narrow views, opinions and actions always find a prominent place in the media, it is important to note that the majority of the members of the *sangha*, are not still actively involved in politics or political activism.

In the 1990s, Sri Lanka witnessed a steady growth of political activism on the part of Buddhist monks. A new generation of young Buddhist monks did not hesitate to engage in various protests in order to defend the rights of the Sinhalese and Buddhists in the face of an ethnic crisis aggravated by the terrorism of the LTTE. On the one hand, their protests can be seen as a by-product of generally unhealthy tendencies in the political and social climate in modern Sri Lanka. On the other hand, monks themselves have increasingly been involved in politically motivated activities. Their political activities have seriously affected monastic practices and have altered the prevalent image of the Buddhist monk as socially and politically aloof.

Though in the early phases of Sri Lankan history, there were cases where individual monks acted bravely in the face of outside threats, their actions were not acts of political activism carried out on collective basis as has been the case in the last decade. Sporadic heroic acts such as the one that Ven. Kudapola allegedly performed in front of the Tooth Relic Temple at the ceremony of signing the Kandyan convention on 2 March 1815 are not common. Kudapola is said to have brought down the Union Jack, which was raised before the signing of the agreement. Kudapola's heroism is recorded in school textbooks and is taught as an example of patriotism that should be cultivated in the face of injustice.

In 2000, the People's Alliance (PA) government of President Chandrika Kumaranatunga proposed the Seventeenth Amendment to the Sri Lankan constitution. However, the constitutional reform package included several other reforms such as the devolution of power from the central government to provincial administration. This constitutional reform package, which was identified as the Seventeenth Amendment, gave birth to tense political debates and agitation. Monks loosely affiliated with the lay political party, the Sihala Urumaya (Sinhala Heritage) and other nationalistic movements, staged protests opposing the Seventeenth Amendment and took a stand threatening 'fasting until death' if the government did not withdraw the constitutional amendments. These protests and agitations were drastic, and in terms of the degree of severity and force, novel in the context of the monastic traditions of Sri Lanka.

The symbolic location for the protest was the Pettah Bus Station in the heart of Colombo. After a long march to Pettah, one young Buddhist monk began a fast to the death. When the national television interviewed Ven. Athuraliye Rathana,[19] an organizer of the march, an active member of the Jathika Sangha Sabhava[20] (National Sangha Council) and an ardent supporter of the new political party, Sihala Urumaya, he told them that they would continue to protest by giving their lives until the complete withdrawal of the amendments. The exact words used by Rathana on that occasion were '*marantika upavasayak*' (a fast ending in death). Even the words that modern activist monks use are striking and demonstrate serious challenges to modern Theravada monasticism. For some young people, both lay and monastic, human life seems to be less important than a noble death in what they perceive as a just cause. Quite often, what they take as a 'just cause' contains a 'political end' whether it is a 'constitutional amendment' or 'a new proposal to revive the educational system.' Another peculiar feature that appears commonly in Sri Lanka is that for any issue there seems to be a protest by opponents and a demonstration by those in favour.[21]

A young monk named Ven. Hadigalle Vimalasara began a fast unto death under the Pettah Bodhi tree.[22] At the time of fasting, Ven. Vimalasara played an active role as the publisher and propagation secretary of the Jathika Sangha Sabhava (National Sangha Council). Ven. Vimalasara explained his intention in fasting: he fasted under the Bodhi tree in order to give his life for the nation. This kind of 'life giving' by a Sri Lankan Buddhist monk in the name of the country and to stop a constitutional amendment had not happened before. Such acts of devotion to the nation for political ends are highly unusual in the context of Buddhist monasticism.

This kind of fast can be seen as a 'spiritual protest'. The modern Sinhala word used to describe such an act is *upavasaya*. According to the *English-Sinhalese Dictionary*, the closest English term for *upavasaya* is 'fast'.[23] As a religious activity, it has the connotation of abandoning regular daily activities, in particular, the abandonment of taking meals. As an indigenous term, however, the *upavasaya* does not seem to have a long linguistic history. Standard classical Sinhala dictionaries such as that of Sorata's *Sri Sumangala Sabdakosaya*, for example, do not record its appearance in any of the medieval Sinhala texts.[24] The absence of references to the term *upavasaya* in Sinhala literature demonstrates its recent origin and modern adoption in Sri Lanka. However, it is worth noting the presence of another important Indic term, which conveys similar spiritual meanings to the term *upavasaya*. For example, Sorata notes that some Sinhala texts such as the *Dharmapradipika* and the *Dahamsarana* used the term *satyakriya* (P. *saccakiriya*)[25] with the meaning of a truthful 'act of making a wish'. In the act of *satyakriya*, the wish of the aspirant comes true due to the inherent power of the virtue that the aspirant possesses.

This kind of non-violent protest is closely related to pan-Indian religious practices known as *saccakiriya* (an act of truth). In the twentieth century such forms of non-violent protests have become popular with Mahatma Gandhi (1869–1948).

Realizing the power and potential of such fasts as expedient means for achieving political ends, modern monastics do not hesitate to use them.

On 8 August 2000, the Sinhala newspaper *Lankadipa* gave full coverage to the death fast including photographs which portrayed the emotional atmosphere under the Pettah Bodhi tree. One of the two photographs on the front page displayed four male adults emotionally venerating the feet of the monk who began the fasting. Their eyes are filled with tears. The other photograph on the left side shows several young monks sitting on the ground with handkerchiefs in their mouths, a gesture of desperation and sorrow. They also have tears in their eyes. The front-page heading read in Sinhala *vyavasthava askaraganna* (withdraw the constitution!), *himinama upavasaya arambayi* (the monk begins the fast!). There is no doubt about the purpose of the fast; protesters wanted the government to withdraw the constitutional amendment. On 8 August, delivering a special message, the young monk promised that he would not rise up from the fasting seat until the proposed amendments were withdrawn. Ven. Vimalasara stated:

> I sat for this fasting not to protect my life. My ambition is to protect the country, the nation and the *sasana*. I will stop this fast only if an acceptable promise arrives that the Government will withdraw the constitutional amendments. Otherwise, I will offer my life for this sovereign country.[26]

Ven. Vimalasara further elaborated the rationale of his past political activities:

> In the name of the nation (*jatiya*), for a number of years, we have carried out various activities to defeat the package. But such activities have become like cutting wood to a running massive river. The constitutional amendments proposed now are much more dangerous than the political proposals of 1995. Even though we tried to defeat this proposal in a non-violent manner, it was unsuccessful. Politicians, who do not listen to the people's voice, did not even listen to the voice of the *mahasangha*. It is not our lives that are precious to us. For us, country, nation and *sasana* are precious. I sacrifice my life to protect the country, nation and religion. As yet the lions of the Sinhabahu lineage have not risen, but they will rise tomorrow or the day after. If there is no acceptable response to the effect of withdrawing the constitutional amendments, I will carry on fasting until my death. I will offer my life. In the name of the life given now, I request everyone to go forward to protect the country, the nation and the *sasana*.[27]

Ven. Vimalasara began fasting on 6 August. During the fast, he refused even drinking water and several times, he fainted. In a weakened state he carried out the last stage of the protest lying on a special seat.[28] To extend support to his fast and as a gesture of public support to the protest, the shops on Olcott Street in Pettah were closed. Thousands of people gathered around the fasting place. In the premises, the *mahasangha* and various speakers explained to the public the details of the protest.

In this example, the image of the monk and his death-fast is used to achieve a political end. The symbolic location selected for the fast is important. Those involved selected a Bodhi tree in a visible public space. The tree itself as a symbol has several layers of meaning for Buddhists in relation to the Buddha's awakening.

The events which followed the fast are also significant. The government withdrew the constitutional amendments and postponed the debate on it in Parliament. As a post-fast event, a photograph on the front page of the Sinhala daily *Lankadipa* recorded the visit of the late Ven. Madihe Pannasiha (1913–2003) to the site giving a soft drink to the recovering death-fast monk Vimalasara.[29] In this case, the activist monks proved that political activism works and can help them to achieve their political goals.

Pressures from the *Sangha* Chiefs and Non-Monastic Quarters

In this climate, pressure from monastic quarters was not uncommon. A few days after the above events, the Mahanayakas (*Sangha* Chiefs) issued a statement saying they would not go to the funeral of those MPs if they changed their political parties in order to cast votes for the constitutional amendments. The context for this statement was the following. On 8 August 2000, Mr Marvin Silva, a UNP member of Parliament, left the opposition during the debate and joined the government. Ronnie de Mel had already left the party.[30] It was believed that if the MPs were paid in cash, they would be ready to change political parties and join the ruling party. To avoid such things happening further, the four Mahanayakas said that they would not come even for the funerals of those MPs.

On 8 August, the four Mahanayakas – Ven. R. Vipassi of the Malvatta, Ven. U. Buddharakkhita of the Asgiriya, Ven. M. Paññasiha of the Amarapura, and Ven. W. Medhalankara of the Amarapura – unanimously agreed to protest by issuing a message to all members of Parliament. The Sinhala daily *Divayina* carried their message on the front page under the heading 'cast [your] vote against the proposed constitutional amendments with courage and sincerely.'[31] The complete message of the Mahanayakas was:

> This is the final message made with strong affection for the country (*desamamakatvaya*) to all members of the Sri Lankan Parliament. The proposed constitutional amendments are harmful and a threat for the country, nation and Buddhism. We draw your attention to our request on 15 June 2000 and would like to request you to cast your vote against the constitutional amendments with courage and sincerity. If you do otherwise, you may have to face the reaction of the Sinhala Buddhist public.[32]

In these communications, one can see the monks interfering in politics by claiming that the amendments are harmful to the country.

The United Sinhala Association (Ekabaddha Sinhala Sanvidhanaya) of Kandy organized a *satyakriya* (P. *saccakiriya*) campaign in front of the Tooth Relic Temple on 7 August 2000. On that occasion, they also burnt the new constitution written by the People's Alliance government. In that *satyakgraha*, the Sangha Council of the Three Fraternities in Kandy (Kanda Udarata Trainikayika Maha Sangha Sabha) issued the following statement:

> This island of the Sinhalese is the place where pure Theravada Buddha *sasana* prevails. The proposed constitutional amendments will betray the nation (*jatidrohi*) and country (*desadrohi*). It will separate the ethnic groups and will divide this one land into eight pieces in order to establish eight Federal Governments. It will destroy the friendship and unity among Sinhalas, Tamils, Muslims and Burghers. It will also lead to the destruction of the Buddha *sasana* and the decline of Sinhala Buddhists while creating prosperity among other ethnic groups and religions. Further, it will be a direct invitation to the Eelam Government. Taking the Three Refuges, we pray that the minor and major deities not to allow the approval of the amendments by resorting to evil means such as giving bribes, the use of power, wealth and cunning behaviour.
>
> Furthermore, due to the influence of an unrighteous Government if members of the Parliament cast votes to approve the new constitution which will betray the nation and country, the divine curse and the curse of Sinhala Buddhists who have been preserving the Buddha *sasana* will fall on their families for seven generations. By doing *satyagraha* in front of the Tooth Relic temple, we request all members of Parliament to think about the future consequences and avoid casting votes in favour of the new Constitution. This will betray the nation and be harmful to the country by encouraging an Eelam Government.[33]

These three responses mentioned above – the monk's fast under the Bodhi tree, the joint message of the four monastic chiefs and the pressures from monastic circles – were crucial in forcing the government to postpone the debate on the constitutional amendment in Parliament. In addition to this monastic political activism, there were several non-monastic groups who expressed their opinions vehemently against the constitutional amendments. All these protests resulted in the government's postponement of voting on the amendments.

Protests of the Janatha Vimukti Peramuna
Buddhist monks were not alone in their protests against the constitutional amendments. Besides monks' protests, political parties such as the Janatha Vimukti Peramuna (JVP) and the United National Party (UNP) also engaged in campaigns of agitation. The revolutionary political party, the Janatha Vimukti Peramuna actively opposed the amendments by organizing a series of events nationwide.

Let me briefly introduce the Janatha Vimukti Peramuna (People's Liberation Front), a political party founded by Rohana Wijeweera in 1966, which has made significant radical contributions by involving Buddhist monks in political activism. Highlighting the JVP's activities in this respect, Sarath Amunugama wrote in 1991, '[o]f all the Sri Lankan political parties, it was the JVP that set out deliberately to mobilize the monks as a vital support group.'[34] On two occasions, in 1971 and 1987–89, the JVP attempted to overthrow the Sri Lankan government by resorting to extreme forms of violence and brutal killings of the innocent including prominent Buddhist monks in 1987–89, in particular. The 1971 insurrection was against the Sri Lanka Freedom Party (SLFP) led coalition government. The 1987–89 revolts were against the UNP government. The JVP strategy was to bring the civil administration to a halt by intimidating public servants and by the use of violence against the private sector. The JVP's power base was the educated youth of the rural poor, mostly the unemployed. Though some have suggested[35] the JVP's strength is concentrated in the *vahumpura*[36] and *batgama*[37] castes, the issue of class plays a prominent role in their revolutionary attitude.

After the insurrection in 1971, the late President J.R. Jayawardene (1906–96) lifted the proscription on the JVP in 1978. On 29 July 1987, when the UNP signed the Indo-Sri Lanka Peace Accord to end the conflict between the LTTE and government forces, the JVP took an extremely nationalist stand.[38] Public resentment against the accord was based on the requirement to merge the Northern and Eastern Provinces to form one province, the restrictions placed on Sri Lanka's freedom to receive foreign military personnel, and the use of Trincomalee harbour. The objection to the accord was primarily led by the JVP, and anti-Indian sentiments were strong in the JVP thinking. Other political parties such the SLFP and Buddhist monks were also involved in the agitation campaign. The JVP was very successful in recruiting Buddhist monks for its armed anti-accord insurrection. Disruptions of the JVP stemming from the accord led to severe threats to peace and instability in Sri Lanka by 1989 and as a result, the UNP government led by President R. Premadasa (1924–93) assassinated Wijeweera in 1989 to remove the terror that the JVP had created all over Sri Lanka.

As a left-wing, Marxist political party, the JVP has gradually entered parliamentary politics since the 1990s. At the general elections held in 1999 and 2001, it secured 10 and 16 out of 225 parliamentary seats respectively. Its profile has grown and at the general election held on 2 April 2004, it secured 39 seats and became the most important partner in forming the United People's Freedom Alliance (UPFA) government. In the UPFA government, the JVP held four ministerial portfolios. However, after a dispute with President Kumaratunga with regard to the distribution of post-Tsunami relief to the LTTE as proposed by the Post Tsunami Operational Management Structure (P-TOMS), the JVP withdrew from the coalition on 16 June 2005.[39] In September 2005, however, the JVP signed a memorandum of understanding containing 12 points with Mr Mahinda Rajapaksa, Prime Minister of the UPFA government since April 2004, who is planning to contest the forthcoming Presidential election on 17 November 2005 as the Sri Lanka Freedom Party

(SLFP) candidate. Like the JVP, the Jathika Hela Urumaya, the only all-monk political party of Sri Lanka, has also expressed support for Mr Rajapaksa in his presidential campaign by signing an electoral pact with him in Kandy on 13 September 2005.[40]

Though Marxist in orientation, at present the JVP leadership takes a keen interest in the national, cultural and religious issues in relation to the current peace negotiations and proposals for devolution of power within Sri Lanka as a solution to the continuing ethnic conflict. Ironically, the JVP parliamentary leader, Mr Wimal Weeravansa, holds the position of co-President of the Deshahitaishi Jatika Vyaparaya (National Patriotic Movement) with Ven. Elle Gunavansa who has been accused by scholars as being a military type of monk because of his patriotic songs written for soldiers combining 'militancy and music'.[41] On 14 November 2004, on the occasion of recognizing the London based Mavubima Surakime Sanvidhanaya (Organization for the Protection of the Motherland) as a branch of the Deshahitaishi Jatika Vyaparaya, both Mr Weeravansa and Ven. Gunavansa appeared on the same stage sharing a common vision of safeguarding the motherland.[42]

Historically, the JVP has been accused of using young Buddhist monks as 'foot soldiers' in their revolutionary, Marxist-oriented liberation campaigns by encouraging them and drawing them into political activism. In the current political climate, the challenge for Sri Lankan Buddhist monasticism is twofold: internally, the foundations of monastic structures have been weakened; externally, politics – in particular, Marxist oriented JVP politics – have penetrated monastic establishments and the lifestyles of young university monks. Sarath Amunugama has already illustrated the way the JVP shrewdly drew a new class of young monks into its active politics and protests.[43] These political influences have dire consequences both on the image of Theravada Buddhist monasticism and on the very survival of monastic practices in Sri Lanka.

On 7 August 2000, the JVP held a political rally in front of the Supreme Court, Colombo. Protesters held posters, which read 'Do not make the judicial system [the] Government's puppet!' (*adhikaranaya anduve rukadayak no karanu!*); 'Democracy is at stake!'; 'We do not want the constitutional amendments which destroy democracy!' (*prajatantravadaya valalana vyavastha mara ugulak epa*); 'No change to the election process!' (*candakrama sansodhanat epa*); 'Withdraw the unfair election revision which aims at 2/3 majority vote!' (*tunen deke balaya sandaha gena ena takkadi candakrama samshodanat epa*).[44]

The one full page advertisement that the JVP published in the Sinhala daily *Lankadipa* on 8 August 2000 shows the explicit political and national interests of the protesters:

Yes, we oppose dividing this Mother Land on the basis of ethnicity; by doing so this land will be turned into an affiliated kingdom. Yes, we oppose dividing the country on the basis of ethnicity rather than unifying Sinhalas, Tamils and Muslims within one country. Yes, we oppose it because it will not solve the ethnic problem and it will further increase it. Instead of one war, it will create seven or eight wars.

This constitution is a death trap, which will divide the people and the country. Yes, we oppose the constitutional amendments since they will affirm Parliamentary dictatorship and will introduce mob rule into the election procedures. The day that our opposition should be brought to the streets is on 9 August. A National Opposition Day! Let's raise black flags in every house, every institution and every city. Let's express opposition in every institution and every place. On 9 August, at 8 a.m., let's gather in our thousands at Boralla Town. "This country is ours. Do not divide it. This country is ours. Do not destroy it." On 9 August, let's say it in a loud, crying voice.[45]

Protesting in various ways, the JVP requested the public to raise black flags in opposition to the constitutional amendments. On 10 August 2000, the JVP also held a public rally at Kagalla in which prominent speakers of the party delivered speeches. Throughout the period of civil unrest, the JVP opposed the constitutional amendments vehemently.

The Sri Lankan government of the SLFP-led People's Alliance (PA) of President Chandrika Bandaranaike Kumaratunga responded to the protests of the *sangha* and the political parties in two ways: (i) it made an important change in the administration by appointing a new Prime Minister, Mr Ratnasiri Wickremanayake, to replace the President's mother, Mrs. Sirimavo Bandaranaike (1916–2000); (ii) it also withdrew the constitutional amendments that it had proposed. On 9 August 2000, the headline of the Sinhala daily *Divayina* reported that the government postponed the debate over the constitutional amendments and cancelled the taking of the votes for the Seventeenth Amendment, which was designed to regulate a new general election process.

Recent Political Agitations

In 2005, the world witnessed the most fearful fast unto death. Two prominent monks holding different political agendas and being sympathizers of two different political parties were involved in the agitation campaign against the controversial Post Tsunami Operational Management Structure (P-TOMS) proposed by the Sri Lankan government. This had international backing to share Tsunami relief aid with the Tamil Tigers after the Tsunami devastation on 26 December 2004 which killed 31,000 in Sri Lanka alone.

First, the Deputy Leader of the Jathika Hela Urumaya (JHU) and parliamentarian monk, Ven. Omalpe Sobhita Thera, led a fast unto death on 6 June 2005 in front of the Tooth Relic Temple in Kandy[46] to protest the government's proposed implementation of the Tsunami aid-sharing deal with the Liberation Tigers of Tamil Eelam. At 9.15 am on Saturday 11 June 2005, Ven. Omalpe Sobhita Thera gave up his fast unto death following assurances given by the *Sangha* Chiefs (*mahanayakas*) of the three main Buddhist orders in Sri Lanka. Once Ven. Omalpe

Sobhita, MP of the JHU ended the fast, the second monk belonging to a monastic organization backed by the JVP, Ven. Dhambara Amila, President of Jathika Sangha Peramuna (National Sangha Front) and Lecturer in Sri Jayawardanapura University, undertook the fast unto death against the proposed implementation in front of the Colombo Fort Railway Station held on 11–15 June 2005.[47] Supporting their political activism, one commentator wrote to the *Lankaweb*:

> Their acts have nothing to do with the religion they profess, but…their acts…highlight the cause for which they undertook that extreme act… Theravada Monks have always stood for the cause of the religion and the people. It is thanks to these Theravada monks that we have the pure teaching of the Buddha, and the Buddha *sasana* itself. The Theravada monks did not pay mere lip service to the cause of protection of the country, the *sasana* or the teachings, they were there in the forefront of the protests, whenever the[ir] presence was necessary. This should be seen in the light of Sri Lanka being the repository of the Buddha's pure teachings, and the only homeland of the Sinhala people.[48]

However, here it is also important to see how the chief monks of Sri Lanka view the efficacy of fast-unto-death campaigns by monastic members. The BBC Sinhala service interviewed the Ven. Udagama Buddharakkhita Mahanayaka Thera of the Asgiriya Chapter of Siyam Nikaya on 11 June 2005, after he had already met President Kumaratunga to discuss the monks' protests. Ven. Buddharakkhita told the *Sandeshaya* programme that after talks with the President he felt that 'there is no need for protest… Disorderly protest is no help to any one. Any protest has to be made only after studying the facts carefully.'[49]

Concluding Remarks

This chapter has discussed Buddhist political activism as a serious challenge to monastic community life in Sri Lanka. Making reference to specific events that occurred in August 2000, it has argued that Theravada Buddhism in Sri Lanka is becoming increasingly immersed in this-worldly affairs and politics. What Walpola Rahula (1907–97) aspired to in 1946 by writing *The Heritage of the Bhikkhu* has generated many unintended consequences for Buddhist practice and community life. While this chapter has outlined one significant monastic and public protest in relation to the Seventeenth constitutional amendment proposed by the People's Alliance government, there are many unexpected events occurring in the monastic community. For instance, in the general election held on 2 April 2004, nine monks of the Jathika Hela Urumaya were elected as Members of Parliament. As a response to the civil war and the ethnic conflict, the involvement of Buddhist monks in politics has taken dramatic turns. If these tendencies continue, it will definitely change the shape of Theravada Buddhist monastic practice in Sri Lanka.

12

THE COST OF PEACE: BUDDHISTS AND CONFLICT TRANSFORMATION IN SRI LANKA

Elizabeth J. Harris

Being victorious one produces enmity. The conquered one sleeps unhappily.
The one at peace, giving up victory and defeat, sleeps happily.[1]
(Dhammapada v. 201)

Can Buddhist principles aid conflict transformation? If they can, why has the ethnic conflict in Sri Lanka, a country where 69 per cent of the population is Buddhist, continued for so many decades? Has 'pure' Buddhism simply been forgotten there? Have the contingencies in Sri Lanka forced Buddhists to make exceptions to moral norms that they might otherwise see as exceptionless? Or are Buddhists in fact making a positive contribution to the making of peace?

There are no simple answers to any of these questions. To explore them, I will use a fourfold paradigm from conflict transformation theory as expressed by Louis Kreisberg in his claim that reconciliation in communal conflict requires antagonistic parties to attain a minimal degree of four beliefs: honest acknowledgement of the terrible aspects of what happened; compassionate acceptance of those who committed injurious conduct and acknowledgement of each other's suffering; belief that injustices are being redressed; anticipation of mutual security and well-being.[2]

I will take each of these 'beliefs' in turn and will ask: is it relevant to the Sri Lankan conflict?; does its content touch Buddhist principles?; are Buddhists in the country using these principles to make peace? The danger in this method is that I may appear to judge Buddhist practice in Sri Lanka against an ahistorical, 'pure', textual Buddhist standard. That is not my intention. After all, the Theravada texts do not give one message on issues connected with peace and violence. Buddhists in Sri Lanka have quoted from them both to justify military methods to end the ethnic conflict and to oppose them.[3] My intention is to appeal to Buddhist principles that live in the Sri Lankan imagination today, many of which happen to be rooted in the texts. My selection of these, however, will not escape subjectivity. It will be informed by my own conviction that the resolution of Sri Lanka's ethnic conflict will only come through a negotiated settlement in which both sides are willing to compromise.

The Sri Lankan conflict

The population of Sri Lanka is between 18 and 19 million. Four religions meet in the country (Buddhism, Hinduism, Islam and Christianity) and two main ethnic and linguistic identities, Sinhala and Tamil, with Muslim identity as a separate, important factor. Buddhists form a majority of 69 per cent and, with only a handful of exceptions, are Sinhala. Hindus are approximately 15 per cent of the population and are Tamil. Christians are spread across both ethnic groups at about 7.5 per cent of the population. Muslims form another 7.5 per cent. There are two main Tamil groups: those who trace their ancestry in Sri Lanka back to early times and those brought to the country in the nineteenth century by the British to work in the central hill plantations. Risking simplification, the North, beyond Vavuniya, and the East of the country are now predominantly Tamil, although post-independence colonization schemes in the East have somewhat modified the demography there. The Sinhala people are concentrated in the South, West and Central parts of the country, and, to a lesser extent, the East.

The roots of Sri Lanka's conflict lie in the country's colonial past, particularly the period of British rule from 1796–1948, when the island was placed under a unified administrative structure, within which the Tamil population proved themselves more willing to work for the British as civil servants than the Sinhalese. Independence in 1948 brought a Sinhala and Tamil English-speaking elite into power, under a Constitution that offered some protection to minorities,[4] against a background of rising communalist political parties in both the North and South.[5] A Sinhala backlash against this ruling elite and the Tamil-dominated civil service, in 1956, gave power to a party that appealed to Sinhala ethnicity, religion and language. Legislation aimed at giving justice to the Sinhalese, but seen by Tamils as discriminatory, followed.

The first serious outburst of violence came in May 1958 when Sinhala mobs sought out attendees bound for a convention of the Tamil Federal Party.[6] Elder Tamil statesmen tried non-violent means of addressing the growing problems without success. They were then overtaken by the militant Tamil youth groups that arose in the 1970s demanding a separate state. After 1983, there was a rapid escalation of violence.[7] By the 1990s, the conflict was between the Sri Lankan state and just one of the separatist militant Tamil groups that had arisen in the North - the Liberation Tigers of Tamil Eelam (LTTE), who claimed that they represented all Tamils. In the conflict people of all communities and religions have suffered.

There has been a ceasefire in the civil war since February 2002. As I write, in January 2005, the ceasefire is fragile. In December 2004, before the tsunami hit the country killing over 30,000 people, some newspapers, provocatively and precipitately, were speaking of a possible return to war.[8]

The conflict betrays traits familiar to any watcher of communal war. Firstly, people on both sides claim minority status. Census results declare the Tamil population of Sri Lanka to be a shrinking minority of less than 18 per cent and the Sinhala people, a majority of 73 per cent. Most Tamils do not defer from this. They see themselves as a minority within a centralized parliamentary structure that cannot be other than Sinhala dominated, unless there is constitutional change. But the perception of some Sinhalese is different. They look across the Palk Straits and, seeing some 50 million Tamils in Tamil Nadu, judge themselves to be the ethnic and linguistic minority in the geopolitical landscape of greater India.

Closely linked to this is that both sides to the conflict also see themselves as the victim. Tamils point to the series of post-independence measures taken by the Sinhala-dominated Parliament that have discriminated against them,[9] and also to systematic state brutality, before and after the arising of militant youth groups in the 1970s, particularly after a draconian Prevention of Terrorism Act in 1979. Numerous moments and actions have etched themselves into Tamil minds, which include: the burning of the Jaffna Public Library by government forces in 1981, an act of cultural genocide, and attacks on Tamils between May and September of the same year;[10] the anti-Tamil pogrom of 1983, when Sinhala gangs killed Tamils and burnt their houses with evident exhilaration, even ecstasy;[11] the bombing of the Roman Catholic Church at Navaly killing 120 in July 1996; the approximately 600 disappearances in the north in 1996–97 under army occupation; and the brutal murder by a Sinhala mob of 27 out of 46 Tamil inmates (suspected of being members of the LTTE) of the Bindunuwewa Rehabilitation Centre, managed by the National Youth Services Council, in the southern town of Bandarawela in October 2000. Such incidents, plus low-level harassment and discrimination, have convinced some that they can never be at home in a united Sri Lanka.

Some Sinhala people, on the other hand, point to the privileged position that Tamils had at Independence, the pre-Independence birth of communalist Tamil political parties and the terrorist attacks by Tamil militants on the South as proof that it is they, not the Tamils, who are the victims. Again, numerous moments remain in the memory: the massacre of 62 Sinhala villagers in the Dollar and Kent Farm government settlements on the borders of the Tamil North in 1984; the gunning down of 146 Buddhist pilgrims at the holy city of Anuradhapura in May 1985; the suicide truck bombing of the Central Bank in Colombo in October 1997; the truck bombing of the Temple of the Tooth, in Kandy in January 1998 killing 13; the killing of eight a few months later at a commercial junction in Colombo; a series of bus bomb explosions in 2000; the killing of Tamil moderates in the South, such as the greatly respected Dr Neelan Tiruchelvam, in July 1999 and LTTE recruitment of child soldiers. Many of these are seen not only as attacks on the Sinhala people but on Buddhism itself.

Thirdly, there is a 'holy land' myth on the Sinhala side, conditioned by narratives in Sinhala historical chronicles, particularly the *Mahavamsa* – a still influential, didactic work, written by the monastic *sangha* in about the fifth century CE, which was given additional prominence when British orientalists seized on it as proof that Sri Lanka had a noble past.[12] It begins with the narrative of three visits made by the Buddha to Sri Lanka in order to bring reconciliation and blessing. One of these was to 'Nagadipa', which scholars, and indeed Buddhist pilgrims, have situated in the North of Sri Lanka.[13] The narrative thus claims the whole of Sri Lanka as the *dhammadipa*, the island of the *dhamma*, a holy island dedicated to the Buddha and his teachings. This is underscored in chapter seven of the *Mahavamsa* when the Buddha, on his deathbed, witnessing the landing in Sri Lanka of Vijaya, the mythical founder of the Sinhala race, directs the god Sakka to protect Vijaya and Sri Lanka, because Buddhism would be established there. For those imbued with the spirit of the *Mahavamsa*, the LTTE demand for a separate state is no less than a threat to the *dhamma*, a threat to the continuation of 'pure' Buddhism in the world.

One fruit of the conflict is a battle over historical truth, with both sides constructing history to prove that they have a right to possess the island or to be in the island. According to Bartholomeusz, this began at the end of the nineteenth century, with both Tamil and Sinhala attempts, in an already charged ethnic context, to bring religion, territory and ethnicity centre stage.[14] In the twentieth century a paradigmatic Sinhala construction is found in a school history primer entitled *Golden Threads*, authored by J.R. Jayawardene, Prime Minister and then President of Sri Lanka. As Sankaran Krishna has pointed out, Jayawardene situates himself in the primer at the peak of a *Mahavamsa*-based chronology that combines myth and history to define Sri Lanka solely through the Sinhala Buddhist race and Sinhala Buddhist history, effectively effacing the history of the Tamils, and other ethnic and religious communities such as the Muslims.[15]

Jayawardene's construction has been repeated up to the present. As late as 2003, A.S. Amarasekera could declare that Sri Lanka should be called 'Sinhale' (an ancient name that had been used for parts of the island), on the grounds that a country should be defined by the identity of the indigenous population, thus marginalizing Tamils as non-indigenous. Failure to insist on this name, he sweepingly declares, 'has brought in its wake the extinction of a civilisation that has existed for two thousand five hundred years.'[16]

Tamil constructions, not surprisingly, are completely different. For instance, Arudpragasam, mapping what he considers to be hidden pages in Sri Lanka's history, compares the Sinhala concept of *Jathiya* (nation), perfectly exhibited in Jayawardene's *Golden Threads*, to the Nazi use of *Volk*, in its exclusion of those considered unworthy of belonging to the nation.[17] He goes on to contest the Sinhala claim that the Sinahalese once controlled the whole island, arguing for Tamil primacy. For instance he claims that the King of Kotte in the South was subservient to the King of Jaffna in the fourteenth century.[18]

The Sri Lankan ethnic conflict, therefore, can be seen as a war between two nationalisms, one of which is couched in religious language, as defence of the *dhammadipa* from external threat. But the conditioning factors behind these nationalisms are not religious. They are rooted in the legacy of colonialism and the country's lack of will to change the centralized model of democracy inherited at independence to allow for devolution of power. The conflict cannot, therefore, be dubbed a religious war. Yet, it is a war in which religion is not innocent, a war in which religious people on both sides have supported violence as politically necessary and expedient.

The telling of Truth

The first of my four tests of conflict resolution capacity, honest acknowledgement of the terrible aspects of what happened, concerns telling truth and perceiving truth. 'Because of the conflict's brutal history, the excesses on both sides will probably need to be publicly acknowledged before healing can take place,' H.L. Seneviratne has declared.[19] I agree with him. The 'terrible aspects' of Sri Lanka's conflict are indeed the excesses that have been committed on all sides and they will have to be recognized and narrated. There are two barriers to this. The first is the tenacity of the different, constructed realities that fuel the conflict, which prevent objectivity. As John Lederach lamented after the destruction of New York's Twin Towers, '[a]lways remember that realities are constructed – conflict is, among other things, the process of building and sustaining very different perceptions and interpretations of reality. This means that we have at the same time multiple realities defined as such by those in conflict.'[20]

The second is the cost of speaking out. Some Sri Lankans who have spoken truth have lost their lives. Dr Rajani Thiranagama, from a Christian Tamil family in the North, was killed by the LTTE in September 1989 because she had co-authored a book that not only exposed government excesses in the North, but also LTTE abuse of human rights.[21] Numerous other assassinations have followed, of people whose only crime was that they dissented from LTTE policy or were dubbed, 'informants'.[22] Then, in the South, in the late 1980s, Sinhala people such as Daya Pathirana, Ven. Raddegoda Saranakara and Ven. Pohoddaramulle Pemaloka, who were either members of what could be called 'the old left' or supporters of justice for the Tamil people through devolution of power, were killed by the militant 'new left': the anti-LTTE, anti-Indian, Sinhala JVP (Janatha Vimukti Peramuna: Peoples' Liberation Party) and its political wing, the DJV (Deshapremi Janatha Vyaapaaraya: Peoples' Patriotic Movement), both of which had supporters within the monastic *sangha*. As I write, the JVP has transformed itself into a member of the ruling coalition party and is no longer involved in assassinations, but it remains opposed to compromise with the LTTE. The LTTE, though, continues to kill those within the Tamil community who oppose its policies.

What can Buddhism offer here? If challenging constructed realities is the first step to telling truth and perceiving truth, Buddhist principles should have much to contribute. At its heart is the proposition that humans create a conceptual prison for themselves through their greed, hatred and delusion. The Buddha is recorded as saying:

> Monks, there are to be seen beings who can admit freedom from suffering from bodily disease for one year, for two years, for three, four, five, ten, twenty, thirty, forty, fifty years; who can admit freedom from bodily disease for even a hundred years. But, monks, those beings are hard to find in the world who can admit freedom from mental disease even for one moment, save only those in whom the *asavas* (corruptions) are destroyed.[23]

These 'corruptions' are fourfold according to classical Buddhism: sense desire (*kamasava*); desire for existence (*bhavasava*); (wrong) views (*ditthasava*); and ignorance (*avijjasava*). Prime among the 'views' that are considered wrong and prime among the components of 'ignorance' is *atta-ditthi*, the ego illusion, the belief that there is an 'I' at the centre of our beings that is separate from all other beings and in need of protection and promotion.

This analysis goes further than saying that our suffering is caused by selfishness. It claims that the way we perceive and use language locks us into addictive patterns of response that prevent us seeing things as they are, creating, according to Buddhist psychologist Caroline Brazier, 'a *cordon sanitaire* between the person and the world,' an 'illusory safety net' which 'is held together by the ever-repeating patterns of habitual behaviours.'[24] And this can also be a corporate phenomenon. A family, a community or a nation can cling to an imprisoning corporate identity that is rooted in false premises.

These habitual behaviours arise at the point of contact between our senses and sense objects. And, as I have argued elsewhere in line with the pioneering work of Bhikkhu Nanananda,[25] there is a point when we can become victim of these conditioned patterns in a process of proliferation (*papanca*) through which our conceptual processes run riot. At this point deliberate choice vanishes and the perceiver becomes the victim of his or her own thought constructions.[26]

The way out of this mental disease, according to Buddhism, is through the threefold path of: morality (*sila*), meditation (*samadhi*) and wisdom (*pañña*). The hardest work lies in the second: *samadhi*, concentration, usually translated as meditation. For it is through meditation practices such as 'bare attention' that the practitioner confronts and perhaps transforms the distorted patterns of thinking that have seared themselves into the psyche.

The above interpretation of Buddhist psychology is one that Sri Lanka gave me. Nanananda's influence was prior to Caroline Brazier's. I took my first steps in 'bare attention' at Nilambe Meditation Centre, in the central hills of Sri Lanka, under the guidance of a Sinhala Buddhist, Godwin Samararatne. It is part of the ever-evolving Sri Lankan tradition. Twentieth-century Sri Lanka saw an upsurge of interest in meditation, the early stages of which have been documented by Bond.[27] But is there evidence that recognition of the imprisoning nature of our conditioned views has been applied to the truth-telling and truth-perceiving that must be part of peacemaking in Sri Lanka?

I believe there is. There is a sizeable number of Buddhists who have come to see Sinhala nationalism as a conditioned 'view' rooted in false thinking, leading to excess. Let me quote again Ven. Professor Kumburugamuve Vajira's words after he led a delegation that included over 20 Buddhist monks to Jaffna in 1999, '[t]he Sangha, as an intellectual and inspirational community must enable the Sinhalese to rid themselves of *avijja* (ignorance) – of misconceptions that they are the superior race on the island and that other ethnic groups have to be subordinate.'[28]

It is perhaps A.T. Ariyaratne, however, who has done the most to encourage meditation as a grassroots response to conflict transformation. Ariyaratne founded Sarvodaya in 1958 as a Shramadana (giving of energy) movement, through which students were encouraged to voluntarily give of their time to help others. As its influence was felt, the emphasis changed to 'village awakening' along Buddhist lines, for the welfare of all. And, then, as the ethnic conflict began to grip the country, there was another movement – towards a universalization of the spiritual message of Sarvodaya in the interests of peace building. In recent years, this has involved drawing people into peace meditations. In August 1999, thousands came to Vihara Maha Devi Park in Colombo for this purpose. Jehan Perera, Media Director of the National Peace Council, described it in this way:

> There was the objective of an emptying of the mind and inner purification that resonated with the highest sentiments of human beings. It contrasts with the hate-filled mobilisation for war, whether in the war shattered north-east or the rest of the country... The people who attended the event will go back to their villages carrying the message of peace imprinted in their consciousness.[29]

In the summer of 2002, Sarvodaya held another meditation, this time in Kandy, adjacent to the Temple of the Tooth, bringing together not only Buddhists but also smaller numbers of Hindus, Christians and Muslims. However, it met opposition. Right-wing Buddhists opposed to peace talks with the LTTE verbally assaulted the meditators, declaring that they were stooges of the LTTE, who had no right to meditate next to the Temple.[30] Police intervention was eventually necessary.[31] Yet, as Bond observes, the publicity given to the meditation and the fact that the meditators were not distracted from their purpose, proved that Sarvodaya possessed spiritual force.[32]

Compassionate acceptance of those who committed injurious conduct and acknowledgement of each other's suffering

Truth-telling is intimately connected to the challenge to antagonists in conflict to recognize that the other has also suffered. Peacemaking in Sri Lanka has repeatedly faltered at this challenge, succumbing to battles of comparative suffering, and cycles of attack and counter-attack. The mob violence that has marked the conflict has often shown a revenge mentality rather than empathy for the 'other'. The LTTE massacre of Buddhists in Anuradhapura in 1985 was in retaliation for the killing of 70 Tamil civilians in the North by the Sri Lankan army.[33] The 1983 anti-Tamil pogrom was in revenge for 13 soldiers killed by the LTTE in the North. And when the Sri Lankan Government in 1957 came to an agreement with Tamil leaders that would have given some devolution of power to Tamil majority areas, it had to renege because of opposition from Buddhists whose wish for a united *dhammadipa* prevented them from understanding how important some form of self-government was to the Tamils. Yet, it is in the territory of this belief, particularly acknowledgement of each other's suffering, that the greatest potential may lie for reconciliation in Sri Lanka, because it is consonant with principles deeply embedded in the Sri Lankan psyche.

One of the legs on which Buddhist morality stands is an argument from empathy, as voiced in these popular verses from the *Dhammapada*:

All tremble at violence; all fear death.
Comparing (others) with oneself,
One should not kill or cause to kill

All tremble at violence, to all life is dear.
Comparing (others) with oneself,
One should not kill or cause to kill[34]

A look under the surface of Sri Lanka's mob violence and cycles of attack and counter-attack reveals a well of empathy ready to be drawn from. In my experience, this empathy has been most evident in Sri Lanka's poorer communities. Ethnic differences broke down in the East of the country after the tsunami of 26 December 2004, when Sinhala Buddhist villagers living inland, hearing of the tragedy, walked to the coast with food on their heads to help their Tamil neighbours. Ethnic differences break down in some of the Colombo slums where Buddhist, Christian, Hindu and Muslim live side by side sharing the same problems: high unemployment, youth disenchantment, poverty, and poor facilities. When in the late 1980s, southern villagers experienced the murderous hand of the military, after the government decided to clamp down on the JVP through extra-judicial killings, they broke down when some, comparing their experience with that of the Tamils thought, 'If the army can do this to us, who are Buddhists and Sinhala, what will it be doing to the Tamils in the North?'

Two keys to the releasing of empathy have been encounter with 'the other' and exposure to facts previously unknown. Activists from multi-faith peace organizations have found, when conducting workshops on the ethnic conflict, that Sinhala villagers have been willing to listen empathetically to the experiences and convictions of Tamil villagers when given the opportunity. Their reaction has been, 'Why didn't we know this!' Their experiences of economic hardship and the *dukkha* (pain) of village life was enough to allow them to empathize with unknown Tamil villagers when the facts were made known.

Empathy has also been encouraged through language learning. The Ven. Dr Kadurugamuve Nagitha Thero, then Head of the Linguistics Department at the University of Kelaniya, staged a Tamil Day in June 1998, where students sung, danced and staged dramas in Tamil. The innovation was that they were all Sinhala, some of them Buddhist monks. All had taken a certificate course in Tamil. Ven. Nagitha, when asked about his reasons for encouraging Sinhala students to learn Tamil, replied, '[w]hen you understand the other side better, you learn to respect the other's cultural identity. Just as much as we are Sinhalese and proud of it, we must learn to respect Tamil culture and their way of life.'[35]

Particularly since the 2001 ceasefire, a number of exchange visits and joint programmes have taken place between people in the North and the South. Members of the Buddhist monastic *sangha* have been instrumental in some of these. One that gained media publicity was a weekend programme, organized by the southern Ranaviru Family Counselling Service. It brought together over a hundred war orphans aged between eight and fifteen years from the North and South, some coming with their one remaining parent. A drama for peace was created and performed in one of Colombo's priority venues. And empathy flowed as Sinhala and Tamil shared their common suffering and hope. One Buddhist widow, whose husband had been a member of the army, was reported as saying, '[w]hen I see Tamil orphans I feel sad for them and I only wish these children could have the world their fathers wished them to have.'[36]

Unfortunately, as with Ariyaratne's peace meditation in Kandy, events such as this have met with opposition. At the beginning of November 2003, a Sinhala-Tamil Art Festival (Sinhala Demala Kala Ulela) was held in Colombo. About two hundred creative writers, artists and actors came from the North and East to share with southern artists in a two-day event organized by activists from different religions based in the South. On the first day, in the second session, supporters of the right-wing, predominantly Buddhist Sihala Urumaya political party burst into the proceedings with sticks and other weapons, claiming that it was an LTTE event. Several of the artists were hospitalized as a result. The event then continued with police protection, members of the Sihala Urumaya continuing to protest, outside, behind police barriers. The newspapers offered photos of these external protests, clearly showing the number of Buddhist monks involved.[37]

In a later conversation with two of the organizers of the event, I was shown about 50 photographs of the violence inside and outside the building. What was striking was that the Sinhala artists defended the Tamils from the onslaught. 'The Tamils saw Sinhala people defending them and for some this changed their view of the Sinhala people,' I was told. The network of creative artists continues.

Belief that injustices are being redressed

In 1999, the National Peace Council, an independent non-government organization, enabled Pradeshiya Sabha (Local Council) politicians from the Matara District
in the predominantly Buddhist South to meet their counterparts in the Batticaloa
District of the predominantly Tamil East. One of the Matara politicians, in an opening conversation, suggested, '[w]e should live in peace.' A woman on the other
side, according to reports of the event, countered this by saying, '[b]efore talking
about peace, it is necessary to talk about rights.'[38]

Empathy with 'the other' who has suffered is not enough by itself if peace is to
be achieved; neither is the uncovering of the excesses perpetrated by the antagonists. Justice and human rights enter. The Tamil people of Sri Lanka, not only the
LTTE, have consistently used the language of rights and justice when speaking of
peace: the right to receive replies to official letters in Tamil rather than Sinhala; the
right to education; the right to live without fear of harassment from the police and
army; the right to have some control over their own lives through substantial devolution of power.

There is controversy over whether Buddhism has a concept of human rights. In
Sri Lanka, some Buddhists have dismissed the concept as a Western import; others
have defended the idea to the extent of legitimizing each article of the Universal
Declaration of Human Rights through supportive Theravada texts.[39] Damien Keown has argued that, although the concept of human rights is not explicitly present
in classical Buddhism, it is implicit, couched in a vocabulary of duties.[40] Searching
then for the most persuasive philosophical underpinning for this, he came up with
human potential to reach the goal of Buddhahood.[41]

I am largely in agreement with Keown but my experience of Buddhism in Sri
Lanka tells me that, in practice, it is not so much human potential to reach the goal
of enlightenment or Buddhahood that underlies respect for the rights of others but
an awareness that human birth is difficult to obtain, as expressed in this *Dhammapada* verse:

> It is difficult to obtain birth as a human;
> Difficult is the life of mortals;
> Difficult is the hearing of the true doctrine;
> Difficult is the arising of the awakened ones.[42]

The verse combines two messages: that each human holds in their hands something that is incredibly precious, 'earned' through wholesome action in a previous
life – an opportunity to progress along the path towards enlightenment; that the
life each human holds, however precious, is a source of pain as well as pleasure, no
easy option once gained. The first is capable of generating respect, for self and
other; the second, compassion and empathy, in a similar way to the *Dhammapada*
verses quoted earlier. And it is these qualities that the Five Precepts call upon:
abstaining from killing any living being; not taking what is not given; not lying; not

indulging in sexual misconduct; not intoxicating the mind. Each one embodies both a refraining from and a commitment to.

In the Sri Lankan context, however, there is a clash of rights. In addition, the 'duties' voiced by some Sinhala people towards Tamils do not mesh with the rights Tamils wish to be honoured. The LTTE claim a right to self-determination in the face of a discriminatory parliamentary system. The more moderate Tamils expect substantial devolution. Political supporters of a unitary state in the South are quite happy to affirm that they have a duty to ensure freedom of religion and culture to Tamils in a united, constitutionally centralized country, but ridicule any form of self-governing authority in the North and East as a violation of their own rights. These include: their right as the majority to insist that Buddhism should have the foremost place; their right to live free from terrorism in their own country; their right to travel and live in all parts of the country; their right to defend Buddhism from attack. And this right to defend has led some Buddhists to waive the respect embedded in the Five Precepts in order to justify war. As I have argued elsewhere, three generic types of justification have been used: appeal to a strand within text and tradition that would appear to modify essentialist, non-violent Buddhist approaches to conflict; the use of utilitarian arguments concerning the greater good; and the denial that fighting a war necessarily has negative karmic consequences.[43] Oliver McTernan, when questioning a monk sympathetic to the Sihala Urumaya, found this:

It is true, he said, that the goal of Buddhism is to live without attachment to land or country, but this can only be achieved when one reaches a high level of spiritual awareness. Meanwhile, Buddhists like others have to live in the real world and to operate on a conventional level. The ideal way to resolve conflicts, he believed, was without arms but if your opponent lacks goodwill then you have no alternative but to deal with the problem in the 'conventional' way.[44]

When McTernan then asked the monk how he could bless soldiers who would be killing people, he replied that the Five Precepts were applicable in 'normal circumstances' but that the situation in Sri Lanka was abnormal and therefore some of these principles had to be suspended.[45]

In the face of the terrorism of the LTTE, the First Precept, not to deprive another human being of life, one that meshes well with the Universal Declaration of Human Rights, is a norm with exceptions for some Buddhists in Sri Lanka. The monk interviewed by McTernan would have given the preciousness of human life little respect in the extreme circumstances facing the country. And he could have pointed to many times in Sri Lanka's recent history where state forces, militant groups and ordinary people had lived by the same conclusion.

Some Buddhist leaders, in the face of this, in order to persuade war-supporters that military methods will feed, not destroy, the conflict, have pointed to the importance of causal analysis. I have quoted before these words, said to me in 1995, by Ven. Delgalle Padumasiri:

> The solutions are crystal clear in Buddhism. The first step is to ask what caused the war in the North and East. Why did the young people take up arms? The same thing happened in the South. The key to the solution is rooted in this basic question. We must tackle the causes.[46]

Ven. Padumasiri could speak from experience. In the 1970s and 1980s, he lived for twelve years in the northern city of Jaffna at the Tissa Viharaya in Kankesan-thurai. When he first moved there, he was harassed, but gradually, through courtesy and his knowledge of Tamil, he won the people over. At that time, there were still Sinhala Buddhists in Jaffna, but he found that more Tamils came to the Vihara than Buddhists. And he experienced the injustices faced by the Tamils at that time: a young lad who lost the chance of employment because the letter calling him for an interview had been in Sinhala; the death of nine Tamils in 1974 at the hands of the police during an international convention of Tamil scholars; the inability of some Tamils to take out a loan because the forms were in Sinhala or English. He could understand, although not condone, why patience ran out because 'rights' were not met, and militancy began.[47]

Anticipation of mutual security and well-being

Recognition of rights, in all conflicts, must go hand in hand with ensuring the security of all. Justice for one party to the conflict will not bring peace if the other parties are thereby discriminated against.

Some people on both sides of the Sri Lankan conflict see the aspirations of the 'other' as threat to their security, and cultural and religious identity. Taking away this sense of threat, or creating a situation in which the removal of threat is anticipated by all, is one of the greatest challenges peacemakers in Sri Lanka face. The strength of the sense of threat on the side of some Buddhists can be seen in the rhetoric of the Jathika Hela Urumaya (JHU), which, as successor to the Sihala Uru-maya, fielded Buddhist monks at the 2004 general election. Interviewed in February 2004 before the elections, Ven. Uduwe Dhammaloka Thera of the Colombo District declared, '[w]e do not see this as contesting elections but as a measure to safeguard the Buddha Sasana and the country from falling into enemy hands.'[48] The 'enemy' was the LTTE, as became obvious when he stated that their main policy was protecting Sri Lanka as a 'Unitary Buddhist State'. He added later that, although their exact policies on the ethnic conflict had not been finalized:

> What has been decided up to now is that this country is a Bauddha Rajjya – where the Dhamma will prevail. There will be no religious or ethnic division and all races and religions will enjoy rights. Even non-Buddhists are happy with the policies, so there will be no need for war.[49]

However beautiful the words, it is difficult to see how this approach can give mutually assured security to Tamils who have suffered in a unitary country and see control over their own affairs as the only way to achieve security.

If there is a Buddhist principle, popularly recognized, underlying the task of bringing this 'belief' to birth, it must be the inseparability between the welfare of self and the welfare of others in the holy life. This is inherent in Theravada Buddhism in the concepts of *anatta* (no self) and *paticcasamupada* (dependent origination), but becomes more obvious in the realm of moral action where Buddhists are encouraged to assess paths of action through asking: Does it harm self? Does it harm others? Does it harm both self and others?[50] But before it is possible to 'know' what will harm others, in a situation of conflict, it is necessary to listen to how the 'others' define their security and their well-being. If this is done, then there is likely to be a cost.

The cost of ensuring these convictions on both sides

The verse from the *Dhammapada* quoted at the very beginning of this chapter voices the principal cost of a negotiated solution to the ethnic conflict that would bring security for all: that neither side should feel defeated; that there should be a win-win situation. This cannot happen without compromise for all sides. This is the unspoken concept behind my fourfold paradigm. If truth is told and perceived; if there is empathetic listening to the suffering of the 'other'; if issues of justice, rights and duties are uncovered; if a win-win situation is imagined – a willingness to compromise must result.

The cost to the LTTE may be to stay with their stated willingness to give up the idea of a separate state in favour federalism, to envisage democratic methods of testing their mandate with the people and to reject extra-judicial killing. The cost to the Sinhala people may be to accept that Jaffna is the cultural capital of the Tamils in a democratic, federal Sri Lanka, and to realize that bringing this to birth would do greater honour to the teaching of the Buddha than clinging to the idea of a unitary state.

Such compromise on both sides will not come easily as this chapter illustrates, even if Buddhist principles to aid this are at hand. The greatest of all religious tools for transformation, however, may simply be the ongoing experience of the *dukkha* (suffering) generated by the conflict – husbands killed in combat, wives blown apart by bombs, children orphaned, homes destroyed, livelihoods torn apart – and empathetic recognition that people on all sides of the conflict have suffered. If compromise could lead to the end of this pain, is there really any choice for those who follow the teaching of the Buddha?

NOTES AND REFERENCES

Introduction

1 Rappaport, R.A., *Ritual and Religion in the Making of Humanity* (Cambridge: Cambridge University Press, 1999), p. 1.

2 Locke, John, 'A Letter Concerning Toleration' in John Horton and Susan Mendus (eds), *John Locke: A Letter Concerning Toleration in Focus* (London and New York: Routledge, 1991), p. 18.

3 Mill, John Stuart, 'On Liberty' in Stefan Collini (ed), *J.S. Mill: On Liberty and Other Writings* (Cambridge: Cambridge University Press, 1989), p. 36.

Chapter One

1 For more information on this, see Israeli, Raphael and Bardenstein, Carol, *Man of Defiance: A Political Biography of Anwar Sadat* (Totowa, NJ: Barnes & Noble, 1985).

2 Knesset records, 20 November 1977.

3 Friedlander, Melvin A., *The Domestic Politics of Peace-Making*, (Boulder CO: Westview, 1983).

4 Rowland, Robert C., *The Rhetoric of Menachem Begin: The myth of redemption through return* (Lanham MA: University Press of America, 1985).

5 Record of speeches given at the conference, published in Bentsur, Eytan, *Making Peace: A First-Hand Account of the Arab-Israeli Peace Process* (Westport CT: Praeger, 2001), Appendix.

6 Landau, Yehezkel, *Healing the Holy Land: Interreligious Peacebuilding in Israel/Palestine*, (Washington D.C.: USIP, 2003); Gopin, Marc, *Holy War, Holy Peace*, (Oxford: Oxford University Press, 2002). See also Küng, Hans, *Judaism* (London: SCM, 1992), pp. 519f and 612f.

7 Hanan Ashrawi has long emphasized the need to separate divisive, nationalistic and fanatical religion from the pragmatic trust-building process between Israelis and Palestinians. A brief reflection of this line of thought can be found in Wallach, John and Wallach, Janet, *The New Palestinians: The emerging generation of leaders* (Rocklin, CA: Prima Publishing, 1992), pp. 36–37. For a sense of the consistent opposition of Shimon Peres to a political role for religion, see his biography, *Battling for Peace: Memoirs* (London: Orion, 1996), e.g. pp. 323–336 His vision of regional confederation also rests on a se-

cular Middle East, aware of the threat of political Islam; see *The New Middle East* (Shaftesbury: Element, 1993), pp. 38–45.

8 Hroub, Khaled, *Hamas: Political thought and practice* (Washington D.C.: Institute for Palestine Studies, 2000); Robinson, G.E., *Building a Palestinian State: the incomplete revolution*, (Bloomington IN: Indiana University Press, 1997).

9 The speech by Rabbi Yosef in August 2000 received extensive coverage from media inside and outside Israel. In 1990, Yosef had been one of the most determined and outspoken rabbinical defenders of the peace process, who had meanwhile lost trust in the will of the Palestinian leadership to prevent acts of terror.

10 See Yadgar, Yaacov, 'SHAS as a struggle to create a new field: A Bourdieuan perspective of an Israeli phenomenon' *Sociology of Religion* 37/4 (Summer 2003) at <http://www.findarticles.com/p/articles/mi_m0SOR/is_2_64/ai_104733010>.

11 Abu-Amr, Ziad, *Islamic Fundamentalism in the West Bank and Gaza: Muslim Brotherhood and Islamic Jihad* (Bloomington IN: Indiana University Press, 1994), 13f.

12 Abu-Amr: *Islamic Fundamentalism*, especially chapter 3.

13 For example Ye'or, Bat *Islam and Dhimmitude: Where Civilisations Collide* (Fairleigh: Dickinson University Press, 2002); Armstrong, Karen, *Jerusalem: One City, Three Faiths* (New York: Ballantine Books, 1997) and *The Battle for God* (New York: Ballantine Books, 2001).

14 Israeli, Raphael, *Fundamentalist Islam and Israel* (Lanham MA: University Press of America, 1993).

15 See discussion in Küng, Hans, *Judaism* (London: SCM Press, 1992), pp. 3–18, 566–583.

16 See, especially, Nüsse, Andrea, *Muslim Palestine: The Ideology of Hamas* (Amsterdam: Harwood Academic, 1998).

17 Ravitsky, Aviezer, *Messianism, Zionism, and Jewish Religious Radicalism* (Chicago: University of Chicago Press, 1996), chapter 3.

18 Ravitsky: *Messianism*, ch. 3.

19 Nüsse: *Muslim Palestine*, p. 14 and p. 129. Comparable developments in militant opinion elsewhere are discussed in Kelsay, John, 'War, Peace and the Imperatives of Justice in Islamic Perspective: What do the 11 September 2001 attacks tell us about Islam and the Just War tradition?', in Paul Robinson (ed), *Just War in Comparative Perspective* (Aldershot: Ashgate, 2003), pp. 76–89.

20 An extended discussion on the Hamas website was published as 'Greater and "Lesser" Jihad?' by Abu Khubayb and Abu Zubayr, at <http://www.ilaam.net/Articles/Slander edJihad.html>.

21 On Hamas, see Nüsse: *Muslim Palestine*, pp. 127–29. On the hardline tendency within Gush Emunim and its successors, which takes the same position, see Keinon, Herb, 'A Divided Soul' in *Jerusalem Post*, 12 December 1997, p. 11f; Sheleg, Yair, 'Rabbi Thau versus Rabbi Thau' in *Ha'aretz*, 29 September 2004. However, a broader Modern Orthodox constituency, with the Chief Rabbi of Great Britain and the Commonwealth, Jonathan Sacks, has applied this strictly to Jerusalem (press reports, January 2001). This qualifies his positive comments about sharing Jerusalem in *Dignity of Difference: How to avoid the clash of civilization* (London and New York: Continuum, 2002), p. 189.

22 See the essays collected in Landau, Yehezkel (ed), *Violence and the Value of Life in Jewish Tradition* (Jerusalem: OzveShalom, 1984).

23 Useful discussion in Peres: *Battling for Peace*, pp. 330–36.

24 The accommodationist and rejectionist strands in the NRP almost reached the point of formal divorce in late 2004, as disengagement from Gaza began to appear a likelihood. Both NRP factions, however, are united in rejecting relations with the Palestinians. A similar formal rejectionism continued to characterize public statements by Hamas leaders after the Sharm el-Sheikh summit of February 2005.

25 An account of Meimad history and aims is given on the party's website at <http://www.meimad.org.il>.

26 Pundak, Ron, 'From Oslo to Taba: What went wrong?' in *Survival* 43/3 (Autumn 2001), p. 42f.

27 Pundak: 'From Oslo to Taba', 42f.

28 Media reports throughout the year 2000; further commentary in Gopin, Marc, *Holy War, Holy Peace* (Oxford: Oxford University Press, 2002).

29 Mendes-Flohr, Paul R. (ed), *A land of two peoples: Martin Buber on Jews and Arabs* (New York: Oxford University Press, 1983).

30 For two examples, one on either side of the Green Line, see <http://www.ariga.com/humanrights/al-liqa.shtml> and <http://www.rhr.israel.net/>.

31 See Ateek, Naim *et al.*, (eds), *Jerusalem: what makes for peace: a Palestinian Christian contribution to peacemaking* (London: Melisende, 1997).

32 Newsletters from IEA 2004, see <www.interfaith-encounter.org>.

33 The organization is discussed briefly in Klein Halevi, Yossi, *At the Entrance to the Garden of Eden* (New York: William Morrow, 2001).

34 See <http://www.coventrycathedral.org.uk/bkground.html>; Paz, Reuven, 'Religion and Politics in Alexandria' *Washington Institute Policy Watch* 599, 1 February 2002.

35 Leading settlers, for instance, increasingly adopted the habit of paying condolence visits to mourning Palestinian families in the early years of the Second Intifada.

36 <http://www.theparentscircle.com>.

Abu-Amr, Z., (1994). *Islamic Fundamentalism in the West Bank and Gaza: Muslim Brotherhood and Islamic Jihad* (Bloomington IN: Indiana University Press)

Armstrong, K., (1997). *Jerusalem: One City, Three Faiths* (New York: Ballantine Books)

―――― (2001). *The Battle for God* (New York: Ballantine Books)

Ateek, N. (1997). *Jerusalem: what makes for peace: a Palestinian Christian contribution to peacemaking* (London: Melisende)

Bat Ye'or (2002). *Islam and Dhimmitude: Where Civilisations Collide* (Madison NJ: Fairleigh Dickinson University Press)

Bentsur, E. (2001). *Making Peace: A First-Hand Account of the Arab-Israeli Peace Process* (Westport CT: Praeger)

Friedlander, M.A. (1983). *The Domestic Politics of Peace-Making* (Boulder CO: Westview)

Gopin, M. (2002). *Holy War, Holy Peace* (Oxford: Oxford University Press)

Hroub, K. (2000). *Hamas: Political thought and practice* (Washington D.C.: Institute for Palestine Studies)

Israeli, R. and Bardenstein, C. (1985). *Man of Defiance: A Political Biography of Anwar Sadat* (Totowa NJ: Barnes & Noble)

Israeli, R. (1993). *Fundamentalist Islam and Israel* (Lanham MA: University Press of America)

Klein Halevi, Y. (2001). *At the Entrance to the Garden of Eden* (New York: William Morrow)

Küng, H. (1992). *Judaism* (London: SCM)

Landau, Y. (1984). *Violence and the Value of Life in Jewish Tradition* (Jerusalem: OzveShalom)

―――― (2003). *Healing the Holy Land: Interreligious Peacebuilding in Israel/Palestine* (Washington D.C.: USIP)

Mendes-Flohr, P.R. (1983). *A land of two peoples: Martin Buber on Jews and Arabs* (New York: Oxford University Press)

Nüsse, A. (1998). *Muslim Palestine: The Ideology of Hamas* (Amsterdam: Harwood Academic)

Peres, S. (1993). *The New Middle East* (Shaftesbury: Element)

―――― (1996). *Battling for Peace: Memoirs* (London: Orion)

Ravitsky, A. (1996). *Messianism, Zionism, and Jewish Religious Radicalism* (Chicago: University of Chicago Press)

Robinson, G.E. (1997). *Building a Palestinian State: the incomplete revolution* (Bloomington IN: Indiana University Press)

Robinson, P. (2003). *Just War in Comparative Perspective* (Aldershot: Ashgate)

Rowland, R.C. (1985). *The Rhetoric of Menachem Begin: The myth of redemption through return* (Lanham MA: University Press of America)

Sacks, J. (2002). *Dignity of Difference: How to avoid the clash of civilization* (London and New York: Continuum)

Swanwick, K. (1988). *Music, Mind and Education* (London: Routledge)

Wallach, J. and Wallach, J. (1992). *The New Palestinians: The emerging generation of leaders* (Rocklin CA: Prima Publishing)

Yadgar, Y. (2003). 'SHAS as a struggle to create a new field: A Bourdieuan perspective of an Israeli phenomenon' *Sociology of Religion* 37/4 (Summer)

Chapter Two

1   Abu-Nimer, M., *Nonviolence and Peace Building in Islam: Theory and Practice* (Gainesville TX: University Press of Florida, 2003), p. 99.

2   Abu-Nimer: *Nonviolence and Peace Building*, p. 98.

3   Henderson Stewart, F., *Honor* (London: University of Chicago Press, 1994), pp. 151–3.

4   Abu-Nimer: *Nonviolence and Peace Building*, p. 107.

5   Halliday, F., *Islam and the Myth of Confrontation: Religion and Politics in the Middle East* (London: I.B.Tauris, 1996), p. 134.

6   Geertz, C., *Islam Observed* (New Haven and London: Yale University Press, 1968), pp. 90–117.

7   Starrett, G., *Putting Islam to Work: Education, Politics and Religious Transformation in Egypt*, (Berkeley, Los Angeles and London: University of California Press, 1998), p. 91.

8   'community/society'; the distinction refers to the transition from a social condition in which and most people live in small, predominantly rural settings and hence most interpersonal communication is face-to-face with familiar others, to one in which, as a result of industrialization and urbanization, most people live in towns and cities and hence much communication occurs at a distance, and most encounters are anonymous.

9   Starrett: *Putting Islam to Work*, pp. 224–5.

10   Starrett: *Putting Islam to Work*, p. 225.

11   Starrett: *Putting Islam to Work*, p. 225.

12   Starrett: *Putting Islam to Work*, p. 39.

13   Starrett: *Putting Islam to Work*, p. 62.

14   Starrett: *Putting Islam to Work*, pp. 135–6.

15   Starrett: *Putting Islam to Work*, p. 139.

16   Starrett: *Putting Islam to Work*, p. 139.

17   Starrett: *Putting Islam to Work*, p. 139.

18   Starrett: *Putting Islam to Work*, p. 153.

19   Starrett: *Putting Islam to Work*, p. 199.

20   McLuhan, H.M., *Understanding Media: the Extensions of Man* (New York: McGraw Hill, 1964), pp. 7–9.

21   Goldberg, E., 'Smashing Idols and the State: The Protestant Ethic and Egyptian Sunni Radicalism' *Comparative Studies in History and Society* 33, pp. 30–2; Starrett: *Putting Islam to Work*, p. 231.

22   Starrett: *Putting Islam to Work*, pp. 232–3.

23   Starrett: *Putting Islam to Work*, p. 93.

24   '*Integralisme*' is the term used in French in place of 'fundamentalism', and refers to a religious outlook which holds that all areas of life ought to be governed by a religious authority (hence 'integrated'). It defines religious authoritarianism in terms of its

approach to politics and morals rather than texts, which is arguably more salient to understanding the impact of these groups on society.

25   Murphy, C., *A Passion for Islam* (New York: Scribner, 2002).
26   Abu-Nimer, M., 'Conflict Resolution in an Islamic Context' in *Peace and Change* 21:1 (1996), p. 22–40.
27   Abu-Nimer: *Nonviolence and Peace Building*, p. 87.
28   Abu-Nimer: *Nonviolence and Peace Building*, p. 87.
29   Abu-Nimer: *Nonviolence and Peace Building*, p. 113.
30   Abu-Nimer: *Nonviolence and Peace Building*, p. 116–7.
31   Abu-Nimer: *Nonviolence and Peace Building*, p. 118.
32   Abu-Nimer: *Nonviolence and Peace Building*, p. 124.
33   Abu-Nimer: *Nonviolence and Peace Building*, p. 122.
34   Abu-Nimer: *Nonviolence and Peace Building*, p. 125.
35   Abu-Nimer: *Nonviolence and Peace Building*, p. 121.
36   Abu-Nimer: *Nonviolence and Peace Building*, p. 119.
37   Abu-Nimer: *Nonviolence and Peace Building*, p. 123.
38   Abu-Nimer, M. and Groves, J., 'Peace Building and Nonviolent Political Movements in Arab-Muslim Communities: A Case Study of the Palestinian Intifada' in *Nonviolence and Peace Building in Islam: Theory and Practice* (Gainesville TX: University Press of Florida, 2003), pp. 128–9.
39   Abu-Nimer and Groves: 'Peace Building and Nonviolent Political Movements', p. 128.
40   Caplan, N., *Futile Diplomacy* (London: Cass, 1983).
41   Wilkes, G., *Land of Promise and Conflict* (Cambridge: CJCR, 2000), p. 130.
42   Abu-Nimer and Groves: 'Peace Building and Nonviolent Political Movements', p. 167.
43   Bush, however, was careful to avoid presenting this 'struggle' in terms of a straightforward clash with Islam: in his speech to Congress on 20 September 2001, he described the terrorists as 'traitors to their own faith' (*The Times*, 21 September 2001, p. 5).

Abu-Nimer, M. (1996). 'Conflict Resolution in an Islamic Context' *Peace and Change* 21:1, pp. 22–40
—— (2003). *Nonviolence and Peace Building in Islam: Theory and Practice* (Gainesville TX: University Press of Florida)
Abu-Nimer, M. and Groves, J. (2003). 'Peace Building and Nonviolent Political Movements in Arab-Muslim Communities: A Case Study of the Palestinian Intifada' in M. Abu-Nimer (ed) *Nonviolence and Peace Building in Islam: Theory and Practice* (Gainesville TX: University Press of Florida)
Beyer, P. (1994). *Religion and Globalization* (London: Sage)
Caplan, N. (1983). *Futile Diplomacy* (London: Frank Cass)
Castells, M. (1997). *The Power of Identity, The Information Age: Economy, Society and Culture* Vol. II (Oxford: Blackwell)
—— (1998). *The End of the Millennium, The Information Age: Economy, Society and Culture* Vol. III (Oxford: Blackwell)
Geertz, C. (1966). 'Religion as Cultural System' in M. Bouton (ed), *Anthropological Approaches to the Study of Religion* (New York: Praeger)
—— (1968). *Islam Observed* (New Haven and London: Yale University Press)
Goldberg, E. (1991). 'Smashing Idols and the State: The Protestant Ethic and Egyptian Sunni Radicalism' *Comparative Studies in History and Society*, pp. 3–35
Habermas, J. (1987). *Theory of Communicative Action Vol. 2: Lifeworld and System: A Critique of Functionalist Reason* (Cambridge: Polity/Blackwell)
Halliday, F. (1996). *Islam and the Myth of Confrontation: Religion and Politics in the Middle East* (London: I.B.Tauris)

McLuhan, H.M. (1964). *Understanding Media: the Extensions of Man* (New York: McGraw Hill)

Murphy, C. (2002). *A Passion for Islam* (New York: Scribner)

Reynolds, V. and Tanner, R. (1995). *The Social Ecology of Religion* (Oxford: Oxford University Press)

Starrett, G. (1998). *Putting Islam to Work: Education, Politics and Religious Transformation in Egypt* (Berkeley, Los Angeles and London: University of California Press)

Stewart, F. Henderson (1994). *Honor* (London: University of Chicago Press)

Wilkes, G. (2000). *Land of Promise and Conflict* (Cambridge: CJCR)

Chapter Three

1   Quoted in 'What is the Legacy of the Holocaust?' by Jonathan Sachs in *The Independent*, Thursday 27 January 2005, p. 8.

2   Raul Hilberg understood that '[a] destruction process of a series of administrative measures that must be aimed at a definite group. The German bureaucracy knew with whom it had to deal: the target of its measures was Jewry' (p. 65). Hilberg explores the processes of destruction that followed once the distinction between 'Aryan' and 'non-Aryan' was allowed in *The Destruction of the European Jews* Vol. 1 (New York and London: Holmes and Meier, 1985), chapters 3 and 4.

3   For a discussion of some of the tensions in relation to equality and difference in Kant's moral theory see Seidler, Victor J., *Kant, Respect and Injustice: The Limits of Liberal Moral Theory* (London: Routledge, 1986). For an exploration of the radicalized assumptions that work within Kant's *Geography* see, for instance, Goldberg, David, *Racist Culture: Philosophy and the Politics of Meaning* (Oxford: Blackwell, 1993), Poliakov, Leon, *The Aryan Myth* (London: University of Sussex Press, 1974) and Gilroy, Paul, *The Black Atlantic: Modernity and Double Consciousness* (Cambridge MA: Harvard University Press, 1993), chapter 1.

4   For some helpful discussions of some of the sources of Christian anti-Semitism see for instance, Little, Franklin, *The Crucifiction of the Jews* (New York: Harper and Row, 1975) and Libowitz, Richard (ed), *Faith and Freedom: A Tribute to Franklin H. Little* (Oxford: Pergamon Press, 1987). For a discussion of anti-Semitisms more broadly within philo-sophical traditions in the West see for instance, Hertzberg, A., *The French Enlightenment and the Jews* (New York: Columbia University Press, 1990), Poliakov, L., *The History of Anti-Semitism*, Vol. 1 (Oxford: Oxford University Press, 1985), and Yovel, Yirmiyahu, *Dark Riddle: Hegel, Nietzsche, and the Jews* (Cambridge: Polity Press, 1998).

5   For an interesting discussion of Jean Paul Sartre's *Anti-Semite and Jew* (New York: Schoken Books, 1968) that also explores later developments in his thinking see Friedlander, Judith, *Vilna on the Sein* (New Haven: Yale University Press, 1990).

6   For an interesting collection that gathers some of Levinas' writings in relation to Judaism and modernity see *Difficult Freedom: Essays on Judaism* (London: The Athone Press, 1990). For some interesting discussion that provides a context for Levinas' thinking see for instance, Bernasconi, Robert and Critchley, Simon (eds), *Re-Reading Levinas* (Bloomington IN: Indiana University Press, 1991), Cohen, Richard A., *Elevations: The Height of the Good in Rosenzweig and Levinas* (Chicago: University of Chicago Press, 1994), Handelman, Susan A., *Fragments of Redemption: Jewish Thought and Literary Theory* (Bloomington IN: Indiana University Press, 1991) and Caygill, Howard, *Levinas and the Political* (London: Routledge, 2002).

7   Quoted in 'The Shadows of Auschwitz' by John Lichfield in *The Independent*, Thursday 27 January 2005, p. 8.

8   *The Independent*, Thursday 27 January 2005, p. 8.

9   For some helpful discussions that help introduce different Zionist traditions see, for instance, Sternhell, Zeev, *The Founding Myths of Israel*, (New Jersey: Princeton University Press, 1999), Selzer, Michael (ed), *Zionism Reconsidered* (London: Macmillan, 1970) and

Shlaim, Avi, *The Iron Wall: Israel and the Arab World* (Harmondsworth: Penguin, 2000).

10   Quoted in *The Independent*, 27 January 2005, p. 8.

11   See for instance some of the discussions that relate in different ways to Adorno's challenge in Bauman, Zygmung, *Modernity and Holocaust* (Cambridge: Polity Press, 1989), Seidler, Victor J., *Shadow of the Shoah: Jewish Identity and Belonging* (Oxford: Berg, 2000) and Cohen, Josh, *Interrupting Auschwitz* (London: Continuum, 2003).

12   For an introduction to these aspects of Simone Weil's writings see Blum, Lawrence and Seidler, Victor J., *A Truer Liberty: Simone Weil and Marxism* where certain aspects of *The Need for Roots* (London: Routledge, 1954) are explored. See also McFarland, Dorothy, *Simone Weil* (New York: Ungar, 1983), Fiori, Gabriela, *Simone Weil: An Intellectual Biography* (Atlanta: University of Georgia Press, 1989), and McLellan, David, *Simone Weil: Utopian Pessimist* (Basingstoke: Macmillan, 1989).

13   These themes are invoked in Walter Benjamin's 'Theses on the Philosophy of History' in Arendt, Hannah (ed), *Illuminations* (London: Fontana, 1970). For a helpful context to these writings see Alter, Robert, *Necessary Angels: Tradition and Modernity in Kafka, Benjamin and Scholem* (Cambridge MA: Harvard University Press, 1991) and Handelman, Susan, *Fragments of Redemption: Jewish Thought and Literary Theory* (Bloomington IN: Indiana University Press, 1991).

14   *The Independent*, Thursday 27 January 2005, p. 8.

15   Gramsci explores the need for Marxism to rethink its rationalist visions of ideology if it is to come to terms with the significance of religious belief in people's lives in *The Prison Notebooks* (London: Lawrence and Wishart, 1971). This is a theme that has been explored in Seidler, Victor J., *Recovering The Self: Morality and Social Theory* (London: Routledge, 1993).

16   Quoted in 'Words can Kill' *Jewish Chronicle*, 9 July 2004.

17   Quoted in 'Words can Kill' *Jewish Chronicle*, 9 July 2004.

18   For some helpful reflections on the relationship between globalization and the emergence of diverse Islamist movements see Turner, Bryan, *Orientalism, Postmodernism and Globalisation* (London: Routledge, 1994), Sayyid, S., *A Fundamental Fear* (London: Zed Books, 2003) and Sardar, Ziauddin, *Orientalism* (Milton Keynes: Open University Press, 1999).

19   *The Guardian*, 7 July 2004, p. 22.

20   *The Guardian*, 7 July 2004, p. 22.

21   Lone, Salim, 'Iraq is Now Another Palestine' in *The Guardian*, 7 July 2004, p. 22.

22   Lone: 'Iraq is Now Another Palestine', p. 22.

23   Lone: 'Iraq is Now Another Palestine', p. 22.

24   Lone: 'Iraq is Now Another Palestine', p. 22.

25   Soans, R., *The Arab-Israeli Cookbook* (London: Aurora Metro Publications, 2004) p. 85.

26   Sagi, Uri, quoted in 'Israelis Challenge Clinton' by Joseph Millis in *Jewish Chronicle*, 9 July 2004, p. 11.

27   Morris, Harvey, 'Remember Zion? How a vision of Utopia became a nightmare' in *Financial Times* magazine, p. 10.

28   Morris: 'Remember Zion?, p. 10.

29   Shalom Joseph Shapira quoted in Reform Synagogues of Great Britain (RSGB), *Forms of Prayer - Days of Awe* (Oxford: Oxford University Press, 1985), p. 891.

30   Kuschel, Karl-Josef, *Abraham: Sign of Hope for Jews, Muslims and Christians* (New York: Continuum, 1995), p. 239.

31   Kuschel: *Abraham*, p. 239.

32   Kuschel: *Abraham*, p. 240.

33   Kuschel in *Abraham: Sign of Hope for Jews, Muslims and Christians* (New York: Continuum, 1995) seeks to develop an 'Abrahamic ecumenism' though in crucial ways he remains within a Christian reading of Jewish sources. But at least he shows the potency of an

appeal to Abraham for at least the religious traditions that emerged historically through his influence.

34 Ben-Chorin, Israeli peace activist, is quoted in Kuschel: *Abraham*, p. 243.

35 Klein, Naomi, 'The grieving parents who might yet bring Bush down' in *The Guardian*, Saturday 10 July 2004, p. 22.

36 Klein: 'The grieving parents who might yet bring Bush down', p. 22.

37 Klein: 'The grieving parents who might yet bring Bush down', p. 22.

38 'George Bush never looked into Nick's eyes' in *The Guardian*, 21 May 2005, p. 22.

39 'George Bush never looked into Nick's eyes', p. 22.

40 *The Guardian*, 21 May 2005, p. 22.

41 *The Guardian*, 21 May 2005, p. 22.

42 *The Guardian*, 21 May 2005, p. 22.

43 *The Guardian*, 21 May 2005, p. 22.

44 Goldhill, Simon, 'Tragic Consequences' in *Jewish Chronicle*, 14 May 2004, p. 31.

45 Goldhill: 'Tragic Consequences', p. 31.

46 McGreal, Chris, 'The day the tanks arrived at Rafah Zoo' in *The Guardian*, 22 May 2004, p. 14.

47 McGreal: 'The day the tanks arrived at Rafah Zoo', p. 14.

48 McGreal: 'The day the tanks arrived at Rafah Zoo', p. 14.

49 McGreal: 'The day the tanks arrived at Rafah Zoo', p. 14.

50 McGreal, Chris, 'Palestinian doctors despair at rising toll of children shot dead by army snipers' in *The Guardian*, Thursday 20 May 2004, p. 15.

51 McGreal: 'Palestinian doctors despair', p. 15.

52 McGreal: 'Palestinian doctors despair', p. 15.

53 McGreal, Chris, 'Ten Die as Israeli Tanks Fire on Peaceful protest' in *The Guardian*, Thursday 20 May 2004, p. 1.

54 *The Guardian*, Thursday 20 May 2004, p.14.

55 McGreal: 'Ten Die as Israeli Tanks Fire on Peaceful protest', p. 1.

56 McGreal: 'The day the tanks arrived at Rafah Zoo', p. 14.

57 Quoted in The Editor (section) in *The Guardian*, Friday 20 May 2004, p. 30.

58 Quoted in The Editor (section) in *The Guardian*, Friday 20 May 2004, p. 30.

59 McGreal, Chris, 'Bulldozers crush hope in Rafah camp' in *The Guardian*, Friday 20 May 2004, p. 18.

60 McGreal: 'Bulldozers crush hope in Rafah camp', p. 18.

61 McGreal: 'Bulldozers crush hope in Rafah camp', p. 18.

62 Steele, Jonathan, 'More carnage in Gaza as the US mutters is disapproval' in *The Guardian*, Friday 20 May 2004, p. 28.

63 Steele: 'More carnage in Gaza', p. 28.

64 Steele: 'More carnage in Gaza', p. 28.

65 Benvenisti, Meron, 'An Old Refrain that stabs the heart' in *The Guardian*, Saturday 22 May 2004, p. 20.

66 Benvenisti: 'An Old Refrain that stabs the heart', p. 20.

67 Benvenisti: 'An Old Refrain that stabs the heart', p. 20.

68 Benvenisti: 'An Old Refrain that stabs the heart', p. 20.

69 Shindler, Colin, 'Has *The Guardian* deserted the Angels?' in *The Jewish Chronicle*, 16 July 2004, p. 22.

70 Shindler: 'Has *The Guardian* deserted the Angels?', p. 22.

71 Shindler: 'Has *The Guardian* deserted the Angels?', p. 22.

72 Berg, Michael, 'George Bush never looked into Nick's eyes' in *The Guardian*, Friday 20 May 2004, p. 28.

73 Berg: 'George Bush never looked into Nick's eyes', p. 28.

74 Berg: 'George Bush never looked into Nick's eyes', p. 28.

75 Berg: 'George Bush never looked into Nick's eyes', p. 28.
76 Berg: 'George Bush never looked into Nick's eyes', p. 28.
77 Berg: 'George Bush never looked into Nick's eyes', p. 28.
78 Interview with Michael Berg: 'Nick Berg's father addresses anti-war rally' in *Jewish Chronicle*, 9 July 2004, p. 7.
79 Interview with Michael Berg: 'Nick Berg's father addresses anti-war rally', p. 7.
80 Interview with Michael Berg: 'Nick Berg's father addresses anti-war rally', p. 7.

Alter, Robert (1991). *Necessary Angels: Tradition and Modernity in Kafka, Benjamin and Scholem* (Cambridge MA: Harvard University Press)

Bauman, Zygmung (1989). *Modernity and Holocaust* (Cambridge: Polity Press)

Benjamin, Walter (1970). 'Theses on the Philosophy of History' in Hannah Arendt (ed), *Illuminations* (London: Fontana)

Bernasconi, Robert and Critchley, Simon (1991). *Re-Reading Levinas* (Bloomington IN: Indiana University Press)

Blum, Lawrence and Seidler, Victor J. (1990). *A Truer Liberty: Simone Weil and Marxism* (London: Routledge)

Caygill, Howard (2002). *Levinas and the Political* (London: Routledge)

Cohen, Josh (2003). *Interrupting Auschwitz* (London: Continuum)

Cohen, Richard A. (1994). *Elevations: The Height of the Good in Rosenzweig and Levinas* (Chicago: University of Chicago Press)

Fiori, Gabriela (1989). *Simone Weil: An Intellectual Biography* (Atlanta: University of Georgia Press)

Friedlander, Judith (1990). *Vilna on the Sein* (New Haven: Yale University Press)

Gilroy, Paul (1993). *The Black Atlantic: Modernity and Double Consciousness* (Cambridge MA: Harvard University Press)

Goldberg, David (1993). *Racist Culture: Philosophy and the Politics of Meaning* (Oxford: Blackwell)

Gramsci, Antonio (1971). *The Prison Notebooks* (London: Lawrence and Wishart)

Handelman, Susan (1991). *Fragments of Redemption: Jewish Thought and Literary Theory* (Bloomington IN: Indiana University Press)

Hertzberg, A. (1990). *The French Enlightenment and the Jews* (New York: Columbia University Press)

Hilberg, Raul (1985). *The Destruction of the European Jews* Vol. 1 (New York and London: Holmes and Meier)

Kuschel, Karl-Josef (1995). *Abraham: Sign of Hope for Jews, Muslims and Christians* (New York: Continuum)

Levinas, E. (1990). *Difficult Freedom: Essays on Judaism* (London: The Athone Press)

Libowitz, Richard (ed) (1987). *Faith and Freedom: A Tribute to Franklin H. Little* (Oxford: Pergamon Press)

Little, Franklin (1975). *The Crucifiction of the Jews* (New York: Harper and Row)

McFarland, Dorothy (1983). *Simone Weil* (New York: Ungar)

McLellan, David (1989). *Simone Weil: Utopian Pessimist* (Basingstoke: Macmillan)

Poliakov, Leon (1974). *The Aryan Myth* (London: University of Sussex Press)

—— (1985). *The History of Anti-Semitism* Vol. 1 (Oxford: Oxford University Press)

Reform Synagogues of Great Britain (RSGB) (1985). *Forms of Prayer - Days of Awe* (Oxford: Oxford University Press)

Sardar, Ziauddin (1999). *Orientalism* (Milton Keynes: Open University Press)

Sartre, Jean Paul (1968). *Anti-Semite and Jew* (New York: Schoken Books)

Sayyid, S. (2003). *A Fundamental Fear* (London: Zed Books)

Seidler, Victor J. (1986). *Kant, Respect and Injustice: The Limits of Liberal Moral Theory* (London: Routledge)

—— (1993). *Recovering The Self: Morality and Social Theory* (London: Routledge)

—— (2000). *Shadow of the Shoah: Jewish Identity and Belonging* (Oxford: Berg)
Selzer, Michael (ed) (1970). *Zionism Reconsidered* (London: Macmillan)
Shlaim, Avi (2000). *The Iron Wall: Israel and the Arab World* (Harmondsworth: Penguin)
Soans, Robin (2004). *The Arab-Israeli Cookbook* (London: Aurora Metro Publications Ltd)
Sternhell, Zeev (1999). *The Founding Myths of Israel.* Translated by David Maisel. (New Jersey: Princeton University Press)
Turner, Bryan (1994). *Orientalism, Postmodernism and Globalisation* (London: Routledge)
Yovel, Yirmiyahu (1998). *Dark Riddle: Hegel, Nietzsche, and the Jews* (Cambridge: Polity Press)

Chapter Four

1   See the more hopeful perspective of Richard Falk who argues that the creation of truly humane global governance depends upon drawing on the 'positive' resources of the world's religion and taking on board the fact that religion is still taken seriously by much of the world's population. Falk, R., *Religion and Humane Global Governance* (New York: Palgrave, 2001).

2   Cf. Juergensmeyer, M., *Terror in the Mind of God: The Global Rise of Religious Violence* (Berkeley: University of California Press, 2000); Appleby, S., *The Ambivalence of the Sacred: Religion, Violence and Reconciliation* (Lanham: Rowman & Littlefield, 2000).

3   The final text of the constitution can be found in *Slovo Kyrgyzstana*, 21 May 1993.

4   See the discussion of Metropolitan Ioann in Ellis, Jane, *The Russian Orthodox Church - Triumphalism and Defensiveness* (London: Macmillan, 1996), pp. 105–9; samples of his writings can be found in *Sovetskaya Rossiya*, 12 September 1992 and 12 November 1992.

5   For a critical view of this proposal see Ikhlov, Evgeny, 'Tsivilizatsyia ili plemya' to be found at <http://portal-credo.ru/site/print.php?act=fresh&id=114>.

6   The analysis of the period 1993–97 draws heavily on chapter 7 of my *The International Politics of Central Asia* (Manchester: Manchester University Press, 1997); another useful discussion can be found in Rubin, B., 'Russian hegemony and state breakdown in the periphery: causes and consequences of the civil war in Tajikistan' in B. Rubin and J. Snyder (eds), *Post-Soviet Political Order: Conflict and State Building* (London: Routledge, 1998), pp. 128–61.

7   See the interview with IRP leader Davlat Usman in *Komsomolets Tadzhikistana*, 20 November 1990.

8   I.Rotar, 'Tajikistan: why can't women wear the hijab for international identity photos?' *Forum 18* (9 June 2004) at <http://www.forum18.org/>.

9   For the analysis of differences within the Islamist community see the website: <http://www.reliefweb.int/w/rwb.nsf/0/7afa780b159d5d24c1256ab7002f055a?OpenDocument>.

10 Those struggling against Russia encompassed a number of ethnic groupings including Chechens and the phrase 'mountain peoples' might be used to encompass this variety.

11 Dunlop, J., *Russia Confronts Chechnya - Roots of a Separatist Conflict* (Cambridge: Cambridge University Press, 1998), p. 149.

12 Kipp, J., 'Putin and Russia's wars in Chechnya' in Dale Herspring (ed), *Putin's Russia*, (Oxford: Rowman & Littlefield, 2003), p. 189.

13 Cf. Lieven, A., *Chechnya: Tombstone of Russian Power* (New Haven: Yale University Press, 1999), p. 363; Evangelista, M., *The Chechen Wars* (Washington D.C.: The Brookings Institute, 2002), pp. 71–72.

14 See the 1999 statement of Patriarch Aleksii at <http://www.russian-orthodox-church.org.ru/ne903111.htm>.

15 Radio Free Europe, 30 September 2004 at <http://www.rferl.org/newsline/2004/09/300904.asp>.

16 For a fuller study see Anderson, John, *Religious Liberty in Transitional Societies* (Cambridge: Cambridge University Press, 2003).

17 Such groups could be tactless as I saw in Moscow in 1994 where a group of American students from Campus Crusade for Christ were standing on the steps of an Orthodox Church one Sunday morning telling the entering worshippers that by following Orthodoxy they were doomed to hell.
18 For examples see Alisheva, A., 'Polikonfessional'nyi Kyrgyzstana' in E. Shukurova (ed), *Renassans ili regress* (Bishkek: 1996), pp. 79–80; *Vechernii Bishkek*, 10 June 1999; in 2004 the citizens of the town of Shopkov in northern Kyrgyzstan protested about the building of a Kingdom Hall for the Jehovah's Witnesses near the local school, arguing that the sectarians would take advantages of naïve children to lure them into the sect. See <http://www.stetson.edu/~psteeves/relnews/0402a.html#11>.
19 For a general survey of their activities see Rashid, A., *Jihad: The Rise of Militant Islam in Central Asia* (New Haven: Yale University Press, 2002), pp. 137–85.
20 Rashid: *Jihad*, p. 139.
21 <http://www.starlightsite.co.uk/keston/kns/2002/020708UZ.htm>.
22 For a general survey see Rashid: *Jihad*, pp.115–36; their own website can be found at <http://www.hizb-ut-tahrir.org/english/>.
23 <http://www.forum18.org/Archive.php?article_id=170>.
24 Khamidov, Alisher, 'Hizb-ut-tahrir faces internal split in Central Asia' *Eurasia Insight* (21 October 2003), can be found at <http://www.eurasianet.org/departments/insight/articles/eav202103.shtml>.
25 This account is based largely on Ellis, J., *The Russian Orthodox Church: Triumphalism and Defensiveness* (London: Macmillan, 1996), pp.152–4.
26 The Baptist statement on his behalf can be found at < http://www.hrwf.net/html/azerbaijan_2004.html#_Toc86134100 >.
27 See the reports in *Forum 18* from 20 October 2003 to 2 July 2004 at <http://www.forum18.org>.
28 See Appleby, S., *The Ambivalence of the Sacred* (Lanham: Rowman & Littlefield, 2000).

Anderson, J. (1994). *Religion, State and Society in the Soviet Union and the Successor States* (Cambridge: Cambridge University Press)
—— (1997). *The International Politics of Central Asia* (Manchester: Manchester University Press)
—— (2003). *Religion Liberty in Transitional Societies* (Cambridge: Cambridge University Press)
Appleby, S. (2000). *The Ambivalence of the Sacred* (Lanham: Rowman & Littlefield)
Dunlop, J. (1998). *Russia Confronts Chechnya - Roots of a Separatist Conflict* (Cambridge: Cambridge University Press)
Ellis, J. (1996). *The Russian Orthodox Church - Triumphalism and Defensiveness* (London: Macmillan)
Evangelista, M. (2002). *The Chechen Wars* (Washington D.C.: The Brookings Institute)
Falk, R. (2001). *Religion and Humane Global Governance* (New York: Palgrave)
Herspring, D. (ed) (2003). *Putin's Russia* (Oxford: Rowman & Littlefield)
Juergensmeyer, M. (2000). *Terror in the Mind of God: The Global Rise of Religious Violence* (Berkeley: University of California Press)
Lieven, A. (1998). *Chechnya: Tombstone of Russian Power* (Cambridge: Cambridge University Press)
Rashid, A. (2002). *Jihad: The Rise of Militant Islam in Central Asia* (New Haven: Yale University Press)
Rubin, B. and Snyder, J. (eds) (1998). *Post-Soviet Political Order: Conflict and State Building* (London: Routledge)
Shukurova, E. (ed) (1996). *Renassans ili regress Bishkek* (Bishkek)
Tishkov, V. (2004). *Chechnya: Life in a War-Torn Society* (Berkeley: University of California Press)

Chapter Five

1 Datta, S.K. and Sharma, R., *Pakistan: From Jinnah to Jihad.* (New Delhi: UBSPD, 2003), p.173.
2 Reeve, S., *Ramzi Yousef, Osama bin Laden and the future of terrorism: The New Jackals* (London: Andre Deutsch, 1999), pp. 66–67.
3 Syed, A.H., 'The Sunni-Shia Conflict in Pakistan' in H. Malik (ed), *Pakistan: Founder's Aspirations and Today's Realities* (Karachi: Oxford University Press, 2001), p. 246.
4 Cole, J.R., and Keddie, N. (eds), *Shi'ism and Social Protest.* (New Haven: Yale University Press, 1986), p. 17.
5 Ahmad, M., 'Revivalism, Islamization, Sectarianism and Violence in Pakistan' in C. Baxter and C. Kennedy (eds), *Pakistan 1997* (Boulder: Westview, 1998), pp. 109–119.
6 Lockman, Z., *Contending Visions of the Middle East* (Cambridge: Cambridge University Press, 2004), p. 42.
7 Nisan, M., *Minorities in the Middle East* (London: McFarland & Company, 2002), p. 83.
8 Cole, J., *Sacred Space and Holy War: The Politics, Culture and History of Shi'ite Islam* (London: I.B.Tauris, 2002), p. 185.
9 Ruthven, M., *Fundamentalism: The Search for Meaning* (Oxford: Oxford University Press, 2004), p. 139.
10 Abisaab, R.J., *Converting Persia: Religion and Power in the Safavid Empire* (London: I.B.Tauris, 2004), p. 34.
11 Zaman, M.Q., *The Ulema in Contemporary Islam* (New Jersey: Princeton University Press, 2002), p. 117.
12 Maley, W., *The Afghanistan Wars* (Basingstoke: Palgrave, 2002.), p. 226.
13 Nojumi, N., *The Rise of the Taliban In Afghanistan* (New York: Palgrave, 2002), p. 119.
14 Kleveman, L., *The New Great Game: Blood and Oil in Central Asia* (London: Atlantic Books, 2003), p. 160.

Abbas, H. (2004). *Pakistan's Drift into Extremism: Allah, the Army and America's War on Terror* (New York: M.E. Sharpe)
Abisaab, R.J. (2004). *Converting Persia: Religion and Power in the Safavid Empire* (London: I.B.Tauris)
Ahmad, M. (1998). 'Revivalism, Islamization, Sectarianism and Violence in Pakistan' in C. Baxter and C. Kennedy (eds), *Pakistan 1997* (Boulder: Westview)
Cole, J. (2002). *Sacred Space and Holy War: The Politics, Culture and History of Shi'ite Islam* (London: I.B.Tauris)
Cole, J.R. and Keddie, N. (eds) (1986). *Shi'ism and Social Protest* (New Haven: Yale University)
Datta, S.K. and Sharma, R. (2003). *Pakistan: From Jinnah to Jihad* (New Delhi: UBSPD)
Hiro, D. (2003). *War Without End: The Rise of Islamist Terrorism and the Global Response* (London: Routlege)
Kleveman, L. (2003). *The New Great Game: Blood and Oil in Central Asia* (London: Atlantic Books)
Kukreja, V. (2003). *Contemporary Pakistan: Political Processes, Conflicts and Crises* (New Delhi: Sage)
Lockman, Z. (2004). *Contending Visions of the Middle East* (Cambridge: Cambridge University Press)
Maley, W. (2002). *The Afghanistan Wars* (Basingstoke: Palgrave)
Nasr, Vali (2004). 'Military Rule, Islamism and Democracy in Pakistan' *The Middle East Journal* Vol. 58 (2) Spring, pp. 195–210
Nisan, M. (2002). *Minorities in the Middle East* (London: McFarland and Company)
Nojumi, N. (2002). *The Rise of the Taliban in Afghanistan* (New York: Palgrave)
Reeve, S. (1999). *Ramzi Yousef, Osama Bin Laden and the Future of Terrorism: The New Jackals* (London: Andre Deutsch)

Ruthven, M. (2004). *Fundamentalism: The Search for Meaning* (Oxford: Oxford University Press)
Syed, A.H. (2001). 'The Sunni–Shia Conflict in Pakistan' in H. Malik (ed), *Pakistan: Founder's Aspirations and Today's Realites* (Karachi: Oxford University Press)
Zaman, M.Q. (2002). *The Ulema in Contemporary Islam* (New Jersey: Princeton University Press)

Chapter Six

1   Rugg, Dean S., *Eastern Europe* (London: Longman, 1985), especially pp. 118–254.
2   It is these landscapes of dislocation that Marc Chagall tried to recapture in his paintings, which takes the viewer his childhood in Vitebsk.
3   Reitlinger, Gerald, *A Tower of Skulls* (London: Duckworth, 1932), p. 269 and p. 275. The title of this book, reminding the reader of the *Čele kula* or tower of skulls of Tamerlane, clearly has an Orientalist aroma.
4   Carmichael, Cathie, *Ethnic Cleansing in the Balkans: Nationalism and the Destruction of Tradition* (London: Routledge, 2002), especially chapter two where the religious terminology is discussed in more detail.
5   Klier, John, 'Russian Jewry on the Eve of the Pogroms' in John Klier and Shlomo Lambroza (eds), *Pogroms: Anti- Jewish Violence in Modern Russian History* (Cambridge: Cambridge University Press, 1991), p. 10.
6   Judge, Edward H., *Easter in Kishinev: Anatomy of a Pogrom* (New York: New York University Press, 1992), pp. 30–32.
7   Klier, John, 'The Pogrom Paradigm in Russian History' in John Klier and Shlomo Lambroza (eds), *Pogroms: Anti-Jewish Violence in Modern Russian History* (Cambridge: Cambridge University Press, 1991), p. 35.
8   Trotsky, Leon, *1905* (Harmondsworth: Penguin, 1973), p. 151.
9   Moranian, Suzanne E., 'The Armenian Genocide and American Missionary Relief Efforts' in Jay Winter (ed), *America and the Armenian Genocide* (Cambridge: Cambridge University Press, 2003), p. 191.
10   Dadrian, Vahakn N., 'Comparative Aspects of Armenian and Jewish Cases of Genocide: a Sociohistorical Perspective' in Alan S. Rosenbaum (ed), *Is the Holocaust Unique? Perspectives on Comparative Genocide* (Colorado: Westview, 1996), p. 114.
11   Dadrian: 'Comparative Aspects', pp. 113–8.
12   Dadrian, Vahakn N., 'The Armenian Genocide: an interpretation' in Jay Winter (ed), *America and the Armenian Genocide* (Cambridge: Cambridge University Press, 2003), p. 57.
13   In the later nineteenth century, traditional superstitions between communities are radicalized by racial theories that delegitimize the presence of certain groups by origins or racial 'attributes'. In the Russian case, anti-Semitism as a discourse was augmented by racial theories, in the case of anti-Armenian sentiments by pan-Turanism and by a kind of Orientalism against Muslims in the Balkans.
14   Thontowi, Jawahir, 'The Islamic Perspective on the war on Terrorism and current Indonesian responses' at <http://www.law.monash.edu.au/castancentre/events/2003/human-rights-2003.html>.
15   Daniel, E. Valentine, *Charred Lullabies. Chapters in an Anthropography of Violence* (Princeton: Princeton University Press, 1996), p. 15.
16   A case for drawing parallels between the situation of Muslims with other religious groups in Europe in this period has been made by Justin McCarthy in his monograph, *Death and Exile, The Ethnic Cleansing of Ottoman Muslims 1821-1922* (Princeton: Darwin Press, 1996).
17   In his forthcoming book, *Genocide in the Age of the Nation State: The Rise of the West and the Coming of Genocide* Vol. II (London: I.B.Tauris, 2005), Mark Levene argues that genocide developed out of modernity and the striving for the nation-state, both essentially

Western experiences and its roots as a phenomenon are to be found prior to the twentieth century.

18   Mango, Andrew, *Atatürk* (London: John Murray, 1999), p. 329.

19   Dwork, Deborah and van Pelt, Robert Jan, *Holocaust: A History* (London: John Murray, 2003), p. 46; Henry Abramson in his monograph, *A Prayer for the Government: Ukrainians and Jews in Revolutionary Times, 1917-1920* (Cambridge MA: Harvard University Press, 1999), p. 110, gives a lower number of 50,000–60,000 from Nakhum Gergel, though he adds that this estimate could be doubled or tripled. This lower estimate still represents approximately 4 per cent of the total population.

20   On the recurrence of violence against Muslims in Bosnia and the symbolic elements within Serbian nationalist discourses, see Sells, Michael, *The Bridge Betrayed: Religion and Genocide in Bosnia*, 2nd ed. (Berkeley: University of California Press, 1998).

21   Thomson, Harry Craufuird, *The outgoing Turk: impressions of a journey through the western Balkans* (New York: D. Appleton and Company, 1897), p. 139.

22   Gondrand, Richard, *La Tragédie de l'Asie Mineure et L'antéantissement de Smyrne 1914-1922* (Marseille: Y Armen, 1935), p. 115.

23   Gorrini, Giacomo, 'Orrendi episodi di ferocia musulmana contro gli armeni' in *il Messaggero*, 25 Agosto 1915.

24   Goldsworthy, Vesna, *Inventing Ruritania: The Imperialism of the Imagination* (New Haven: Yale University Press, 1998), p. 37.

25   Nassibian, Akaby, *Britain and the Armenian Question 1915-1923* (Beckenham: Croom Helm, 1984), p. 64.

26   Schaller, Dominik 'Die Rezeption des Völkermordes an den Armeniern in Deutschland' in Hans-Lukas Kieser and Dominik J. Schaller (eds), *Der Völkermord an den Armeniern und die Shoah* (Zurich: Chronos Verlag, 2002), p. 532.

27   Blumenkranz, Bernhard *et al.*, *Histoire des Juifs en France* (Toulouse: Edouard Privat, 1972), p. 381.

28   On Orientalism in the description of violence see Jezernik, Božidar, *Dežela, kjer je vse narobe. Prispevki k etnologiji Balkana* (Ljubljana: Znanstveno in publicistično središče, 1998), particularly pp. 146–167.

29   Price, M. Philips, *War and Revolution in Asiatic Russia* (London: George Allen and Unwin, 1918), p. 128.

30   Dourmoussis, E., *La verité sur un drame historique. La catastrophe de Smyrne, September 1922* (Paris: Librarie Caffin, 1928), p. 80A.

31   Horton, George, *The Blight of Asia* (Indianapolis: Bobbs-Merrill Co., 1926), pp. 136–37. An account of the systematic extermination of Christian populations by Mohammedans with the true story of the burning of Smyrna, etc.

32   Kasaba, Reşat, 'İzmir 1922: A Port City Unravels' in Leila Fawaz and C. A. Bayly (eds), *Modernity and Culture from the Mediterranean to the Indian Ocean, 1890-1920* (New York: Columbia University Press, 2002), p. 220.

33   Yriarte, Charles, *Bosnie et Herzégovine: souvenirs de voyage pendant l'insurrection* (Plon: Paris, 1876), p. 151.

34   Spierenburg, Pieter, 'Masculinity, Violence and Honor: An Introduction' in Pieter Spierenburg (ed), *Men and Violence: Gender, Honor and Rituals in Modern Europe and America* (Ohio: Ohio State University Press, 1998), p. 4.

35   Kennedy-Pipe, Caroline and Stanley, Penny, 'Rape in War. Lessons of the Balkan Conflicts in the 1990s' in Ken Booth (ed), *The Kosovo Tragedy. The Human Rights Dimension* (London: Frank Cass, 2001), p. 69.

36   McCarthy: *Death and Exile*, p. 72.

37   Naimark, Norman M., *Fires of Hatred. Ethnic Cleansing in Twentieth Century Europe* (Cambridge MA: Harvard University Press, 2001), p. 33.

38   Karakasidou, Anastasia N., *Fields of Wheat, Hills of Blood: Passages to Nationhood in Greek*

Macedonia 1870-1990 (Chicago: University of Chicago Press, 1997), pp. 151–52.

39 Price, Walter Harrington Crawfurd, *The Balkan Cockpit: the Political and Military Story of the Balkan Wars in Macedonia* (London: T. Werner Laurie, 1914), p. 179.

40 Dobson, Charles, 'Appendix: The Smyrna Holocaust' in Lysimachos Oeconomos, *The Tragedy of the Christian Near East* (London: Anglo-Hellenic League, 1923), p. 28.

41 Anon, *An Authentic Account of the Occurrences in Smyrna and the Aidan District (on the occupation by the Greeks)* (London: Cole and Co, 21 May 1919), p. 3.

42 Appadurai, Arjun, 'Dead Certainty: Ethnic Violence in the Era of Globalization' *Development and Change* Vol. 29 No. 4 (October 1998), p. 920.

43 Conversi, Daniele, 'Nationalism, Boundaries and Violence' *Millenium: Journal of International Studies* Vol. 28 No. 3 (1999), p. 583; this argument has also been made about Bosnia in particular by Misha Glenny in *The Fall of Yugoslavia: The Third Balkan War* (Harmondsworth: Penguin, 1992), p.169.

44 Verkaaik, Oskar, 'Fun and violence. Ethnocide and the effervescence of collective aggression' *Social Anthropology* 11: 1 (2003), p. 21.

45 Nassibian: *Britain and the Armenian Question*, p. 40.

46 Schwandner-Sievers, Stephanie, 'The enactment of "tradition". Albanian constructions of identity, violence and power in times of crisis' in Bettina E. Schmidt and Ingo W. Schröder (eds), *Anthropology of Violence and Conflict* (London: Routledge, 2001), p. 97.

47 Stefanović, Djordje, 'Seeing the Albanians through Serbian Eyes. The Inventors of the Tradition of Intolerance and their Critics 1804-1939' *European History Quarterly* No. 3. Vol. 35 (2005), p. 475.

48 Khrushchev, Nikita, *Khrushchev remembers* Vol. 1 (London: Deutch, 1971 p. 267); with an introduction, commentary and notes by Edward Crankshaw; translated and edited by Strobe Talbott.

49 Judge: *Easter in Kishinev*, p. 57.

50 Waxman, Meyer, *A History of Jewish Literature* Vol. 4 Part 1 (New York: Thomas Yoseloff, 1960).

51 Allcock, John B., *Explaining Yugoslavia* (London: Hurst, 2000) p. 398.

52 Lambroza, Shlomo, 'The pogroms of 1903-1906' in Klier and Lambroza (eds): *Pogroms*, p. 205.

53 Trotsky: *1905*, pp. 150–51.

54 Dobson: 'Appendix: The Smyrna Holocaust', p. 28. Similarly in 1821, the Greek Patriarch of Constantinople, Gregorius, was hanged in his sacred vestments after celebrating the Easter Day mass to the horror of the Christian public of Europe. Marriott, J.A.R., *The Eastern Question: an Historical Study in European Diplomacy* 4th ed. (Oxford: Clarendon Press, 1940), p. 205.

55 Kennan, George F., *The Other Balkan Wars. A 1913 Carnegie Endowment Inquiry in Retrospect with a New Introduction and Reflections on the Present Conflict* (Washington D.C.: Carnegie Endowment for International Peace, 1993), p. 324.

56 Price: *Balkan Cockpit*, p. 355.

57 McCarthy: *Death and Exile*, p. 75.

58 Harris, Rendel J. and Harris, Helen B., *Letters From the Scenes of the Recent Massacres in Armenia* (London: James Nisbet, 1897), p. 32–33. Similarly, Jews were thrown into the Dneister river in 1941 with constant taunts about wanting to see the miracle of the Red Sea re-enacted. Levene, Mark, 'The Experience of Genocide: Armenia 1915-1916 and Romania 1941-42' in Hans-Lukas Kieser and Dominik J. Schaller (eds), *Der Völkermord an den Armeniern und die Shoah* (Zurich: Chronos Verlag, 2002), p. 450.

59 'Der Konsul in Trapezunt (Bergfeld) an die Botschaft Konstantinopel' *Telegraphischer Bericht*, Trapezunt den 2 Juli 1915 at <http://www.armenocide.net>.

60 This point has been argued with some force in Rubinstein, William D., *Genocide* (London: Longman, 2004), especially pp. 11–44.

61   Miller, Donald E. and Miller, Lorna Touryan, 'The Armenian and Rwandan genocides: some preliminary reflections on two oral history projects with survivors' *Journal of Genocide Research* Vol. 6 No. 1 (March 2004), p. 137.

62   Bailey, William Frederick, *The Slavs of the War Zone* (New York: E.P. Dutton, 1916), p. 256.

63   Preface by the editor in Günther Schlee (ed), *Imagined Differences: Hatred and the Construction of Identity* (New York: Palgrave, 2004), p. v.

64   Levene, Mark, 'The changing face of mass murder: massacre, genocide and post-genocide' *International Social Science Journal* Vol. 54 No. 174 (2002), p. 446, 451 fn. 6.

65   Djilas, Milovan, *Wartime: With Tito and the Partisans* (New York: Harcourt Brace Jovanovich, 1977), p. 11.

66   Lieberman, Ben, 'Nationalist Narratives, Violence between Neighbors and Ethnic Cleansing: A Case of Cognitive Dissonance?' in *Journal of Genocide Research* (forthcoming); Rubinstein: *Genocide*, p. 261.

67   Akbari, Suzanne Conklin, 'The Jews in Late Medieval Literature' in Ivan Davidson Klamar and Derek J. Penslar (eds), *Orientalism and the Jews* (Waltham MA: Brandeis University Press, 2005), p. 36.

68   Senderovich, Aleksandr, 'How Dostoyevsky's 'Jew' is made: Judeophobia and the Problems of National Identity', paper presented at the American Association for the Advancement of Slavic Studies (Boston, 5 December 2004). I am also indebted to remarks made by Harriet Lisa Murav in discussions on the subject of Dostoyevsky's anti-Semitism.

69   Judge: *Easter in Kishinev*, p. 40.

70   Orwell, George, 'Antisemitism in Britain', originally published in the *Contemporary Jewish Record* in April 1945 and reprinted in Sonia Orwell and Ian Angus (eds), *The Collected Essays, Journalism and Letters of George Orwell. Vol. 3. As I Please 1943-1945* (Harmondsworth: Penguin, 1970), p. 381.

71   It has been argued that violence against animals can develop into violence against man. For a discussion of this view, see Passmore, John, 'The Treatment of Animals' *Journal of the History of Ideas* Vol. 36 No. 2 (April–June, 1975), p. 201.

72   Morgenthau, Henry, *Ambassador Morgenthau's Story* (Garden City NY: New Age Publishers, 1918), pp. 322–323.

73   Hilderbrand, Emile, 'Kemal Promises More Hangings of Political Antagonists in Turkey' in *Los Angeles Examiner*, 1 August, 1926.

74   The Jews often responded to persecution by emigrating or joining leftist parties. On this phenomenon see Rogger, Hans, *Russia in the Age of Modernisation and Revolution, 1881-1917* (London: Longman, 1983), pp. 199–207.

75   Vitte, S. Iu., *Vospominaniia: Tsarstvovanie Nikolaia II* Vol. 1 (Berlin 1922), pp. 188–89, quoted in Aronson, I. Michael, 'The Attitudes of Russian Officials in the 1880s towards Jewish Assimilation and Emigration' *Slavic Review* 34 No. 1 (March 1975), p. 3.

76   Godelier, Maurice, 'Infrastructures, Societies and History' *Current Anthropology* Vol. 19 No. 4 (December 1978), pp. 763–771.

Abramson, Henry (1999). *A Prayer for the Government: Ukrainians and Jews in Revolutionary Times 1917-1920* (Cambridge MA: Harvard University Press)

Akbari, Suzanne Conklin (2005). 'The Jews in Late Medieval Literature' in Ivan Davidson Klamar and Derek J. Penslar (eds), *Orientalism and the Jews* (Waltham MA: Brandeis University Press)

Allcock, John B. (2000). *Explaining Yugoslavia* (London: Hurst)

Anon (1919). *An Authentic Account of the Occurrences in Smyrna and the Aidan District (on the occupation by the Greeks)* (London: Cole and Co)

Appadurai, Arjun (1998). 'Dead Certainty: Ethnic Violence in the Era of Globalization'

Development and Change Vol. 29 No. 4 (October), pp. 905–925

Aronson, I. Michael (1975). 'The Attitudes of Russian Officials in the 1880s towards Jewish Assimilation and Emigration' *Slavic Review* 34 No. 1 (March), pp. 1–18

Bailey, William Frederick (1916). *The Slavs of the War Zone* (New York: E.P. Dutton)

Blumenkranz, Bernhard *et al.* (1972). *Histoire des Juifs en France* (Toulouse: Edouard Privat)

Carmichael, Cathie (2002). *Ethnic Cleansing in the Balkans: Nationalism and the Destruction of Tradition* (London: Routledge)

Conversi, Daniele (1999). 'Nationalism, Boundaries and Violence' *Millenium: Journal of International Studies* Vol. 28 No. 3, pp. 553–584

Dadrian, Vahakn N. (1996). 'Comparative Aspects of Armenian and Jewish Cases of Genocide: a Sociohistorical Perspective' in Alan S. Rosenbaum (ed) *Is the Holocaust Unique? Perspectives on Comparative Genocide* (Colorado: Westview)

—— (2003). 'The Armenian Genocide: an interpretation' in Jay Winter (ed), *America and the Armenian Genocide* (Cambridge: Cambridge University Press)

Daniel, E. Valentine (1996). *Charred Lullabies: Chapters in an Anthropography of Violence* (Princeton: Princeton University Press)

Djilas, Milovan (1977). *Wartime: With Tito and the Partisans* (New York: Harcourt Brace Jovanovich)

Dobson, Charles (1923) 'Appendix: The Smyrna Holocaust' in Lysimachos Oeconomos, *The Tragedy of the Christian Near East* (London: Anglo-Hellenic League)

Dourmoussis, E. (1928). *La verité sur un drame historique. La catastrophe de Smyrne, September 1922* (Paris: Librarie Caffin)

Dwork, Deborah and van Pelt, Robert Jan (2003). *Holocaust: A History* (London: John Murray)

Glenny, Misha (1992). *The Fall of Yugoslavia: The Third Balkan War* (Harmondsworth: Penguin)

Godelier, Maurice (1978). 'Infrastructures, Societies and History' *Current Anthropology* Vol. 19 No. 4. (December), pp. 763–771

Goldsworthy, Vesna (1998). *Inventing Ruritania: The Imperialism of the Imagination* (New Haven: Yale University Press)

Gondrand, Richard (1935). *La Tragédie de l'Asie Mineure et L'antéantissement de Smyrne 1914-1922* (Marseille: Y Armen)

Gorrini, Giacomo (1915). 'Orrendi episodi di ferocia musulmana contro gli armeni' *il Messaggero* (25 agosto)

Harris, Rendel J. and Harris, Helen B. (1897). *Letters From the Scenes of the Recent Massacres in Armenia* (London: James Nisbet)

Hilderbrand, Emile (1926). 'Kemal Promises More Hangings of Political Antagonists in Turkey' *Los Angeles Examiner* (1 August)

Horton, George (1926). *The Blight of Asia. An account of the systematic extermination of Christian populations by Mohammedans...with the true story of the burning of Smyrna, etc.* (Indianapolis: Bobbs-Merrill Co.)

Jezernik, Božidar (1998). *Dežela, kjer je vse narobe. Prispevki k etnologiji Balkana.* (Ljubljana: Znanstveno in publicistično središče)

Judge, Edward H. (1992). *Easter in Kishinev: Anatomy of a Pogrom* (New York: New York University Press)

Karakasidou, Anastasia N. (1997). *Fields of Wheat, Hills of Blood: Passages to Nationhood in Greek Macedonia 1870-1990* (Chicago: University of Chicago Press)

Kasaba, Reşat (2002). 'İzmir 1922: A Port City Unravels' in Leila Fawaz and C.A. Bayly (eds), *Modernity and Culture from the Mediterranean to the Indian Ocean 1890-1920* (New York: Columbia University Press)

Kennan, George F. (1993). *The Other Balkan Wars: A 1913 Carnegie Endowment Inquiry in*

Retrospect with a New Introduction and Reflections on the Present Conflict (Washington D.C.: Carnegie Endowment for International Peace)

Kennedy-Pipe, Caroline and Stanley, Penny (2001). 'Rape in War: Lessons of the Balkan Conflicts in the 1990s' in Ken Booth (ed), *The Kosovo Tragedy: The Human Rights Dimension* (London: Frank Cass)

Khrushchev, Nikita (1971). *Khrushchev remembers* Vol. 1. Translated and edited by Strobe Talbott. (London: Deutch)

Klier, John (1991). 'The Pogrom Paradigm in Russian History' in John Klier and Shlomo Lambroza (eds), *Pogroms: Anti-Jewish Violence in Modern Russian History* (Cambridge: Cambridge University Press)

——— (1991). 'Russian Jewry on the Eve of the Pogroms' in John Klier and Shlomo Lambroza (eds), *Pogroms: Anti-Jewish Violence in Modern Russian History* (Cambridge: Cambridge University Press)

Lambroza, Shlomo (1991). 'The pogroms of 1903-1906' in John Klier and Shlomo Lambroza (eds), *Pogroms: Anti-Jewish Violence in Modern Russian History* (Cambridge: Cambridge University Press)

Levene, Mark (2002). 'The changing face of mass murder: massacre, genocide and post-genocide' *International Social Science Journal* Vol. 54 No. 174, pp. 443–452

——— (2002). 'The Experience of Genocide: Armenia 1915-1916 and Romania 1941-42' in Hans-Lukas Kieser and Dominik J. Schaller (eds), *Der Völkermord an den Armenien und die Shoah* (Zurich: Chronos Verlag)

——— (2005). *Genocide in the Age of the Nation State: The Rise of the West and the Coming of Genocide* Vol. II (London: I.B.Tauris)

Lieberman, Ben (forthcoming). 'Nationalist Narratives, Violence between Neighbors and Ethnic Cleansing: A Case of Cognitive Dissonance?' *Journal of Genocide Research*

Mango, Andrew (1999). *Atatürk* (London: John Murray)

Marriott, J.A.R. (1940). *The Eastern Question: an Historical Study in European Diplomacy* 4th ed. (Oxford: Clarendon Press)

McCarthy, Justin (1996). *Death and Exile, The Ethnic Cleansing of Ottoman Muslims 1821-1922* (Princeton: Darwin Press)

Miller, Donald E. and Miller, Lorna Touryan (2004). 'The Armenian and Rwandan genocides: some preliminary reflections on two oral history projects with survivors' *Journal of Genocide Research* Vol. 6 No. 1 (March), pp. 135–140

Moranian, Suzanne E. (2003). 'The Armenian Genocide and American Missionary Relief Efforts' in Jay Winter (ed), *America and the Armenian Genocide* (Cambridge: Cambridge University Press)

Morgenthau, Henry (1918). *Ambassador Morgenthau's Story* (Garden City NY: New Age Publishers)

Naimark, Norman M. (2001). *Fires of Hatred: Ethnic Cleansing in Twentieth Century Europe* (Cambridge MA: Harvard University Press)

Nassibian, Akaby (1984). *Britain and the Armenian Question 1915-1923* (Beckenham: Croom Helm)

Orwell, George (1970). 'Anti–Semitism in Britain' in Sonia Orwell and Ian Angus (eds), *The Collected Essays, Journalism and Letters of George Orwell Vol. 3. As I Please 1943-1945* (Harmondsworth: Penguin), pp. 378–388

Passmore, John (1975). 'The Treatment of Animals' *Journal of the History of Ideas* Vol. 36 No. 2 (April–June), pp. 195–218

Price, Walter Harrington Crawfurd (1914). *The Balkan Cockpit: the Political and Military Story of the Balkan Wars in Macedonia* (London: T. Werner Laurie)

Price, M. Philips (1918). *War and Revolution in Asiatic Russia* (London: George Allen and Unwin)

Reitlinger, Gerald (1932). *A Tower of Skulls* (London: Duckworth)

Rogger, Hans (1983). *Russia in the Age of Modernisation and Revolution, 1881-1917* (London: Longman)

Rubinstein, William D. (2004). *Genocide* (London: Longman)

Rugg, Dean S. (1985). *Eastern Europe* (London: Longman)

Sells, Michael (1998). *The Bridge Betrayed: Religion and Genocide in Bosnia* 2nd ed. (Berkeley: University of California Press)

Schaller, Dominik (2002). 'Die Rezeption des Völkermordes an den Armeniern in Deutschland' in Hans-Lukas Kieser and Dominik J. Schaller (eds), *Der Völkermord an den Armeniern und die Shoah* (Zurich: Chronos Verlag)

Schlee, Günther (ed) (2004). *Imagined Differences: Hatred and the Construction of Identity* (New York: Palgrave)

Schwandner-Sievers, Stephanie (2001). 'The enactment of 'tradition'. Albanian constructions of identity, violence and power in times of crisis' in Bettina E. Schmidt and Ingo W. Schröder (eds), *Anthropology of Violence and Conflict* (London: Routledge)

Senderovich, Aleksandr (2004). 'How Dostoyevsky's 'Jew' is made: Judeophobia and the Problems of National Identity', paper presented to the American Association for the Advancement of Slavic Studies 5 December (Boston)

Spierenburg, Pieter (1998). 'Masculinity, Violence and Honor: An Introduction' in Pieter Spierenburg (ed), *Men and Violence: Gender, Honor and Rituals in Modern Europe and America* (Ohio: Ohio State University Press)

Stefanović, Djordje (2005). 'Seeing the Albanians through Serbian Eyes. The Inventors of the Tradition of Intolerance and their Critics 1804-1939' *European History Quarterly* No. 3 Vol. 35, pp. 465-492

Thomson, Harry Craufuird (1897). *The outgoing Turk: impressions of a journey through the western Balkans* (New York: D. Appleton and Company)

Thontowi, Jawahir (2003). 'The Islamic Perspective on the war on Terrorism and current Indonesian responses' at <http://www.law.monash.edu.au/castancentre/events/2003/human-rights-2003.html>

Trotsky, Leon (1973). *1905* (Harmondsworth: Penguin)

Verkaaik, Oskar (2003). 'Fun and violence. Ethnocide and the effervescence of collective aggression' *Social Anthropology* 11/1, pp. 3–22

Waxman, Meyer (1960). *A History of Jewish Literature* Vol. 4 Part 1 (New York: Thomas Yoseloff)

Yriarte, Charles (1876). *Bosnie et Herzégovine: souvenirs de voyage pendant l'insurrection* (Paris: Plon)

Chapter Seven

1   Thucydides, *History of the Peloponnesian War*, trans. Rex Warner (London: Penguin, 1972), p. 80.

2   Markey, D., 'Prestige and the Origins of War: Returning to Realism's Roots' *Security Studies* 8:4 (1999), p. 135.

3   Kagan, D., *On the Origins of War and the Preservation of Peace* (New York: Anchor, 1995), p. 8.

4   Huizinga, J., *Homo Ludens: A Study of the Play Element in Culture* (London: Routledge & Kegan Paul, 1949), p. 90.

5   See for instance, Berger, P., 'On the Obsolescence of the Concept of Honour' in M. Sandel (ed), *Liberalism and its Critics* (Oxford: Basil Blackwell, 1984), pp. 149–158. See also Blok, Anton, 'Rams and Billy Goats: A Key to the Mediterranean Concept of Honour' *Man* 16 (1981), pp. 427–40.

6   See Bowman, J., 'Whatever Happened to Honor?' for The Bradley Lecture to the American Enterprise Institute (10 June 2002) at <http://www.jamesbowman.net/articleDetail.asp?pubID=1169>.

7   A similar discrediting of the language of honour took place in the late Roman Republic,

but 'the emotions of honour…were never more powerful than when they could no longer be expressed' – Barton, C., *Roman Honor: The Fire in the Bones* (Berkeley: University of California Press, 2001), p. 10.

8 Miller, W.I., *Humiliation and Other Essays on Honor, Social Discomfort, and Violence* (Ithaca: Cornell University Press, 1993), pp. ix–x. For similar comments, see Braudy, L., *The Frenzy of Renown: Fame and its History* (New York: Vintage, 1997), pp. 7–8, 54 and 609. The modern obsession with status is analysed in de Botton, A., *Status Anxiety* (London: Hamish Hamilton, 2004) and Marmot, M., *Status Syndrome: How Your Social Standing Directly Affects Your Health and Life Expectancy* (London: Bloomsbury, 2004).

9 Axinn, S., *A Moral Military* (Philadelphia: Temple University Press, 1989), p. 42.

10 Ignatieff, M., *The Warrior's Honor: Ethnic War and the Modern Conscience* (New York: Metropolitan, 1997), p. 116.

11 O'Neill, B., *Honor, Symbols, and War* (Ann Arbor: University of Michigan Press, 2001), p. 85.

12 O'Neill: *Honor, Symbols, and War*, p. 106.

13 O'Neill: *Honor, Symbols, and War*, p. 106.

14 George W. Bush cited in *The North Bay Nugget*, Thursday 5 September 2002, p. A.10.

15 Jack Straw, speaking on Channel 4 News, Thursday 23 January 2003.

16 Pitt-Rivers, J., 'Honor' *Encyclopedia of the Social Sciences* (New York: Macmillan, 1968), pp. 503–4.

17 van Wees, H., *Status Warriors: War, Violence and Society in Homer and History* (Amsterdam: J.C. Gieben, 1992), p. 69.

18 Peristiany, J.G., *Honor and Shame: The Values of a Mediterranean Society* (Chicago: University of Chicago Press, 1968), p. 30.

19 Aristotle, *Ethics*, trans. J. Thompson (London: Penguin, 1976), p. 284.

20 Taylor, C., 'The Politics of Recognition' in A. Gutman (ed), *Multiculturalism: Examining the Politics of Recognition* (Princeton: Princeton University Press, 1994), pp. 32–3.

21 Rawls, J., 'Self Respect, Excellences, and Shame' in R. Dillon (ed), *Dignity, Character, and Self-Respect* (New York and London: Routledge, 1995), p. 125.

22 Gilbert, P., *New Terror, New Wars* (Edinburgh: Edinburgh University Press, 2003), p. 67.

23 de Troyes, Chrétien, *Arthurian Romances*, trans. William W. Kibler (London: Penguin, 1991), p. 358.

24 Wyatt-Brown, B., *The Shaping of Southern Culture: Honor, Grace and War, 1760s to 1880s* (Chapel Hill: University of North Carolina Press, 2001), p. 178.

25 This explanation of the American Civil War is given in Wyatt-Brown, B., *The Shaping of Southern Culture, and Southern Honor: Ethics and Behavior in the Old South* (New York and Oxford: Oxford University Press, 1982). Also, Olson, C., *Political Culture and Secession in Mississippi: Masculinity, Honor, and the Antiparty Tradition* (New York: Oxford University Press, 2000).

26 Crowther, E.R., 'Holy Honor: Sacred and Secular in the Old South' *The Journal of Southern History* Vol. 58 No. 4 (1992), p. 620.

27 Crowther: 'Holy Honor', p. 620.

28 Cited in Magnet, J., 'His Grasp of Spin is Chilling' in *The Daily Telegraph*, Friday 16 November 2001, p. 23.

29 Braudy, L., *From Chivalry to Terrorism: War and the Changing Nature of Masculinity* (New York: Alfred A. Knopf, 2003), p. 547.

30 Abu Gheith, S., 'In the Shadow of the Lances' at <http://www.memri.org/bin/articles.cgi?Area=middleeast&ID=SP38802>.

31 St Augustine cited in Brown Watson, C., *Shakespeare and the Renaissance Concept of Honour* (Princeton: Princeton University Press, 1960), p. 30.

32 Thomas Aquinas, *Summa Theologiae* Vol. 42 (New York: Blackfriars, 1972), p. 135.

33 Aquinas: *Summa Theologiae*, p. 137.

34 de Charny, G., 'The Book of Chivalry' in R. Kaeuper and E. Kennedy (eds), *The Book of Chivalry of Geoffroi de Charny: Text, Context, and Translation* (Philadelphia: University of Pennsylvania Press, 1996), p. 131.

35 Painter, S., *French Chivalry: Chivalric Ideas and Practice in Mediaeval France* (Baltimore: The John Hopkins University Press, 1940), p. 90.

36 Painter: *French Chivalry*, p. 90.

37 Contamine, P., *War in the Middle Ages*, (Oxford: Basil Blackwell, 1984), pp. 266–7.

38 See Martindale, J., 'Peace and War in Early Eleventh-Century Aquitaine' in C. Harper-Bill and R. Harvey (eds), *Medieval Knighthood IV* (Cambridge: The Boydell Press, 1992), pp. 147–176.

39 Bernard of Clairvaux, 'De laude novae militiae' in H. Chickering and T.H. Seiler (eds), *The Study of Chivalry: Resources and Approaches* (Kalamazoo: Medieval Institute Publications, 1988), p. 162.

40 Painter: *French Chivalry*, p. 71.

41 Lull, R., *The Booke of the Ordre of Chyvalry*, trans. William Caxton (London: Oxford University Press, 1926), p. 67.

42 Lull: *The Book of the Ordre of Chyvalry*, pp. 66–74.

43 Froissart, J., *Chronicles*, trans. Geoffrey Brereton (London: Penguin, 1978), p. 251.

44 Vale, Malcolm, *War and Chivalry: Warfare and Aristocratic Culture in England, France and Burgundy at the End of the Middle Ages* (London: Duckworth, 1981), p. 88.

45 Vale: *War and Chivalry*, p. 92.

46 Lull: *The Book of the Ordre of Chyvalry*, pp. 24–5.

47 Kaeuper and Kennedy: *The Book of Chivalry of Geoffroi de Charny*, p. 43.

48 Strickland, M., *War and Chivalry: The Conduct and Perception of War in England and Normandy, 1066-1217* (Cambridge: Cambridge University Press, 1996), p. 55.

49 Contamine: *War in the Middle Ages*, p. 302.

50 Chanson d' Aspremont' cited in Kaeuper, R., *Chivalry and Violence in Medieval Europe* (Oxford: Oxford University Press, 1999), p. 233.

51 Strickland: *War and Chivalry*, p. 97.

52 Keen, M., 'Chivalry, Nobility, and the Man-at-Arms' in C. Allmand (ed), *War, Literature, and Politics in the Late Middle Ages* (Liverpool: Liverpool University Press, 1976), p. 45.

53 See L. Calhoun, 'The Injustices of Just Wars' *Peace Review* 12 (2000), pp. 449–455; Booth, K., *The Kosovo Tragedy: The Human Rights Dimension* (London: Frank Cass, 2001), pp. 314 –324.

54 See Dearey, P., 'Catholicism and the Just War Tradition: The Experience of Moral Value in Warfare' in P. Robinson (ed), *Just War in Comparative Perspective* (Aldershot: Ashgate, 2003), pp. 24–39.

55 Matthew 5: 9.

Abu Gheith, S. (2002). 'In the Shadow of the Lances' at <http://www.memri.org/bin/articles.cgi?Area=middleeast&ID=SP38802>

Aquinas, T. (1972). *Summa Theologiae* (New York: Blackfriars)

Aristotle (1976). *Ethics* (London: Penguin)

Axinn, S. (1989). *A Moral Military* (Philadelphia: Temple University Press)

Barton, C. (2001). *Roman Honor: The Fire in the Bones* (Berkeley: University of California Press)

Berger, P. (1984). 'On the Obsolescence of the Concept of Honour' in M. Sandel (ed), *Liberalism and its Critics* (Oxford: Basil Blackwell)

Bernard of Clairvaux (1988). 'De Laude Novae Militiae' in H. Chickering and T. Seiler (eds), *The Study of Chivalry: Resources and Approaches* (Kalamazoo: Medieval Institute Publications)

Blok, A. (1981). 'Rams and Billy Goats: A Key to the Mediterranean Concept of Honour' *Man* Vol. 16, pp. 427–440

Booth, K. (2001). *The Kosovo Tragedy: The Human Rights Dimension* (London: Frank Cass)

Bowman, J. (2002). 'Whatever Happened to Honor?' The Bradley Lecture to the American Enterprise Institute at <http://www.jamesbowman.net/articleDetail.asp?pubID=1169>

Braudy, L. (1997). *The Frenzy of Renown: Fame and its History* (New York: Vintage)

—— (2003). *From Chivalry to Terrorism: War and the Changing Nature of Masculinity* (New York: Alfred A. Knopf)

Calhoun, L. (2000). 'The Injustices of Just Wars' *Peace Review* Vol. 12, pp. 449–55

Contamine, P. (1984). *War in the Middle Ages* (Oxford: Basil Blackwell)

de Botton, A. (2004). *Status Anxiety* (London: Hamish Hamilton)

de Charny, G. (1996). 'The Book of Chivalry' in R. Kaeuper and E. Kennedy (eds), *The Book of Chivalry of Geoffroi de Charny: Text, Context and Translation* (Philadelphia: University of Pennsylvania Press)

de Troyes, C. (1991). *Arthurian Romances* (London: Penguin)

Dearey, P. (2003). 'Catholicism and the Just War Tradition: The Experience of Moral Value in Warfare' in P. Robinson (ed), *Just War in Comparative Perspective* (Aldershot: Ashgate)

Froissart, J. (1978). *Chronicles* (London: Penguin)

Gilbert, P. (2003). *New Terror, New Wars* (Edinburgh: Edinburgh University Press)

Huizinga, J. (1949). *Homo Ludens: A Study of the Play Element in Culture* (London: Routledge & Kegan Paul)

Ignatieff, M. (1998). *The Warrior's Honor: Ethnic War and the Modern Conscience* (New York: Metropolitan)

Kaeuper, R. (1999). *Chivalry and Violence in Medieval Europe* (Oxford: Oxford University Press)

Kagan, D. (1995). *On the Origins of War and the Preservation of Peace* (New York: Anchor)

Keen, M. (1976). 'Chivalry, Nobility, and the Man-at-Arms' in C. Allmand (ed), *War, Literature, and Politics in the Late Middle Ages* (Liverpool: Liverpool University Press)

Lull, R. (1926). *The Booke of the Ordre of Chyvalry* (London: Oxford University Press)

Magnet, C. (2001). 'His Grasp of Spin is Chilling' in *The Daily Telegraph* (16 November)

Markey, D. (1999). 'Prestige and the Origins of War: Returning to Realism's Roots' *Security Studies* Vol. 8 No. 2 (Summer)

Marmot, M. (2004). *Status Syndrome: How Your Social Standing Directly Affects Your Health and Life Expectancy* (London: Bloomsbury)

Miller, W. (1993). *Humiliation and Other Essays on Honor, Social Discomfort, and Violence* (Ithaca: Cornell University Press)

O'Neill, B. (2001). *Honor, Symbols, and War* (Ann Arbor: University of Michigan Press)

Olson, C. (2000). *Political Culture and Secession in Mississippi: Masculinity, Honor, and the Anti-Party Tradition* (New York: Oxford University Press)

Painter, S. (1940). *French Chivalry: Chivalric Ideas and Practice in Mediaeval France* (Baltimore: The John Hopkins University Press)

Peristiany, J. (1965). *Honour and Shame: The Values of a Mediterranean Society* (London: Weidenfeld & Nicolson)

Pitt-Rivers, J. (1968). 'Honor' *Encyclopedia of the Social Sciences* (New York: Macmillan), pp. 503–4

Rawls, J. (1995). 'Self-Respect, Excellences, and Shame' in R. Dillon (ed.), *Dignity, Character, and Self-Respect* (New York and London: Routledge)

Strickland, M. (1996). *War and Chivalry: The Conduct and Perception of War in England and Normandy, 1066-1217* (Cambridge: Cambridge University Press)

Taylor, C. (1994). 'The Politics of Recognition' in A. Gutman (ed), *Multiculturalism: Examining the Politics of Recognition* (Princeton: Princeton University Press)

Vale, M. (1981). *War and Chivalry: Warfare and Aristocratic Culture in England, France and Burgundy at the End of the Middle Ages* (London: Duckworth)

van Wees, H. (1992). *Status Warriors: War, Violence and Society in Homer and History* (Amsterdam: J.C. Gieben)

Watson, Curtis Brown (1960). *Shakespeare and the Renaissance Concept of Honour* (Princeton: Princeton University Press)

Wyatt-Brown, B. (1982). *Southern Honor: Ethics and Behavior in the Old South* (New York and London: Oxford University Press)

—— (2001). *The Shaping of Southern Culture: Honor, Grace, and War* (Chapel Hill: University of North Carolina Press)

Chapter Eight

1 For overviews of this particular episode, see Blumenthal, U.-R., *The Investiture Controversy: Church and Monarchy from the Ninth to the Twelfth Century* (Philadelphia: University of Pennsylvania Press, 1988) and Morris, C., *The Papal Monarchy. The Western Church from 1050 to 1250* (Oxford: Clarendon Press, 1989). There is an interesting collection of essays in Schmid, K. (ed), *Reich und Kirche vor dem Investiturstreit* (Sigmaringen: Thorbecke, 1985).

2 A good conspectus is to be found in Po-Chia Hsia, R., *The World of Catholic Renewal, 1540-1770* (Cambridge: Cambridge University Press 1998) and Wright, A.D., *The Early Modern Papacy from the Council of Trent to the French Revolution, 1564-1789* (London: Longman, 2000).

3 As McLeod, H., *Secularisation in Western Europe, 1848-1914* (Basingstoke: Macmillan, 2000), p. 1, remarks, secularization, before the French Revolution simply meant the takeover of clerical land.

4 The words come from Article 1 of the Constitutional Act of 1793 as reproduced in Hardman, J. (ed), *The French Revolution. The Fall of the Ancien Régime to the Thermidorean Reaction, 1785-1795* (London: Edward Arnold, 1981), p. 166.

5 On immigration especially, see Caron, V., *Uneasy Asylum. France and the Jewish Refugee Crisis, 1933-1942* (Stanford: Stanford University Press, 1999), whereas notions of citizenship are famously explored in Weber, E., *Peasants into Frenchmen* (Stanford: Stanford University Press, 1977).

6 Still one of the most accessible studies on this period is McManners, J., *Church and State in France, 1870-1914* (London: SPCK, 1972).

7 Gibson, R., *A Social History of French Catholicism, 1789-1914* (London: Routledge 1989), p. 131.

8 Larkin, M., *Church and State after the Separation Affair* (London: Macmillan, 1974), recently published in French as *L'Eglise et l'état* (Toulouse: Privat, 2004).

9 Latreille, A., *De Gaulle, la liberation et l'église catholique* (Paris: Cerf, 1975).

10 See Beattie, N., 'Yeast in the Dough? Catholic Schooling in France, 1981-1995' in K. Chadwick (ed), *Catholicism, Politics and Society in Twentieth-Century France* (Liverpool: Liverpool University Press, 2000), pp. 197–218.

11 For a brief introduction to this issue, see Davie, G., 'Religion and Laïcité' in M. Cook and G. Davie (eds), *Modern France. Society in Transition* (London: Routledge, 1999), pp. 207–8; Bauberot, J., 'The Two Thresholds of Laicization' in R. Bhargava (ed), *Secularism and its Critics* (Oxford: Oxford University Press, 1998), pp. 94–136; and Gemie, S., 'Stasi's Republic: the School and the Veil' *Modern and Contemporary France* 12:3 (2004), pp. 387–398.

12 On this point, see Rémond, R., *Religion and Society in Modern Europe* (Oxford: Blackwell, 1999) who talks about the move from a 'sacral' state to a 'concordatory regime'.

13 See Plongeron, B., *Les Défis de la modernité 1750-1840* Vol. 10 of J-M. Mayeur *et al* (eds), *Histoire du Christianisme des origines à nos jours* (Paris: Desclée, 1997), p. 432.

14 On the experiences of religion in Communist-dominated Europe, see Chadwick, O., *The Christian Church and the Cold War* (Harmondsworth: Penguin, 1992) and Bociurkiw, B.R. and Strong, J.W. (eds), *Religion and Atheism in Eastern Europe* (London: Macmillan 1975).

15 The key study on this is Michaud, C., *L'Eglise et l'argent sous l'ancien régime. Les receveurs généraux du clergé de France aux XVIe-XVIIe siècles* (Paris: Fayard, 1991).

16 On the orders generally, see Beales, D., *Prosperity and Plunder. European Catholic Monasteries in the Age of Revolution, 1650-1815* (Cambridge: Cambridge University Press, 2003). On the 1766 Commission, see Chevallier, P., *Loménie de Brienne et l'ordre monsatique, 1760-89* (Paris: Bibliothèque de la Société d'histoire Ecclésiastique de la France, 1959) and McManners, J., *Church and Society in Eighteenth-Century France* Vol. 1 (Oxford: Oxford University Press, 1999), chapter 19.

17 Jansenism is exhaustively explored in Van Kley, D., *The Jansenists and the Expulsion of the Jesuits from France, 1757-1765* (New Haven: Yale University Press, 1975) and his *The Religious Origins of the French Revolution. From Calvin to the Civil Constitution, 1560-1791* (New Haven: Yale University Press, 1996). See too Williams, W.H., 'The Significance of Jansenism in the History of the French Catholic Clergy in the Pre-Revolutionary Era' *Studies in Eighteenth-Century Culture* Vol. 7 (1978), pp. 289–306; and Doyle, W.O., *Jansenism* (Basingstoke: Macmillan, 2000).

18 Palmer, R.R., *Catholics and Unbelievers in Eighteenth-Century France* (Princeton: Princeton University Press, 1939) and McMahon, D.M., *Enemies of the Enlightenment and the Making of Modernity* (Oxford: Oxford University Press, 2001). See too Barnett, S.J., *The Enlightenment and Religion: The Myths of Modernity* (Manchester: Manchester University Press, 2003).

19 McManners: *Church and Society in Eighteenth-Century France* Vol. 1, p. 3.

20 On the diffusion of ideas, see the many works of Darnton, R., notably *The Forbidden Best-Sellers of Pre-Revolutionary France* (New York: Norton, 1995); *The Business of Enlightenment. A Publishing History of the Encyclopédie, 1775-1800* (London: The Belknap Press 1968); and *The Literary Underground of the Old Regime* (Cambridge MA: Harvard University Press, 1982).

21 On this event, Fitzsimmons, M.P., *The Night the Old Regime Ended: August 4, 1789, and the French Revolution* (Pennsylvania: Pennsylvania State University Press, 2003).

22 The debates can be followed first-hand in Mavidal, M.J. *et al.* (eds), *Archives Parlementaires de 1781 à 1806, première série* Vols. 16–17 (Paris: Imprimerie Nationale, 1879–1990); cited hereafter as AP.

23 Still useful on the plight of the religious orders is Aulard, A., *Le Christianisme et la Révolution française* (Paris: Alcan 1910).

24 There is no single recent work on the Civil Constitution, but Sciout, P., *Histoire de la constitution civile du clergé* (Paris: no publisher, 1872) is a mine of information. For a recent summary, see Aston, N., *Religion and Revolution in France, 1780-1804* (Basingstoke: Macmillan, 2000), chapter 7.

25 Quoted in Aston: *Religion and Revolution in France*, p. 144. See also Miller, D.C., 'A-G. Camus and the Civil Constitution of the Clergy' *Catholic Historical Review* 76 (1990), pp. 408–9.

26 Speech on 30 May 1790, *Moniteur* Vol. 4, p. 500.

27 Thirty of the bishops in the Assembly put their names to the document in October 1790: *Exposition des principes sur la Constitution de Clergé* (Paris, 1790).

28 The objections to the holding of a Church Assembly were succinctly noted by a contemporary observer, Granié, P., *Histoire de l'Assemblée constituante de France écrite pour un citoyen des Etats-Unis* (Paris: no publisher, 1797), pp. 145–47. For the argument that a clerical Assembly would have swallowed the reforms, see Aston: *Religion and Revolution in France*, pp. 144–46 and McManners, J., *The French Revolution and the Church* (London: SPCK, 1969), pp. 41–2.

29 Tackett, T., *Religion, Revolution and Regional Culture in Eighteenth-Century France: The Ecclesiastical Oath of 1791* (Princeton: Princeton University Press, 1986).

30 On the counter-revolution, Godechot, J., *The Counter-Revolution. Doctrine and Action*

1789-1804 (London: Routledge and Kegan Paul, 1972) is out of date but provides the best overall synthesis. On the clerical emigration, see Greer, D., *The Incidence of Emigration during the French Revolution* (Cambridge MA: Harvard University Press, 1951) and for the numbers in England see Bellenger, D-A., *The French Exiled Clergy in the British Isles after 1789: An Historical Introduction and Working List* (Bath: Downside Abbey, 1986).

31 Quoted in Plongeron: *Les Défis*, p. 366. See also his, 'L'Eglise et les déclarations des droits de l'homme au XVIIe siècle' *Nouvelle Revue Théologique* 101 (1979), p. 363. Pius VI singled out for condemnation the election of clerics by 'laymen, heretics, infidels and Jews'.

32 Aston: *Religion and Revolution*, p. 161.

33 Louis' concerns are detailed in his declaration of 20 June 1791 in AP Vol. 17, pp. 378–83, reproduced in Roberts, J.M. and Cobb, R.C., *French Revolution Documents* Vol. 1 (Oxford: Basil Blackwell, 1966), pp. 297–310.

34 See Blanning, T.C.W., *The Origins of the French Revolutionary Wars* (London: Longman, 1986).

35 On Federalism, there is no general study but see the excellent Edmunds, W.D., *Jacobinism and the Revolt of Lyon, 1789-93* (Oxford: Oxford University Press, 1990); Hanson, P., *Provincial Politics in the French Revoltion: Caen and Limoges, 1789-1794* (Baton Rouge: Louisiana State University Press, 1999) and Forrest, A., *Society and Politics in Revolutionary Bordeaux* (Oxford: Oxford University Press, 1975). On the Vendée, see Martin, J.-C., *La Vendée et la France* (Paris: Gallimard, 1986); Gérard, A., *La Vendée, 1789-1793* (Seysell: Perrin, 1992); Sutherland, D.M.G., *The Chouans. The Social Origins of Popular Counter-Revolution in Upper Brittany, 1770-1796* (Oxford: Clarendon Press, 1982); Tilly, C., *The Vendée* (Cambridge MA: Harvard University Press, 1964) and Le Goff, T.J.A., *Vannes and its Region: A Study of Town and Country in Eighteenth-Century France* (Oxford: Clarendon Press, 1981)

36 On the tendency during the eighteenth century to provide causal explanations in terms of conspiracy see Cobb, R., *Police and the People. French Popular Protest, 1789-1820* (Oxford: Clarendon Press, 1970) and Coward, B. and Swann, J. (eds), *Conspiracies and Conspiracy in Early Modern Europe. From the Waldensians to the French Revolution* (Aldershot: Ashgate, 2005).

37 On the September massacres, see Rudé, G., *The Crowd in the French Revolution* (Oxford: Oxford University Press, 1959).

38 On the refugees in England, see Carpenter, K., *Refugees of the French Revolution. Emigrés in London, 1789-1802* (Basingstoke: Macmillan, 1999).

39 See Vovelle, M., *The Revolution Against the Church. From Reason to the Supreme Being* (Cambridge: Polity, 1991).

40 Tallett, F., 'Dechristianising France. The Year II and the Revolutionary Experience' in F. Tallett and N. Atkin (eds), *Religion, Society and Politics in France since 1789* (London: Tauris 1991), p. 10. On abdicating and marrying priests see also Reinhard, M., *Les prêtres abdicataires pendant la revolution française* (Paris: Imprimerie Nationale, 1965); Langlois, C., and Le Goff, T., 'Jalons pour une sociologie des prêtres mariés' in *Voies nouvelles pour l'histoire de la Révolution française* (1978), pp. 281–312; de la Gorce, P., *Histoire de la Révolution française* Vol. 3 (1923–25), pp. 361–63.

41 Mathiez, A., *Les Origines des cultes révolutionnaires* (Paris: Bibliothèque d'histoire moderne, 1904) remains the standard work. See also Ozouf, M., *La Fête révolutionnaire* (Paris: Gallimard, 1976); Soboul, A., 'Sentiment religieux et cultes populaires pendant la Révolution: saintes, patriotes et martyrs de la liberté' *Annales historiques de la Révolution française* 29 (1957), pp. 193–213; Sicard, A., *A la recherche d'une religion civile* (Paris: Lecoffre, 1895); Vovelle, M., *Les Métamorphoses de la fête en Provence, 1750-1820* (Paris: Falmmarion, 1976).

42 On the cult of the Supreme Being, see Aulard, A., *Le Culte de la raison et le culte de l'Etre Suprême* (Paris: Alcan, 1892).

43 On schooling, see Palmer, R.R., *The Improvement of Humanity. Education and the French Revolution* (Princeton: Princeton University Press, 1985) and the older Barnard, H.C., *Education and the French Revolution* (Cambridge: Cambridge University Press, 1969).

44 See Desan, S., *Reclaiming the Sacred: Lay Religion and Popular Politics in Revolutionary France* (Ithaca: Cornell University Press, 1990).

Ardura, B. (2001). *Le Concordat entre Pie VII et Bonaparte* (Paris: Cerf)

Aston, N. (2000). *Religion and Revolution in France, 1780-1804* (Basingstoke: Macmillan)

Atkin, N. and Tallett, F. (eds) (1991). *Religion, Society and Politics in France since 1789* (London: I.B.Tauris)

—— (eds) (1996). *Catholicism in Britain and France since 1789* (London: I.B.Tauris)

—— (eds) (2003). *Priests, Prelates and People: A History of European Catholicism since 1750* (London: I.B.Tauris)

Aulard, A. (1892). *Le Culte de la raison et la Culte de l'Etre Suprême, 1794-94: essai historique* (Paris: Alcan)

Aulard, A. (1910). *Le Christianisme et la Révolution française* (Paris: Alcan)

Chadwick, K. (ed) (2000). *Catholicism, Politics and Society in Twentieth-Century France* (Liverpool: Liverpool University Press)

Fitzsimmons, M.P. (2003). *The Night the Old Regime Ended. August 4, 1789, and the French Revolution* (Pennsylvania: Pennsylvania State University Press)

Gibson, R. (1989). *A Social History of French Catholicism, 1789-1914* (London: Routledge)

Larkin, M. (1974). *Church and State after the Dreyfus Affair* (London: Macmillan)

Le Goff, J. and Rémond, R. (eds) (2001). *Histoire de la France religieuse Vol. 3, Du Roi Très Chrétien à la laïcité républicaine* (Paris: Seuil)

Lebrun, F. (1980). *Histoire des catholiques en France du Xve siècle à nos jours* (Toulouse: Privat)

Lemaitre, N. (2002). *Histoire des curés* (Paris: Fayard)

Mathiez, A. (1904). *Les Origines des cultes révolutionnaires* (Paris: Société Nouvelle de Librairie et d'Edition)

McLeod, H. (2000). *Secularisation in Western Europe, 1848-1914* (Basingstoke: Macmillan)

McManners, J. (1969). *The French Revolution and the Church* (London: SPCK)

—— (1972). *Church and State in France, 1870-1914* (London: SPCK)

—— (1998–99). *Church and Society in Eighteenth-Century France* 2 Vols. (Oxford: Clarendon Press)

Ozouf, M. (1976). *La Fête révolutionnaire* (Paris: Gallimard)

Plongeron, B. (1969). *Conscience religieuse en revolution. Regards sur l'historiographie religieuse de la Révolution française* (Paris: Picard)

—— (1973). *Théologie et politique au siècle des Lumières, 1770-1820* (Geneva: Droz)

—— (1988). *La Vie quotidienne du clergé français au XVIIIe siècle* (Paris: Hachette)

—— (1997). *Les Défis de la modernité 1750-1840* Vol. 10 of Mayeur, J-M. (eds) *Histoire du Christianisme* (Paris: Desclée)

Quinet, E. (1984). *Le Christianisme et la Révolution française* (Paris: Fayard)

Rémond, R. (1999). *Religion and Society in Modern Europe* (Oxford: Blackwell)

Rogier, L-R. *et al.* (eds) (1966). *Nouvelle Histoire de l'Eglise Vol. 4, Siècle de Lumières, Révolutions, Restaurations* (Paris: Seuil)

Tackett, T. (1986). *Revolution and Regional Culture in Eighteenth-Century France. The Ecclesiastical Oath of 1791* (Princeton: Princeton University Press)

Van Kley, D. (1996). *The Religious Origins of the French Revolution. From Calvin to the Civil Constitution, 1560-1791* (New Haven: Yale University Press)

Vovelle, M. (1976). *Piété baroque et déchristianisation. Les attitudes devant la mort en Provence au XVIIIe siècle* (Paris: Seuil)

—— (1991). *The Revolution Against the Church. From Reason to the Supreme Being* (Cambridge: Polity)

—— (2001). *Les Métamorphoses de la fête en Provence, 1750-1820* (Paris: Falmmarion)

Chapter Nine

1   Phayer, Michael, *The Catholic Church and the Holocaust, 1930-1965* (Indianapolis: Bloomington, 2000), p. 213.
2   Croatian Fascists.
3   Kertzer, David, *Unholy War: The Vatican's Role in the Rise of Modern Anti-Semitism* (London: Pan Books, 2001), p. 7.
4   Kertzer: *Unholy War*, p. 27.
5   Kertzer: *Unholy War*, p. 130.
6   Kertzer: *Unholy War*, p. 137.
7   Kertzer: *Unholy War*, p. 145.
8   Kertzer: *Unholy War*, p. 221.
9   Kertzer: *Unholy War*, pp. 234–236.
10 The first scholarly life of Benedict XV in English is Pollard, John F., *The Unknown Pope: Benedict XV (1914-1922) and the Pursuit of Peace* (London: Geoffrey Chapman, 1999). However, whilst Pollard emphasizes Benedict's hostile reaction to Jewish settlement in Palestine, he gives far less information about the Pope's more friendly attitude towards European Jewry than Kertzer does.
11 Goldhagen, Daniel Jonah, *A Moral Reckoning: The Role of the Catholic Church in the Holocaust and Its Unfulfilled Duty of Repair* (London: Little, Brown and Company, 2002), p. 81.
12 Kertzer: *Unholy War*, p. 251.
13 Kertzer: *Unholy War*, p. 249–63.
14 Goldhagen: *A Moral Reckoning*, pp 80–81.
15 Phayer: *The Catholic Church and the Holocaust*, p. 203.
16 Passelecq, Georges and Suchesky, Bernard, *The Hidden Encyclical of Pius XI* (New York, San Diego and London: Harcourt Brace and Company 1997), p. xix and 167.
17 For a far more detailed discussion of these issues, see Pollard, John F., *The Vatican and Italian Fascism, 1929-32: A study in conflict* (Cambridge: Cambridge University Press, 1985).
18 With deep concern.
19 See for example Zuccotti, Susan, *Under His Very Windows: The Vatican and the Holocaust in Italy* (New Haven and London: Yale University Press, 2000), pp. 8–57.
20 Zuccotti: *Under His Very Windows*, pp. 34–35.
21 Zuccotti: *Under His Very Windows*, p. 45.
22 Pius XI quotation taken from Zuccotti: *Under His Very Windows*, p. 45.
23 Zuccotti: *Under His Very Windows*, p. 45.
24 Pignatti's report to the Italian foreign ministry, quoted in Chadwick, Owen, *Britain and the Vatican during the Second World War* (Cambridge: Cambridge University Press, 1986), p. 34.
25 Chadwick: *Britain and the Vatican*, p. 25.
26 Chadwick: *Britain and the Vatican*, p. 24.
27 Zuccotti: *Under His Very Windows*, p. 51.
28 Zuccotti: *Under His Very Windows*, p. 52.
29 Pacelli quotation taken from Cornwell, John, *Hitler's Pope: The Secret History of Pius XII*, (London: Viking, 1999), p. 70.
30 Pacelli quotation taken from Cornwell: *Hitler's Pope*, p. 70.
31 Kertzer: *Unholy War*, p. 241.
32 Cornwell: *Hitler's Pope*, pp. 70–71.
33 Cornwell: *Hitler's Pope*, pp. 74–75.

34 Cornwell: *Hitler's Pope*, pp. 94–95.

35 Cornwell: *Hitler's Pope*, p.95.

36 Osborne quoted in Chadwick: *Britain and the Vatican*, p. 290.

37 Cornwell: *Hitler's Pope*, pp. 185–86.

38 Cornwell: *Hitler's Pope*, pp. 185.

39 Chadwick: *Britain and the Vatican*, pp. 26–27.

40 Zuccotti: *Under His Very Windows*, p. 54.

41 Quotations from Cazzani taken from Zuccotti: *Under His Very Windows*, pp. 55.

42 Zuccotti: *Under His Very Windows*, p. 1.

43 Zuccotti: *Under His Very Windows*, p. 112.

44 Kertzer: *Unholy War*, p. 289.

45 Zuccotti: *Under His Very Windows*, pp. 156–57; Katz, Robert, *Fatal Silence: The Pope, the Resistance and the German Occupation of Rome* (London: Weidenfeld and Nicolson, 2003), p. 80.

46 Zuccotti: *Under His Very Windows*, p. 159.

47 Zuccotti: *Under His Very Windows*, p. 159.

48 Zuccotti: *Under His Very Windows*, p. 162.

49 Zuccotti: *Under His Very Windows*, p. 163.

50 Quoted in Zuccotti: *Under His Very Windows*, pp. 163–64.

51 Zuccotti: *Under His Very Windows*, p. 164.

52 Weiszacker quotation taken from Zuccotti: *Under His Very Windows*, p. 164.

53 Weiszacker quotations taken from Zuccotti: *Under His Very Windows*, p. 164.

54 The Italian version was published in 1965, and the English language version in 1966.

55 Graham quotation taken from Zuccotti: *Under His Very Windows*, p. 165.

56 Zuccotti: *Under His Very Windows*, p. 165.

57 For a more detailed account, see Zuccotti: *Under His Very Windows*, pp. 277–90.

58 Zuccotti: *Under His Very Windows*, p. 279.

59 Zuccotti: *Under His Very Windows*, pp. 279–80.

60 Letter quoted in Zuccotti: *Under His Very Windows*, p. 280.

61 Letter quoted in Zuccotti: *Under His Very Windows*, p. 281.

62 Letter quoted in Zuccotti: *Under His Very Windows*, p. 282.

63 Quoted in Zuccotti: *Under His Very Windows*, p. 282.

64 Feinstein, Wiley, *The Civilization of the Holocaust in Italy: Poets, Artists, Saints, Anti-Semites* (London: Associated University Presses, 2003). This book seems to seek to create a negative stereotype of the entire Catholic population of Italy, broadly similar to Goldhagen's vision of the Germans as 'Hitler's willing executioners'. Given Feinstein's hard-line Orthodox Judaism and fanatical Zionism, it is rather strange that he has no qualms of conscience about working for the Loyola University of Chicago, named after the founder of the Jesuit Order, whose historical record of anti-Semitism he rightly lambasts; indeed, given his equation between anti-Semitism and European/American civilization, it is hard to understand why he remains amongst the Diaspora, for whose assimilationism and growing secularism he has such evident contempt.

65 Zuccotti: *Under His Very Windows*, p. 163.

66 Zuccotti: *Under His Very Windows*, p. 301.

67 Zuccotti: *Under His Very Windows*, p. 301.

68 Robert Katz, author of *Death in Rome* (1967) and *Black Sabbath* (1969), an American resident in Italy, seems to have played the leading role here.

69 The play itself preceded *Nostra Aetate*. *Der Stellvertreter* was first performed in Berlin on 20 February 1963, before being premiered in London on 25 September 1963 as *The Representative*, and in New York on 26 February 1964 as *The Deputy*. Rolf Hochhuth was a German Protestant, aged 32 in 1963. The play was published in Italian by Feltrinelli in 1964 as *Il Vicario*.

Chadwick, O. (1986). *Britain and the Vatican during the Second World War* (Cambridge: Cambridge University Press)

Cornwell, J. (1999). *Hitler's Pope: The Secret History of Pius XII* (London: Viking)

Feinstein, W. (2003). The *Civilization of the Holocaust in Italy: Poets, Artists, Saints, Anti-Semites* (London: Associated University Presses)

Goldhagen, D.J. (2002). *A Moral Reckoning: The Role of the Catholic Church in the Holocaust and Its Unfulfilled Duty of Repair* (London: Little, Brown and Company)

Katz, R. (2003). *Fatal Silence: The Pope, the Resistance and the German Occupation of Rome* (London: Weidenfeld and Nicolson)

Kertzer, D.I. (2003). *Unholy War: The Vatican's Role in the Rise of Modern Anti-Semitism* (London: Pan Books)

Passelecq, G. and Suchecky, B. (1997). *The Hidden Encyclical of Pius XI.* Translated by Steven Rendall. (New York, San Diego and London: Harcourt Brace and Company)

Phayer, M. (2000). *The Catholic Church and the Holocaust, 1930-1965* (Bloomington: Indiana University Press)

Pollard, J.F. (1985). *The Vatican and Italian Fascism, 1929-32: A Study in Conflict* (Cambridge: Cambridge University Press)

—— (1999). *The Unknown Pope: Benedict XV (1914-1922) and the Pursuit of Peace* (London: Geoffrey Chapman)

Zuccotti, S. (2000). *Under His Very Windows: The Vatican and the Holocaust in Italy* (New Haven and London: Yale University Press)

Chapter Ten

1   During apartheid, the South African population was divided into four racial categories: African (also called Bantu, Native), Coloured, Asian (Indian), and White (European). Historians acknowledge that these categories only incompletely capture the complexity of ethnic and other identities in the South African context. The Coloured population originated from the inter-mixture of former slaves in the Cape and Bantu, Khoikhoi, Malay, and European peoples.

2   Shell, R.C.-H., 'Islam in Southern Africa, 1652-1998' in N. Levtzion and R.L. Pouwels (eds), *The History of Islam in Africa* (Athens OH: Ohio University Press, 2000), pp. 327–348.

3   Similarly, how Africans may have interacted with the large population of Muslim Indians who entered Natal at the turn of the twentieth century is also unclear.

4   As some indication of the demographic distribution in the Cape, in 1944 Africans comprised only 6 per cent of the total population of Cape Town. Whites were 47 per cent, Coloureds 46 per cent, and Asians 1 per cent of the population (Cape Town City Council Medical Officer of Health, 1944).

5   This is detailed in works by Gaitskell (1962) and Brandel-Syrier (1990), as well as in my doctoral dissertation (2002).

6   Masakhane Muslim Community, 'Islam in the African Townships of the Cape' *Annual Review of Islam in South Africa* No. 5 (December 2002), pp. 50–51.

7   Ismael Gqamane: interview 28 April 2004.

8   Ismael Gqamane: interview 28 April 2004.

9   Sitoto, T.F., 'Imam Essa Al-Seppe and "The Emerging and Unorganised African Muslim sector"' *Annual Review of Islam in South Africa* No. 5 (December 2002), pp. 43–46.

10 The following analysis has been informed by Terence Ranger's (1993) work on the 'local and the global' in African responses to Christianity.

11 Lee, R., 'Conversion or Continuum?: The Spread of Islam Among African Women in Cape Town' *Social Dynamics* Vol. 27 No. 2 (2001), pp. 62–85.

12 Lee: *Conversion or Continuum?*, pp. 65–68; Lee, R., 'Locating "Home": Strategies of Settlement, Identity-formation and Social Change Among African Women in Cape Town,

1948–2000' D.Phil. dissertation, University of Oxford (2002), pp. 211–212.

13 New forms of evangelical Christianity, transplanted from the United States, may also be benefiting from the same disaffection with the established Church.

14 The following is primarily based on two sets of interviews, the first set collected from 2000–2001 and the second set collected in April of 2004. The first interviews were conducted largely within the framework of my doctoral fieldwork, and focused primarily on the conversion narratives of recent female converts. Some of that research was written into an article published in a South African journal (2001). The second, more recent set of interviews was comprised of a smaller sample of conversion narratives from African men. Sixteen female converts, five male converts and male and female leaders/organizers in the Muslim community were interviewed for this research.

15 Rushda: interview 20 October 2000; Lee (2001).

16 The following findings are detailed in a previous article, Lee (2001).

17 Unfortunately, there are no census figures to support this, and bodies such as the Moslem Judicial Council have not undertaken a census of the African Muslim population in South Africa. However, this observation was confirmed by various officials working within the African Muslim community.

18 Lee: *Conversion or Continuum?*, pp. 62–85.

19 Lee (2001); Quick: interview 14 February 2001.

20 Lee: *Conversion or Continuum?*, pp. 62–85.

21 Women's group interview: 21 October 2000.

22 Women's group interview: 2000.

23 Gqamane: interview 31 January 2001; Lobi: interview 15 February 2001.

24 Ismail Ngqoyiyana: interview 8 January 2001.

25 Men's group interview: 27 April 2004.

26 Ismael Gqamane: interview 28 April 2004.

27 Men's group interview: 2004.

28 Men's group interview: 2004.

29 Men's group interview: 2004.

30 Ismael Gqamane: interview 28 April 2004.

Bickford-Smith, V. (1995). *Ethnic Pride and Racial Prejudice in Victorian Cape Town: Group Identity and Social Practice, 1875-1902* (Cambridge: Cambridge University Press)

Brandel-Syrier, M. (1962). *Black Woman in Search of God* (London: Butterworth)

Cape Town City Council Medical Officer of Health (1944). *Annual Report* (South Africa)

Central Statistical Service (1996). *Census 1996: Community Profile Databases with GIS* (South Africa)

Etherington, N. (1996). 'Recent Trends in the Historiography of Christianity in Southern Africa' *Journal of Southern African Studies* Vol. 22 No. 2 (June), pp. 201–219

Fisher, H. (1973). 'Conversion Reconsidered: Some Historical Aspects of Religious Conversion in Black Africa' *Africa* Vol. 13 No. 1, pp. 27–39

Gaitskell, D. (1990). 'Devout Domesticity?: A Century of African Women's Christianity in South Africa' in C. Walker (ed), *Women and Gender in Southern Africa to 1945* (Cape Town: David Philip)

Greenbank, K. (1999). 'Urban Growth, Apartheid and Social Organisation in Cape Town, 1939-1955' Ph.D. Dissertation (University of Cambridge)

Holst-Petersen, K. (ed) (1987). *Religion, Development and African Identity* (Uppsala: Scandinavian Institute of African Studies)

Horton, R. (1971). 'African Conversion' *Africa* Vol. 41, pp. 85–108

Jeppie, S. (1989). 'I.D. Du Plessis and the Re-invention of the Malay' (Cape Town: University of Cape Town Centre for African Studies)

—— (2001). 'Reclassifications: Coloured, Malay, Muslim' in Z. Erasmus (ed), *Coloured by*

History, Shaped by Place: New Perspectives on Coloured Identities in Cape Town (Cape Town: Kwela Books)

Lee, R. (2002). 'Locating "Home": Strategies of Settlement, Identity-formation and Social Change Among African Women in Cape Town, 1948-2000' D.Phil. Dissertation (University of Oxford)

—— (2001). 'Conversion or Continuum?: The Spread of Islam Among African Women in Cape Town' *Social Dynamics* Vol. 27 No. 2, pp. 62–85

Masakhane Muslim Community (2002). 'Islam in the African Townships of the Cape' *Annual Review of Islam in South Africa* No. 5 (December), pp. 50–51

Ranger, T. (1993). 'The Local and the Global in Southern African Religious History' in R. W. Hefner (ed), *Conversion to Christianity: Historical and Anthropological Perspectives on a Great Transformation* (Berkeley: University of California Press)

Sanneh, L. (1993). *Encountering the West, Christianity and the Global Cultural Process: The African Dimension* (Maryknoll: Orbis Books)

—— (1994). 'Translatability in Islam and in Christianity in Africa: A Thematic approach' in W.E.A. van Beek, T.D. Blakely and D.L. Thomson (eds), *Religion in Africa: Experience and Expression* (Portsmouth: New Hampshire: Heinemann)

Shell, R.C.-H. (2000). 'Islam in Southern Africa, 1652-1998' in N. Levtzion and R.L. Pouwels (eds), *The History of Islam in Africa* (Athens OH: Ohio University Press)

Shell, R.C.-H., (1994). 'The "Tower of Babel": The Slave Trade and Creolization at the Cape (1652-1834)' in E. Eldridge and F. Morton (eds), *Slavery in South Africa: Captive Labor on the Dutch Frontier* (Boulder CO: Westview)

Sitoto, T.F. (2002). 'Imam Essa Al-Seppe and "The Emerging and Unorganised African Muslim sector"' *Annual Review of Islam in South Africa* No. 5 December, pp. 43–46

Chapter Eleven

1   The attacks of the troops of the Turk Muhammad Ghuri on two major Buddhist Universities – Nalanda (1197 CE) and Vikramashila (1203 CE) – were important factors in weakening Buddhist institutions, community life and education in India. However, there were also internal forces such as the gradual assimilation of Buddhism by Hinduism, which intensified the process of the disappearance of Buddhism from India.

2   Sri Lanka had strong relationships with Burma beginning from the eleventh century and with the rest of Southeast Asia in the subsequent centuries.

3   For example, most recently in 1753 when Siamese monks headed by Ven. Upali arrived in Sri Lanka to higher-ordain the *sangharaja* Valivita Saranankara (1698–1777).

4   See the conference papers of Madoluvave Sobhita, Athuraliye Rathana and Asanga Tilakaratne in 'Bath Conference on Buddhism and Conflict in Sri Lanka', published in the *Journal of Buddhist Ethics* 10 (2003) at <http://www.jbe.gold.ac.uk/10/bath-conf.html>. See also Deegalle, Mahinda (ed), *Buddhism, Conflict and Violence in Modern Sri Lanka* (London: Routledge, 2006).

5   The triggering event of the July riots of 1983 was the killing of 9 soldiers by the LTTE.

6   Ven. Madoluvave Sobhita highlights the LTTE violations as follows: '[T]he MoU had already been broken more than 500 times. Even last week a ship of armaments came in and the forces were unable to stop it.' See <http://www.dailymirror.lk/2003/01/02/News/1.html>.

7   See Deegalle, Mahinda, 'Politics of the Jathika Hela Urumaya Monks: Buddhism and Ethnicity in Contemporary Sri Lanka' *Contemporary Buddhism* 5 (2) (2004), pp. 86–88 for a brief discussion of the history of Sihala Urumaya in relation to the ethnic problem in Sri Lanka.

8   Quoted in the Sihala Urumaya homepage at <http://sihalaurumaya.s5.com/SUforlanka.htm>.

9   Some of the monks also question the impartiality of the Norwegian mediators. At

the book launch in Colombo on 20 December 2002, Ven. Professor Bellanwila Wimala-ratana remarked, '[w]e have a doubt regarding the role of the Norwegian Government in the peace process. I think it is not impartial. They don't meet the Maha Sangha and other parties.' <http://www.dailymirror.lk/2003/01/02/News/1.html>.

10 The interview with Thilak Karunaratna and other officers of the Sihala Urumaya on 29 July 2003.

11 The papers of the 'Bath Conference on Buddhism and Conflict in Sri Lanka' were translated into Sinhala and published as Deegalle, Mahinda (ed), *Budusamaya saha Sri Lankave Janavargika Ghattanaya* (Buddhism and the Ethnic Conflict in Sri Lanka) (Oslo: The Buddhist Federation of Norway, 2003). When the book launch was held at the Mahaweli Centre Auditorium in Colombo on 20 December 2002, the entire discussion was focused on the use of the Sinhala term *Ghattanaya* on the cover page of the book. Most of the respondents failed to recognize the grammatical point at issue in those words: since the Sanskrit-derived term *Janavargika* was appropriately used with another Sanskrit derived term, *Ghattanaya*, it was grammatically accurate. The words had been chosen with the recommendation of a prominent Sinhala linguist in Sri Lanka, but most critics failed to realize the grammatical issue at hand in the title: as the editor of the volume, I was making an attempt to avoid the inappropriate use of Pali, Sanskrit and Sinhala terms together. The responses to the book title show the nature of criticism leveled at academic works on the basis of mere miscomprehension of names and titles of books without really reflecting upon the issue in depth. For the *Daily Mirror* report on the book launch see 'Conference, Book Launch Disturb Buddhists' at <http://www.dailymirror.lk/2003/01/02/News/1.html>.

12 Personal communication with the members of the Sihala Urumaya and the Jathika Hela Urumaya.

13 Though I have not focused in this paper on the newly formed all-monk political party, the Jathika Hela Urumaya (f. 2004), popular sentiment about Buddhism has been the main impetus in sending nine Buddhist monks to Parliament in the election held on 2 April 2004. For a background on the JHU and its political agenda, see Deegalle, Mahinda, 'Politics of the Jathika Hela Urumaya Monks: Buddhism and Ethnicity in Contemporary Sri Lanka' *Contemporary Buddhism* 5 (2) (2004), pp. 83–103 and Deegalle, Mahinda, 'Religious Concerns in Buddhist Responses to Sri Lanka's Ethnic Turmoil' in Ian Harris (ed), *Buddhism, Power, and Political Order in Theravada Buddhist Asia* (London: Routledge, forthcoming).

14 Madoluvave Sobhita Thera, 'Yehen Ivasa Vadarana Sekva!' in *Vinivida* No. 13 (May 1988), p. 15, quoted in Amunugama, Sarath, 'Buddhaputra and Bhumiputra?: Dilemmas of Modern Sinhala Buddhist Monks in Relation to Ethnic and Political Conflict' *Religion* 21 (1991), p. 129.

15 For photographs of the LTTE's slaughtering of 34 Buddhist monks see <http://www.sinhale.com>. Some may find the graphic nature of this website disturbing.

16 Mahanama Thera, *The Mahavamsa or The Great Chronicle of Ceylon*, trans. by Wilhelm Geiger (Colombo: Ceylon Government Information Department, 1950), p. 6.

17 For more details on the LTTE's attack on the Sri Maha Bodhi premises see <http://www.lankaweb.com/news/items/160598-1.html>.

18 The LTTE suicide bomber targeted the Tooth Relic Temple, damaged the building, killed 13 people and injured 20 innocents. See <http://www.slmfa.gov.lk/foreignpolicy.asp?mode=viewitemdetails&ID=222>.

19 Athuraliye Rathana was elected to the Sri Lankan Parliament in the general election held on 2 April 2004 from the newly formed monastic party the Jathika Hela Urumaya.

20 This was established in 1997 with the aim of unifying the voices of Buddhist monks in the face of national threats. It was an organization of progressive monks who had

affiliations with all three major monastic fraternities – Siyam Nikaya (f.1753), Amarapura Nikaya (f.1803) and Ramanna Nikaya (f.1864).

21 For example, on several occasions the activists affiliated with the National Sangha Front (Jathika Sangha Peramuna) of the JVP, Jathika Sangha Sammelanaya (National Sangha Assembly) and National Movement Against Terrorism (on 9 September 2004) burned the Norwegian flag in front of the Norwegian Embassy as a protest against Norwegian mediation in the peace process. Ironically, the monks who do not approve of the un-Buddhist conduct of those monks have mounted pro-peace demonstrations in front of the Norwegian Embassy. As a gesture of good will, Ven. Madampagama Assaji, President of the Inter Religious Peace Foundation (IRPF), who earlier had responded to Mr Wimal Weerawansa of the JVP that 'peace is not a cup of poison' for Buddhist monks (see http://www.infolanka.com/ubb/Forum1/HTML/007166.html), organized a peace protest in front of the Norwegian Embassy and handed over a Norwegian flag to Mr Erik Solheim, the special envoy in charge of the peace process in Sri Lanka, in September 2004. Occasionally, the activists have asserted the innocence of the Buddhist monks in the act of burning the Norwegian flag. For example, in April 2000, the National Movement Against Terrorism 'denied reports that Buddhist priests were involved in burning the Norwegian flag, but said that it was a Buddhist priest who removed a half burnt Norwegian flag from the roadside'. On the issue of burning the Norwegian flag, the editorial of the *Daily News* (10 April 2000) remarked: 'There is no escape from the horror of war. A conflict of this scale cannot be ended by military means alone. If we crush the terrorists militarily and yet fail to address the grievances of the minority communities that led to ethnic strife, the battle will still not [be] over. Major national parties are holding talks on Constitutional reforms with a view of reaching a southern consensus. It is distressing to note that some extremists' elements are vehemently opposed to a peaceful settlement of the ethnic conflict. Last week we saw how petty minded they can be. A demonstration organised by the National Movement Against Terrorism (NMAT) and certain sections of the Maha Sangha ended with the burning of the Norwegian flag. Burning a National Flag cannot be condoned under any circumstances — how would we feel if a foreigner torched the Lion Flag? If they do not want peace, what is the alternative? What is their plan for winning the war? It is encouraging to note that many religious dignitaries, including leading members of the Maha Sangha have urged Norway to continue its mediatory role.'

22 Though the Pettah Bodhi Tree has no intrinsic historical significance, because of its very visible location in front of the Central Bus Station in Colombo it has become a good theatrical location for displaying public protests.

23 Malalasekera, G.P., *English Sinhalese Dictionary* (Colombo: M.D. Gunasena, 1978), p. 338.

24 Valivitiye Sorata Thera, *Sri Sumangala Shabdakoshaya* (Mt. Lavinia: Abhaya Prakashakayo, 1970).

25 Valivitiye Sorata Thera: *Sri Sumangala Shabdakoshaya*, p. 1024.

26 *Divayina*, 9 August 2000, p. 1 [My translation].

27 *Divayina*, 9 August 2000, p. 10 [My translation].

28 See the photograph on p. 10 in *Divayina*, 9 August 2000.

29 *Lankadipa*, 10 August 2000, p. 1.

30 *Lankadipa*, 8 August 2002, p. 1, recorded that another two MPs – Dickson J. Perera (People's Alliance) and Harindra Corea (United National Party) – changed sides during the debate on the Constitutional Amendments.

31 *Divayina*, 9 August 2000, p. 1 [My translation].

32 *Divayina*, 9 August 2000, p. 1 [My translation].

33 *Divayina*, 9 August 2000, p. 1 [My translation].

34 Amunugama: 'Buddhaputra and Bhumiputra?' *Religion* 21 (1991), p. 130.

35 Gunawardena, C.A., *Encyclopedia of Sri Lanka* (New Delhi: Sterling Publishers Private Limited, 2003), pp. 162–63.
36 A Sinhala disadvantaged caste whose profession is jaggery making.
37 A Sinhala caste, also known as *padu*, whose profession is to provide food for elephants, carry palanquins, and work as smelters of iron. Clough, B., *Sinhalese English Dictionary* (Colombo: Wesleyan Mission Press, 1892), p. 41.
38 Rohana Wijeweera, founder of the JVP, has discussed the problem of the ethnic problem in his book *Demala Ilam Aragalayata Visanduma Kumakda?* (Colombo: Niyamuva Prakashana, 1986).
39 BBCSinhala.com (17 June 2005) at <http://www.bbc.co.uk/sinhala/news/story/2005/06/050617_monks_president.shtml>
40 BBCSinhala.com (13 September 2005) at <http://www.bbc.co.uk/sinhala/news/story/2005/09/050913_jhu_slfp.shtml>.
41 See Seneviratne, H.L., *The Work of Kings: The New Buddhism in Sri Lanka* (Chicago and London: The University of Chicago Press, 1999), p. 242. Seneviratne gives a selection of Ven. Gunavansa's military songs on pp. 272–76.
42 *Lankavitti*, 10 November 2004, p. 1. The meeting was held at Acton Town Hall.
43 See Amunugama: 'Buddhaputra and Bhumiputra?' *Religion* 21 (1991), pp. 115–39.
44 *Lankadipa*, 8 August 2000, p. 1 [My translation].
45 *Lankadipa*, 8 August 2000, p. 15 [My translation].
46 BBCSinhala.com (6 June 2005) at <http://www.bbc.co.uk/sinhala/news/story/2005/06/050606_jhu_fast.shtml>.
47 BBCSinhala.com (25 June 2005) at <http://www.bbc.co.uk/sinhala/news/story/2005/06/050615_monk_abduction.shtml>.
48 Perera, Charles, 'Venerable Omalpe Sobhita, Venerable Dhambara Amila: Deaths, Suicide, and Fasts unto Death' at Lankaweb: <http://www.lankaweb.com/news/items05/250605-2.html>.
49 BBCSinhala.com (12 June 2005) at <http://www.bbc.co.uk/sinhala/news/story/2005/06/050611_monk.shtml>.

Amunugama, Sarath (1991). 'Buddhaputra and Bhumiputra?: Dilemmas of Modern Sinhala Buddhist Monks in Relation to Ethnic and Political Conflict' *Religion* 21, pp.115–39
Clough, B. (1892). *Sinhalese English Dictionary* (Colombo: Wesleyan Mission Press)
Deegalle, Mahinda (ed) (2003). 'Bath Conference on Buddhism and Conflict in Sri Lanka' *Journal of Buddhist Ethics* 10 at <http://www.jbe.gold.ac.uk>
—— (2003). *Budusamaya saha Sri Lankave Janavargika Ghattanaya* (Oslo: The Buddhist Federation of Norway)
—— (2004). 'Politics of the Jathika Hela Urumaya Monks: Buddhism and Ethnicity in Contemporary Sri Lanka' *Contemporary Buddhism* 5 (2), pp. 83–103
—— (ed) (2006). *Buddhism, Conflict and Violence in Modern Sri Lanka* (London: Routledge)
Gunawardena, C.A. (2003). *Encyclopedia of Sri Lanka* (New Delhi: Sterling Publishers Private Limited)
Mahanama Thera (1950). *The Mahavamsa or The Great Chronicle of Ceylon*. Translated by Wilhelm Geiger. (Colombo: Ceylon Government Information Department)
Malalasekera, G.P. (1978). *English Sinhalese Dictionary* (Colombo: M.D. Gunasena)
Seneviratne, H.L. (1999). *The Work of Kings: The New Buddhism in Sri Lanka* (Chicago and London: The University of Chicago Press)
Sorata Thera, Välivitiye (1970). *Sri Sumangala Sabdakosaya* (Mt. Lavinia: Abhaya Prakasakayo)
Wijeweera, Rohana (1986). *Demala Ilam Aragalayata Visanduma Kumakda?* (Colombo: Niyamuva Prakasana)

Chapter Twelve

1   My translations from the *Dhammapada* are taken from Norman, K.R., T*he Word of the Doctrine* (Oxford: Pali Text Society, 1977), p. 30.

2   Kriesberg, L., 'Coexistence and the Reconciliation of Communal Conflicts' in E. Weiner (ed), *The Handbook of Interethnic Coexistence* (New York: Continuum, 1998), p. 185.

3   Two studies that have probed this are Bartholomeusz, T., *In Defense of Dharma: Just-War Ideology in Buddhist Sri Lanka* (London: RoutledgeCurzon, 2002) and Harris, E.J., 'Buddhism and the Justification of War: a Case Study from Sri Lanka' in P. Robinson (ed), *Just War in Comparative Perspective* (Aldershot: Ashgate, 2003).

4   Section 29 (2) b of the Soulbury Constitution provided that no legislation enacted by Parliament could 'make persons of any community or religion liable to disabilities or restrictions to which persons of other communities or religions are not liable'. The next clause was similar in form but with reference to the conferring of privileges.

5   For example the All Ceylon Tamil Congress, from which the Tamil Federal Party split, and the Sinhala Maha Sabha.

6   See Vittachi, T., *Emergency 58* (London: Andre Deutsch, 1958).

7   In July 1983, an ambush by Tamil militants in the North killed 13 soldiers, triggering a largely pre-planned pogrom of anti-Tamil violence in the South and central parts of the island. Thousands of Tamils emigrated, having lost all their possessions, thus internationalizing the issue.

8   See for example 'Peace at stake: shocks and surprises' and 'LTTE ready for war, says Balasingham' in *The Sunday Times*, 5 December 2004, pp. 10 and 11; Athas, I., 'No War, no peace - for how long?' in *The Sunday Times*, 19 December 2004, p. 11.

9   For example: The 'Sinhala Only' Act of 1956 which made Sinhala the national language, linguistically crippling Tamil speakers; the rescinding of agreements in 1957 and 1965/66 that would have given some regional devolution to majority Tamil areas; measures taken by the University Grants Commission in the 1960s and 1970s to reduce the number of Tamil students entering university.

10 See *1981–The Year of Racial Violence* (Kandy: Movement for Inter-Racial Justice and Equality, 1983)

11 See for instance, Roberts, M., *Exploring Confrontation: Sri Lanka: Politics, Culture and History*, (Reading: Harwood Academic Publishers, 1994), pp. 317–25.

12 The process began with the following publications: Upham, E., *The Mahavansi, The Raja Ratnacari and The Raja-Vali forming the Sacred and Historical Books of Ceylon. Also a Collection of Tracts illustrative of the Doctrine and Literature of Buddhism translated from the Sinhalese*, 3 Vols., (London: Parbury Allen & Co, 1833); Turnour, G., *The First Twenty Chapters of the Mahawanso; and a Prefatory Essay on Pali Buddhistical Literature* (Colombo: Cotta Church Mission Press, 1836).

13 See Guruge, A.W.P., *Mahavamsa: the Great Chronicle of Sri Lanka* (Colombo: Associated Newspapers of Ceylon, 1989), p. 724.

14 Bartholomeusz, T., 'First Among Equals: Buddhism and the Sri Lankan State' in I. Harris (ed), *Buddhism and Politics in twentieth-century Asia* (London and New York: Continuum, 1999) p. 174.

15 Krishna, S., *Postcolonial Insecurities: India, Sri Lanka, and the Question of Nationhood* (New Delhi: Oxford University Press, 1999), pp. 36–48.

16 Amarasekara, A.S. (Lt. Col.), 'Original Land of Sinhale' in *The Sunday Times Plus*, 23 November 2003, p. 4.

17 Arudpragasam, A.R., *The Traditional Homeland of the Tamils: the missing pages of Sri Lankan history* (Kotte: Kanal Publications, 1996), p. 3.

18 Arudpragasam: *The Traditional Homeland*, p. 58.

19 Seneviratne, H.L., 'Religion and Conflict: The Case of Buddhism in Sri Lanka' in D.

Davies (ed), *Faith-Based Diplomacy: Trumping Realpolitik* (Oxford: Oxford University Press, 2003), p. 89.

20 Lederach, J.P., *The Challenge of Terror: A Travelling Essay*, written on 16 September 2001, circulated electronically.

21 The book was Hoole, R. *et al.*, *The Broken Palmyra: The Tamil Crisis in Sri Lanka - An Inside Account* (Claremont: The Sri Lanka Studies Institute, 1988).

22 A good source of information is Hoole, R., *Myths, Decadence and Murder: Sri Lanka, the Arrogance of Power* (Colombo: University Teachers for Human Rights Jaffna, 2001).

23 *Anguttara Nikaya*, ii, 143 taken from Woodward, F.L., *The Book of Gradual Sayings* Vol. II (Oxford: Pali Text Society), p. 146.

24 Brazier, C., *Buddhist Psychology* (London: Constable and Robinson, 2003), p. 33.

25 Nanananda, B., *Concept and Reality in Early Buddhist Thought* (Kandy: Buddhist Publication Society, 1971).

26 Harris, E.J., 'Buddhism and the Justification of War' in P. Robinson (ed), *Just War in Comparative Perspective* (Aldershot: Ashgate, 2003), pp. 103–05.

27 Bond, G.D., *The Buddhist Revival in Sri Lanka: Religious Tradition, Reinterpretation and Response*, (Columbia: University of South Carolina Press, 1988), pp. 130–239.

28 Gunasekere, L., 'Sangha must guide Sinhalese on path to power sharing - Vajira Thera' in the *Sunday Observer*, 23 May 1999, p. 7, quoted in E.J. Harris, 'Buddhism in War: a study of cause and effect from Sri Lanka' *Culture and Religion* 2 (2) (2001), p. 203.

29 Perera, J., 'Business Leaders can take lesson from Sarvodaya' distributed by e-mail, 30 August 1999.

30 The perspective of these protestors was admirably summed up several months before the meditation by a southern Sinhala journalist, a Buddhist I suspect, writing under the name Kumbakarna. Branding those who called for peace talks traitors, he continued, '[w]hat is required at the moment is a clear understanding of the nature of the problem facing the country today. Instead of allowing the terrorists and their sympathisers to mislead us into believing that there is an 'ethnic problem' and that it can be solved by 'negotiations', it must be understood that what does exist is a campaign of enormous proportions aimed at the establishment of an independent Tamil state in Sri Lanka... The only way it can be defeated is by fighting against it in every way that it manifests itself. As far as terrorism is concerned, that means unrelenting military pressure. Sorry, Sri Lanka, but there are no short-cuts.' See Kumbakarna, 'Talking peace and giving pieces' in *The Sunday Times*, 21 February 1999, p. 13.

31 Bond, G.D., *Buddhism at Work: Community Development, Social Empowerment and the Sarvodaya Movement* (Bloomfield: Kumarian Press, 2004), pp. 97–98.

32 Bond: *Buddhism at Work*, p. 98.

33 Hoole: *Myths, Decadence and Murder*, p. 80.

34 *Dhammapada* v. 129–30, p. 20.

35 Dissanayake, T., '"Malar Kothu" from Sinhala students' in *The Sunday Times Plus*, 14 June 1998, p. 1.

36 de Silva, N., 'North, South children come together for peace' in *The Sunday Times*, 7 October 2001, p. 6.

37 For example, a picture of Buddhist monks waving Sri Lankan flags and attempting to remove police barriers with the caption 'Moving away from the moderate path' in *The Sunday Leader*, 2 November 2003, p. 1.

38 Perera, J., 'Neither Peace nor Rights can be achieved unilaterally', article circulated electronically by the National Peace Council, 20 September 1999; 'Waging Peace against War: Sri Lanka's National Peace Council Builds New Relationships' in *People Building Peace: 35 Inspiring Stories from Around the World* (Utrecht: The European Centre for Conflict Prevention), p. 170.

39 For example, Perera, L.P.N., *Buddhism and Human Rights* (Colombo: Karunaratne & Sons, 1991).
40 Keown, D., 'Are There Human Rights in Buddhism?' in D. Keown *et al.*, *Buddhism and Human Rights* (Richmond: Curzon, 1998), p. 22.
41 Keown: 'Are There Human Rights in Buddhism?', p. 25.
42 *Dhammapada* v. 182, p. 28.
43 Harris: 'Buddhism and the Justification of War', p. 95.
44 McTernan, O., *Violence in God's Name: Religion in an Age of Conflict* (London: Darton, Longman and Todd, 2003), p. 99.
45 McTernan: *Violence in God's Name*, p. 99.
46 See Harris, E.J., *What Buddhists Believe* (Oxford: Oneword, 1998), pp. 112–14.
47 See Ven. Delgalle Padumasiri Thera, 'My Experiences in Jaffna', a pamphlet published by Vimukti Dharma Kendra, Sri Lanka, 1985.
48 Fernando, S., 'We will restore dignity based on principles of the *Dhamma*' in *The Sunday Times*, 22 February 2004, p. 11.
49 Fernando: 'We will restore dignity based on principles of the *Dhamma*', p.11.
50 See for instance *Majjhima Nikaya* I 414–20 taken from Bhikkhu Nanamoli and Bhikkhu Bodhi, *The Middle Length Discourses of the Buddha* (Boston: Wisdom, 1995), pp. 523–526.

Amarasekara, A.S. (2003). 'Original Land of Sinhale' in *The Sunday Times Plus* (23 November) (Colombo)

Arudpragasam, A.R. (1996). *The Traditional Homeland of the Tamils: the missing pages of Sri Lankan history* (Kotte: Kanal Publications)

Athas, I. (2004). 'No War, no peace- for how long?' in *The Sunday Times* (19 December) (Colombo)

Bartholomeusz, T. (1999). 'First Among Equals: Buddhism and the Sri Lankan State' in I. Harris (ed), *Buddhism and Politics in twentieth-century Asia* (London and New York: Continuum)

—— (2002). *In Defense of Dharma: Just-War Ideology in Buddhist Sri Lanka* (London: RoutledgeCurzon)

Bond, G.D. (1988). *The Buddhist Revival in Sri Lanka: Religious Tradition, Reinterpretation and Response* (Columbia: University of South Carolina Press)

—— (2004). *Buddhism at Work: Community Development, Social Empowerment and the Sarvodaya Movement* (Bloomfield: Kumarian Press)

Brazier, C. (2003). *Buddhist Psychology* (London: Constable and Robinson)

De Silva, K.M. (1981). *A History of Sri Lanka* (Oxford: Oxford University Press)

de Silva, N. (2001). 'North, South children come together for peace' in *The Sunday Times* (7 October)

Dewaraja, L. (1994). *The Muslims of Sri Lanka: one thousand years of ethnic harmony* (Colombo: The Lanka Islamic Foundation)

Dissanayake, T. (1998). 'Malar Kothu from Sinhala students' in *The Sunday Times Plus* (14 June) (Colombo)

Fernando, S. (2004). 'We will restore dignity based on principles of the Dhamma' in *The Sunday Times* (22 February)

Gunasekera, L. (1999). 'Sangha must guide Sinhalese on path to power sharing - Vajira Thera' in *The Sunday Observer* (23 May) (Colombo)

Guruge, A.W.P. (1989). *Mahavamsa: the Great Chronicle of Sri Lanka* (Colombo: Associated Newspapers of Ceylon)

Harris, E.J. (1994). *Violence and Disruption in Society: A Study of the Early Buddhist Texts* (Kandy: Buddhist Publication Society Wheel Publication No. 392/393)

—— (1998). *What Buddhists Believe* (Oxford: Oneworld)

—— (2001). 'Buddhism in War: a study of cause and effect from Sri Lanka' *Culture and Religion* 2 (2)

—— (2003). 'Buddhism and the Justification of War' in P. Robinson (ed), *Just War in Comparative Perspective* (Aldershot: Ashgate)

Hoole, R. *et al.* (1988). *The Broken Palmyra: The Tamil Crisis in Sri Lanka: An Inside Account* (Claremont: The Sri Lanka Studies Institute)

Hoole, R. (ed) (2001). *Myths, Decadence and Murder: Sri Lanka, the Arrogance of Power* (Colombo: University Teachers for Human Rights, Jaffna)

Keown, D. (1998). 'Are There Human Rights in Buddhism?' in D. Keown, C.S. Prebish and W.R. Husted (eds), *Buddhism and Human Rights* (Richmond: Curzon)

Kriesberg, L. (1998). 'Coexistence and the Reconciliation of Communal Conflicts' in E. Weiner (ed), *The Handbook of Interethnic Coexistence* (New York: Continuum)

Krishna, S. (1999). *Postcolonial Insecurities: India, Sri Lanka, and the Question of Nationhood* (New Delhi: Oxford University Press)

Kumbakarna (1999). 'Talking Peace and giving pieces' in *The Sunday Times* (21 February) (Colombo)

McTernan, O. (2003). *Violence in God's Name: Religion in an Age of Conflict* (London: Darton, Longman and Todd)

Nanamoli, Bhikkhu and Bodhi, Bhikkhu (1995). *The Middle Length Discourses of the Buddha: A New Translation of the Majjhima Nikaya* (Boston: Wisdom)

Nanananda, B. (1971). *Concept and Reality in Early Buddhist Thought* (Kandy: Buddhist Publication Society)

Narayan Swamy, M.R. (1994). *Tigers of Lanka: From Boys to Guerillas* (Delhi: Konark Publishers)

Norman, K.R. (trans.) (1997). *The Word of the Doctrine (Dhammapada)* (Oxford: Pali Text Society)

Padumasiri, D. (1985). *My Experiences in Jaffna* (Sri Lanka: Vimukti Dharma Kendra)

Perera, J. (1999). *Neither Peace nor Rights can be achieved unilaterally* (Electronic Circulation: National Peace Council, Colombo) (20 September)

Perera, L.P.N. (1991). *Buddhism and Human Rights* (Colombo: Karunaratne & Sons)

Roberts, M. (1994). *Exploring Confrontation: Sri Lanka: Politics, Culture and History* (Reading: Harwood Academic Publishers)

Rupasinghe, K. (ed) (1998). *Negotiating Peace in Sri Lanka: Efforts, Failures and Lessons* (London: International Alert)

Schmidt-Leukel, P. (2004). 'War and Peace in Buddhism' in *War and Peace in World Religions: The Gerard Weisfield Lectures 2003* (London: SCM)

Seneviratne, H.L. (2003). 'Religion and Conflict: The Case of Buddhism in Sri Lanka' in D. Johnston (ed), *Faith-Based Diplomacy: Trumping Realpolitik* (Oxford: Oxford University Press)

Social Scientists Association (1984). *Ethnicity and Social Change in Sri Lanka* (Colombo)

Tambiah, S.J. (1992). *Buddhism Betrayed?: Religion, Politics, and Violence in Sri Lanka* (Chicago and London: University of Chicago Press)

The European Centre for Conflict Prevention (1999). 'Waging Peace against War: Sri Lanka's National Peace Council Builds New Relationships' in *People Building Peace: 35 Inspiring Stories from Around the World* (Utrecht)

Vittachi, T. (1958). *Emergency 58* (London: Andre Deutsch)

Wilson, A. Jeyaratnam (2000). *Sri Lankan Tamil Nationalism: Its origins and development in the nineteenth and twentieth centuries* (New Delhi: Penguin)

Woodward, F.L. (trans.) (1992). *The Book of the Gradual Sayings* Vol. II (Oxford: Pali Text Society)

CONTRIBUTORS

Tobias Abse is Lecturer in Modern European History at Goldsmiths College, University of London. He is the author of *Sovversivi e fascisti a Livorno: Lotta politica e sociale 1918-1922* (1991) and numerous articles on twentieth-century Italian history and politics.

John Anderson is currently Head of the School of International Relations at the University of St Andrews. His research interests lie in post-Soviet Central Asia and the relationship between religion and democracy. He is the author of *Religion, State and Politics in the Soviet Union and the Successor States* (1994), *The International Politics of Central Asia* (1997), *Kyrgyzstan: Central Asia's Island of Democracy?* (1999), *Religious Liberty in Transitional Societies: The Politics of Religion* (2003), and editor of *Religion, Democracy and Democratization* (2005).

Nicholas Atkin is Professor of Modern European History at the University of Reading. He has published extensively on the history of the French Catholic Church and is currently researching a book on British tourism to France in the nineteenth and twentieth centuries. Along with Frank Tallett, he authored *Priests, Prelates and People: A History of European Catholicism since 1750* (2003).

Cathie Carmichael teaches modern European History at the University of East Anglia. Most of her research and published work has been on the former Yugoslavia with a focus on regional identity, nationalism and violence. She is the co-author of *Slovenia and the Slovenes* (2000), co-editor of *Language and Nationalism in Europe* (2000) and author of a short monograph, *Ethnic Cleansing in the Balkans: Nationalism and the Destruction of Tradition* (2002). She is currently writing a book on violence and European nationalism 1870–1945, which has been inspired in part by recent work on comparative genocide.

Mahinda Deegalle is Senior Lecturer in the Study of Religions, School of Historical and Cultural Studies at Bath Spa University, United Kingdom. His research focuses on Buddhism in Sri Lanka and Japan and religion in peace-making. His publications include *Pali Buddhism* (1996), *Buddhism, Conflict and Violence in Modern Sri Lanka* (2006), and *Popularizing Buddhism: Preaching as Performance in Sri Lanka* (2006).

Elizabeth J. Harris is an Honorary Lecturer at the University of Birmingham and Secretary for Inter Faith Relations for the Methodist Church in Britain. Her research focuses on Theravada Buddhism, the nineteenth century encounter between Buddhism and the West, and contemporary Buddhism in Sri Lanka. Her books and monographs include *Violence and Disruption in Society: A Study of the Early Buddhist Texts* (1994), *What Buddhists Believe* (1998), *Ananda Metteyya: The First British Emissary of Buddhism* (1998) and *Theravada Buddhism and the British Encounter* (2006).

David Herbert is Senior Lecturer in Religious Studies at the Open University (Cambridge, UK). He was Visiting Lecturer in Reconciliation Studies at the Irish School of Ecumenics, Trinity College Dublin (Belfast) from 2004–5. His research focuses on religion, social cohesion and conflict, with particular reference to Muslim and Christian traditions in Europe and the Middle East. His books include *Religion and Civil Society: Rethinking Public Religion in the Modern World* (2003) and *Religion and Social Transformations* (2001).

Saleem Khan taught Mughal and British Commonwealth history at the University of North London and has recently delivered a paper at the Annual Conference of the Political Studies Association (2005) on Intra-Sunni conflict in Pakistan. His doctoral thesis focuses on the role of religion in the politics of Pakistan.

Rebekah Lee is Lecturer in the Department of History at Goldsmiths College, University of London. Her research focuses on gender and urbanization in southern Africa. Her work considers African women's lives in Cape Town, South Africa during the apartheid and post-apartheid period. She has published articles on African women's involvement in home renovations, in informal forms of community justice, and in the growth of Islam in African communities. She is currently writing a generational history of African women in urban South Africa.

Paul Robinson is Lecturer in Security Studies and Deputy Director of the Institute of Applied Ethics at the University of Hull. He has published numerous books and articles on military history, military ethics, and international affairs. His books include *The White Russian Army in Exile 1920-1941* (2002), *Just War in Comparative Perspective* (2003), *Doing Less with Less: Making Britain More Secure* (2005), and *Military Honour and the Conduct of War: From Ancient Greece to Iraq* (forthcoming).

Victor J. Seidler is Professor of Social Theory in the Department of Sociology, Goldsmiths College, University of London. He writes and researches in the area of sociological theory, social and political theory, ethics and gender theory, particularly in relation to issues of men and masculinities. His writings include *Kant, Respect and Injustice* (1986), *The Moral Limits of Modernity: Love, Inequality and Oppression* (1991), *Unreasonable Men: Masculinity and Social Theory* (1993), *Recovering The Self: Morality and Social Theory* (1994) and *Transforming Masculinities* (2005).

Frank Tallett is Senior Lecturer in Early Modern European History at the University of Reading. His twin research interests are in early-modern warfare and the history of French Catholicism under the old regime. His books include *War and Society in Early Modern Europe, 1495-1715* (1992/2001), *Priests, Prelates and People: A History of European Catholicism since 1750* (2003), *The Right in France from the Revolution to Le Pen* (2003), *Catholicism in Britain and France since 1789* (1996) and *Religion, Society and Politics in France since 1789* (1991).

George R. Wilkes is a Fellow and Director of Studies in Social and Political Sciences at St. Edmund's College, Cambridge. He directs a programme on justice, war and religion at the Von Hügel Institute, and lectures at Cambridge and Edinburgh universities. His research focuses on war, ethics and Jewish-Christian-Muslim conflict and encounter, particularly since 1880. His recent publications include 'Judaism and Justice in War' in Paul A. Robinson (ed), *Just War in Comparative Perspective* (2003) and 'Legitimation and Limits in Jewish Equivalents of Just War Thinking' in Linda Hogan (ed), *Religions and the Politics of Peace and Conflict* (forthcoming).

INDEX